Winning More Business

Gregory A. Garrett
& Reginald J. Kipke

Preface by: Dr. Curtis R. Cook, PMP
President, Novations Project Management

CCH INCORPORATED
Chicago

A WoltersKluwer Company

Copyright Notice

Printed in the United States of America.

Notice of Trademarks

Product No.: 0-5325-300

ISBN: 0-8080-0933-8

Contents

Preface

This book goes far beyond merely writing persuasive business proposals - it discusses in detail, from beginning to end, what it takes to win more business in the new supply environment! This book takes a holistic approach to winning more business by developing a comprehensive Capture Management Life-Cycle Model, with 3 phases and 10 key stages. Every stage of the Capture Management Life-Cycle is thoughtfully examined with detailed inputs, tools, techniques, templates, outputs, best practices and successful case studies – from winning companies worldwide.

Gregory A. Garrett and Reginald J. Kipke, authors of this book, have successfully integrated the collective best practices of both the public and private sectors in how to professionally and ethically win more business in the new supply environment. At a time when outsourcing is at an all-time record-high and still growing, the authors have focused on how suppliers must create value for their customers. Today, nearly all organizations are focused on reducing their costs, delivering quality products, services and/or solutions on-time, and developing innovative breakthroughs for their customers.

The book begins, Chapter 1, with an excellent discussion of how to create value for customers, the financial impact of customer loyalty, and the barriers to developing successful business partnerships. Next, Chapter 2 offers a comprehensive Capture Management Life-Cycle Model, which is provided to serve as a framework for examination of the 3 phases and 10 stages of capture management. Chapters 3 – 8 provide a detailed review of all of the key actions required in each of the phases and stages of the Capture Management Life-Cycle. Chapter 9 provides a wealth of knowledge about the information systems and tools, which are commercially available to improve the effectiveness and cost-efficiency of capture management. Chapter 10 discusses Going Global, the opportunities and challenges a company faces when choosing to do business internationally. Chapter 10 is a must read for any company involved in multi-national enterprises.

In addition, to the Capture Management Life-Cycle Model, the detailed processes, inputs, tools, techniques, templates, outputs, best practice, and case studies, the book has three excellent Appendices. Appendix A provides a one-of-a-kind Capture Management Organizational Assessment Tool (CMOAT). This tool alone is worth the price of the book. CMOAT helps companies quickly assess their current ability or capacity to win business, plus assess their past performance. Appendix B provides an outstanding glossary of key terms related to capture management. Appendix C provides a well-documented bibliography of source material. Finally, the book concludes with a user-friendly index to facilitate future references.

Clearly, Garrett and Kipke have created a practical, proven and professional guide of how to win more business. Garrett and Kipke have gone well beyond the norm to share their vast knowledge and experience to benefit all of us. *The Capture Management Life-Cycle: Winning More Business* will serve as an excellent handbook or resource for everyone involved in marketing, sales, account management, bid/proposal management, contract management, supply chain management and project management from novice to experienced professional for many years to come! Simply stated, this book is a must read for all professionals who want to Win More Business!!!

Dr. Curtis R. Cook, PMP
President, Novations Project Management

Dedications

To Carolyn, Christopher, Scott and Jennifer for their love and support!

To Martha, Elizabeth and John for their love and support!

Acknowledgements

Special thanks to Barbara Hanson for her outstanding administrative support.

Special thanks to Dennis Ward for his creative inspiration.

Tremendous appreciation to Aaron M. Broaddus and the entire **CCH** INCORPORATED team for their excellent work – editing, formatting, design, layout, marketing and more!

Thanks to Curtis R. Cook for writing an excellent Preface for this book and his many years of support and friendship.

Thanks to Dr. William C. Pursch for his many years of support and friendship.

About the Authors

Gregory A. Garrett is a respected international educator, author, consultant, and industry executive. During the past 20 years he has successfully managed more than $25 Billion in business opportunities. He has served as a lecturer for The George Washington University Law School and School of Business and Public Management. He has provided training and consulting services to major corporations, small businesses, and government organizations in more than 40 countries. Previously, Mr. Garrett was Executive Director of Global Business for ESI International where he led sales, consulting, and business training programs for numerous Fortune 100 Companies and multi-national organizations worldwide, including: ABB, AT&T, BellSouth, Boeing, CSM, IBM, Lucent Technologies, Motorola, NCR, Nippon Telephone and Telegraph, Northrup-Grumman, U.S. Department of Defense, U.S. Trade Development Agency and the United Nations. Currently, he is President and CEO Garrett Consulting Services.

Mr. Garrett is a Certified Professional Contracts Manager (CPCM), Fellow, winner of two national awards for his contributions to the contract management profession and a Member of the Board of Advisors of the National Contract Management Association. He is a Certified Project Management Professional (PMP), and recipient of the Eric Jenett – International Project Management Excellence Award from the Project Management Institute. Mr. Garrett is a frequent speaker for numerous professional associations and member of the Association of Proposal Management Professionals. He has authored or co-authored two other books, Managing Contracts for Peak Performance (NCMA, 1991), and World Class Contracting (CCH, 2003), plus authored more than 40 published articles in a variety of professional magazines and journals. He resides in Oakton, VA with his wife Carolyn and three children – Christopher, Scott and Jennifer.

Reginald J. Kipke is most recently Capture Management Director at one of the world's largest communications technology companies providing Bids & Proposal (B&P) support for all wireless sales in the North America Region. A respected industry professional with over 20 years of sales, business management, program management and B&P experience in both the government and private sectors, he has successfully managed over $10 billion in business opportunities.

Mr. Kipke has directed capture and proposal management opportunities with such Fortune 500 companies as Verizon Wireless, AT&T Wireless, Sprint PCS, Cingular, Qwest, and Nextel. He has supported projects with the Department of Defense, numerous Federal Civilian and Intelligence Agencies, as well as governments and commercial enterprises in the Middle East, Europe and Pacific Rim. Mr. Kipke has led the start-up of capture management and program management organizations at Lucent Technologies, Avaya (formerly Business Communications Systems) and AT&T.

Mr. Kipke is a Certified Project Management Professional (PMP), and a graduate of The George Washington University Masters Certificate Program in Federal Project Management. He holds an MBA from Marymount University and a Bachelors in Finance & Economics from the University of Maryland. He resides in Great Falls, VA with his wife Martha. They are the proud parents of their adult children Elizabeth and John.

Introduction

The purpose of this book is to help business professionals understand the totality of actions which influence whether or not a supplier is successful in Winning More Business. Said more simply, this books states what it takes to win in today's highly demanding business environment! Suppliers often focus too much on developing expensive, artful, and well-worded bids/proposals and not enough on building trust, setting-expectations, and delivering on commitments.

This book uses a simple and highly effective Capture Management Life-Cycle Model – composed of 3 phases, 10 stages, and more than 35 key actions to win more business. Winning more business is all about changing potential opportunities into business reality – through proven professional and ethical business practices. Every phase and stage of the Capture Management Life-Cycle is examined in detail with specific inputs, tools, techniques, templates, outputs, and best practices. Numerous real-world case studies are interwoven into the discussion of the phases and stages of the Capture Management Life-Cycle.

A special feature of the book is the extensive use of graphics, process diagrams, examples, tables, and forms to illustrate the vital aspects of what it takes to win more business. Plus, the book contains an extensive discussion of information systems and tools to facilitate cost-effective business practices. An extra bonus, the book contains a Capture Management Organization Assessment Tool (CMOAT), so you can evaluate your organization's capabilities and performance potential.

Finally, the book contains a robust glossary of key terms involved with sales, solicitations, bids/proposals, negotiations, contracts, and project management – the key elements of capture management. A Bibliography of related source materials and a detailed index complete this comprehensive text.

We hope you enjoy reading the book and using it as a reference tool to help your organization be more successful!

Regards,

Gregory A. Garrett and Reginald J. Kipke

chapter

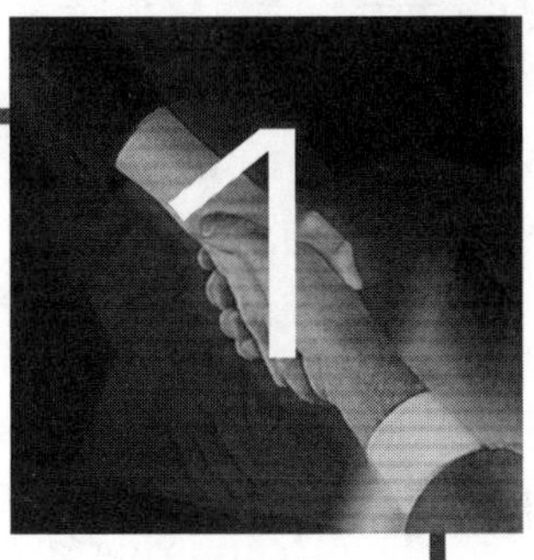

What it Takes to Win More Business

Introduction

In both the public and private sectors, customers are far more knowledgeable about their rights, have higher expectations regarding the quality of products and services, have little tolerance for poor performance, are quick to change their minds, and frequently complain if they do not get what they want when they want it. Thus, capturing a customer's business and achieving customer loyalty is like learning to dance with a partner who keeps setting a faster pace, changing the music, and varying the dance steps at the same time.

Learning to dance with customers is vital in today's new supply environment. Suppliers must listen to the music of their customers and end-customers to ensure they truly understand what the customer needs so that they can proactively offer products, services, or business solutions to meet or exceed expectations. Customer intimacy is important; however, like dancing you need to establish with your partner how close is appropriate so you do not overstep your boundaries, or step on their foot.

Just like dancing, customer/partner feedback is critical. You must know the difference between a partner's needs and desires. You must know how to treat your partner, so you do not start out or end up on the wrong foot. Business partners, like dance partners, must work together to achieve success, otherwise, one or both will stumble and fall.

Recognizing that the music keeps changing, just like technologies, requires suppliers to be flexible and react quickly. Product innovation is essential to help suppliers keep pace with the music of business and the beat of each industry in our global economy.

Despite these major challenges, some companies and organizations are very successful at learning to dance with their customers, thus improving execution and achieving customer loyalty. One of the key ingredients to becoming a successful customer dance partner is the use of capture management.

The focus of this book is to provide an in-depth understanding of capture management. Specifically, the book focuses on how winning organizations obtain high bid capture rates, provide consistent high performance and maintain world-class customer loyalty.

This book uses a three phased "Capture Management Life-Cycle" Model discussed in Chapter 2 to illustrate the stages or dance steps required for a supplier to win more business, improve execution and achieve high customer loyalty. This chapter discusses the importance of learning how to dance with customers, which is critical to winning new business, the key elements of creating value and the economics of customer loyalty. Each subsequent chapter of the book examines one or more of the phases and stages of the Capture Management Life-Cycle model.

Bottom line – Learning to dance with customers, thus winning more business and achieving Customer Loyalty, is not the action of just the sales manager or bid/proposal manager, rather winning new business and achieving customer loyalty is about a joint buyer-seller team effort like dance partners – including everyone involved in determining the customer's needs or requirements, developing a capture management plan, submitting winning bids/proposals, negotiating and documenting the deal, to the individuals who ensure the deal is delivered as promised and those who provide on-going customer service. Integrating the discipline of customer-focused capture management in a supplier's organization, in a flexible and cost-effective manner, is critical to business success!

Capture management is vital to successfully dancing with customers and delivering on promises. Capture management provides the teamwork, processes, tools and discipline, the dance steps, to allow organizations to develop winning bids, honor their commitments and create long-lasting customer loyalty.

Creating Value for Customers — "What it Takes to Win"

Suppliers of products, services and/or business solutions must create value for their customers, otherwise, the customers will select a new dance partner. Value creation drives today's business, which causes organizations to form partnerships. Creating value for customers over a sustained period of time, at a fair and reasonable market-based price is why customers want to dance with a supplier. So, what exactly are the key elements of creating value?

There are several key elements, which are typically linked to creating value for customers resulting in high performance and greater customer loyalty.

Figure 1-1 illustrates some of the key elements, which affect a customer's perception of value, thus either increasing or decreasing their loyalty to a dance/business partner. As is illustrated in Figure 1-1, trust is critical to winning new business and achieving customer loyalty, and many factors can and do affect how trust is gained or lost. It is important to note that perceptions, more than facts, in some cases will dramatically impact customer loyalty. Thus, winning new business and achieving customer loyalty is a blend of art and science – like demonstrating the concept of rigid-flexibility when dancing a tango or when developing a capture plan while the customer continually changes its requirements.

Figure 1-1.

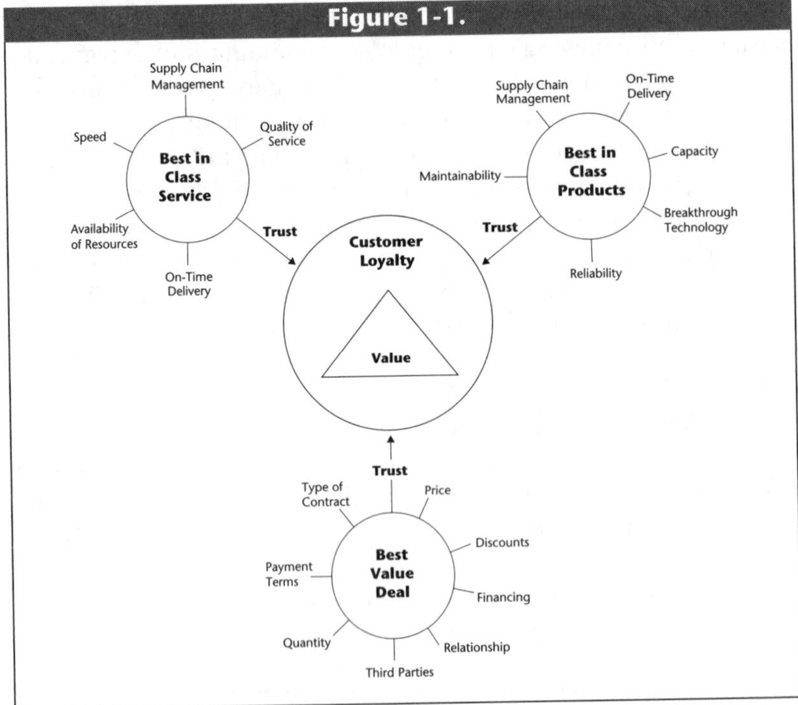

The Economics of Customer Loyalty

Why should you care about customer loyalty?

According to numerous business surveys, raising customer retention rates by five percentage points could increase the value of an average customer by 25 to 100 percent.

Figure 1-2, shows the increase in the net present value of an average customer in a number of different industries when the customer retention rate increase by five percentage points. For example, if a life insurance company can hold on to another 5 percent of its customers each year, then total lifetime profits from a typical customer will rise, on average, by 90 percent.

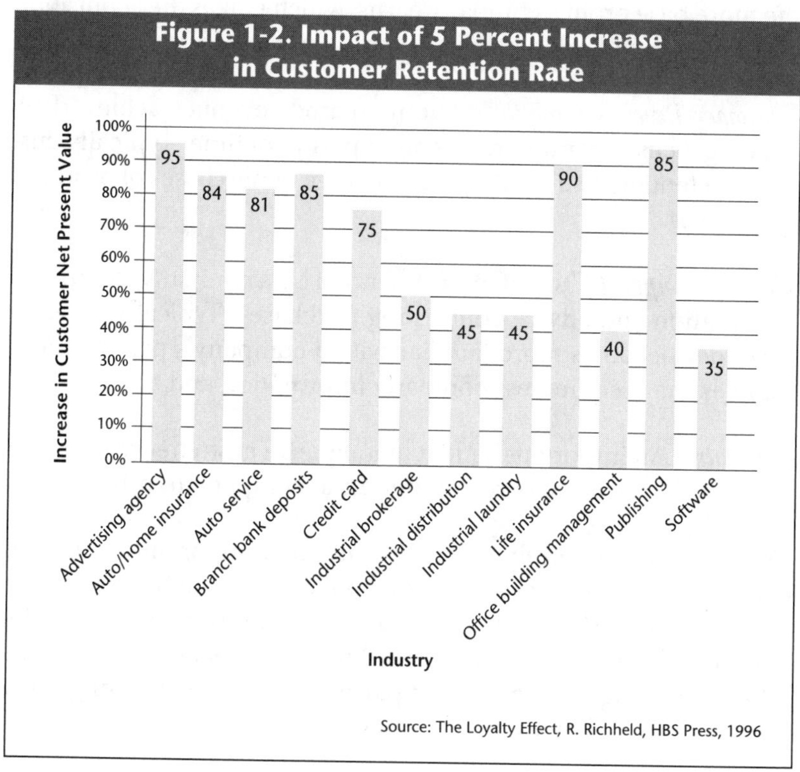

Suppose two companies are competitors and one company has a customer retention rate of 90 percent, the other with a rate of 85 percent. If both companies obtain new customers at the rate of 15 percent per year, the first will have a 5 percent net growth, while the other will have none. Over 14 years, the first company will double in size, but the other company will have no growth.

Why Customer Loyalty Means Higher Profits

According to studies conducted by Bain & Company, Inc., while every company is unique, of course, listed below are five common elements, which are proven to have important company economic effects as a result of customer loyalty.

Acquisition Cost – The money invested up front to bring in new customers. For example: advertising, commissions on sales, proposal preparation costs, sales force overhead costs, etc.

Base Profit – The money a company is paid by a customer, which exceeds the company's costs. The longer you maintain a customer, the more base profit a company earns, which makes the acquisition cost investment look better.

Customer Revenue Growth – The increased revenues achieved by keeping a customer for an extended period of time. Typically customer retention results in expanded range of purchases of products or services.

Customer Support Costs – Costs expended by a company to provide information and advice concerning purchases. Typically, when a customer becomes more familiar with a company's products and services they require less company information and advice.

Referrals – An important benefit of long-term customer retention is that satisfied customers recommend the company to others.

The aforementioned five elements all have important economic effects on a company as a result of their ability or inability to retain customers. Clearly, when a company provides proven value to its customers it retains more of them. Thus, the greater the customer loyalty, keeping the same dance partner, the greater the long-term revenue and profits a supplier can earn.

Assessing Customer Base Net Present Value (NPV)

Every organization needs a means of measuring the impact of various pricing and investment alternatives in order to make important business decisions which will potentially impact customer retention. If organizations are penny-wise and pound-foolish they may elect not to invest in important improvements in customer service or supply chain management which might increase short-term costs, but result in reduced operating expenses and increased revenues and profits in the future. The measurement of customer Net Present Value (NPV), the lifetime customer revenue stream discounted by the investment costs (acquisition costs and customer support costs) and operations costs, is a crucial aspect of building a customer business case.

The following Figure 1-3 illustrates the major components of determining Net Present Value (NPV) for your customer-base.

Figure 1-3 Customer-Base NVP

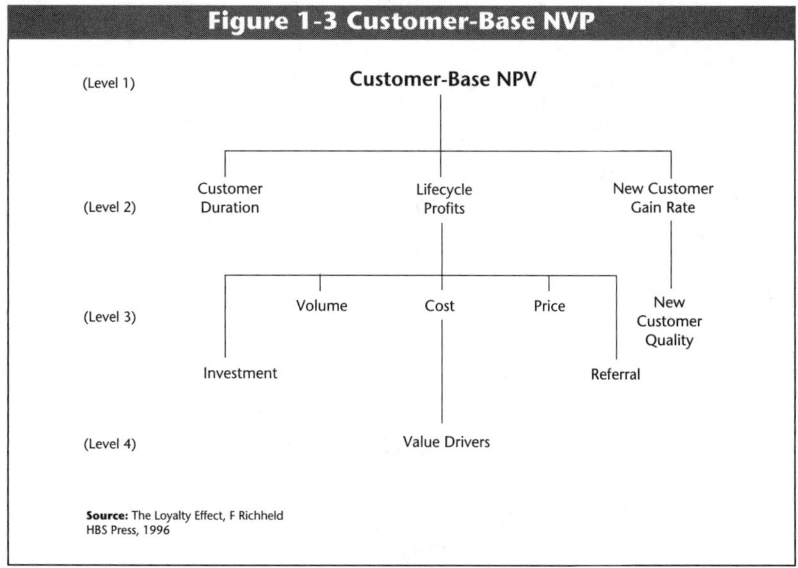

Source: The Loyalty Effect, F Richheld HBS Press, 1996

In order for an organization to calculate NPV for a customer and in turn their entire customer base, an organization must have a system for measuring the three key factors, contained in Figure 1-3: customer duration, life-cycle cash flow and new customer gain rate. Creating and providing value is the key to mutual business success – suppliers must create value for their customers – while customers provide value to suppliers.

VALUE CHALLENGES: INADEQUATE CUSTOMER VALUE

There are numerous reasons why customers become dissatisfied with their dance partners/suppliers. The following diagram, Figure 1-4, illustrates several of the major causes of inadequate customer value. While every industry has certain unique aspects, the major causes to inadequate customer value are pretty much the same everywhere.

Figure 1-4. Inadequate Customer Value

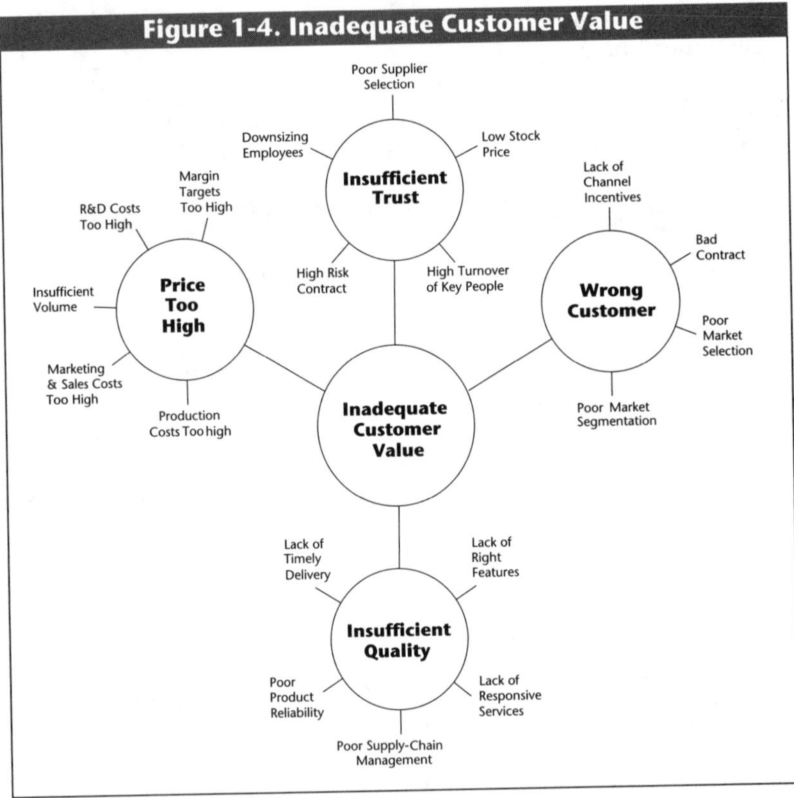

Figure 1-4 illustrates some of the many challenges an organization typically faces in creating real value for its customers.

Barriers to Effective Supplier Partnerships

In addition to the many challenges an organization typically faces in creating value for its customers, there are numerous barriers to forming effective supplier partnerships. According to the A.T. Kearney, 1997 CEO Global Business Study (see Figure 1-5), the three major reasons why companies have difficulty in forming successful business partnerships are:

- Too many other competing initiatives
- Comfortable relationships with existing suppliers
- Lack of cross-business unit cooperation

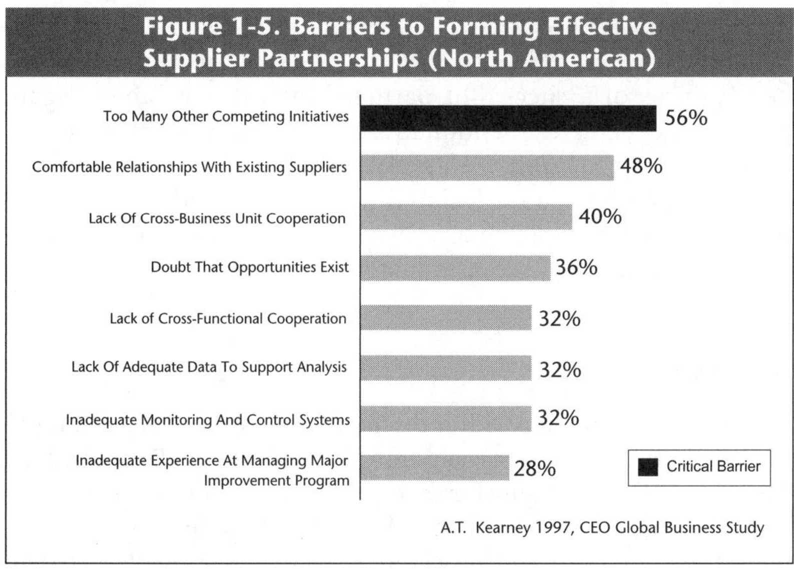

Likewise, according to the Center of Advanced Purchasing Studies' (CAPS) 1998 report titled "The Future of Purchasing and Supply – A Five and Ten Year Forecast," most CEOs worldwide have not placed supplier relationships high enough on their agendas. In fact, the report states that few CEOs have looked to suppliers as a source of competitive advantage and only rarely have they summoned the imagination to empower procurement to support their customers. Particularly in North America, nearly 60 percent of CEOs are content with cost reduction alone from supplier relationships (see Figure 1-6). Only 7 percent of the CEOs surveyed make the connection between supplier relationships and their customers.

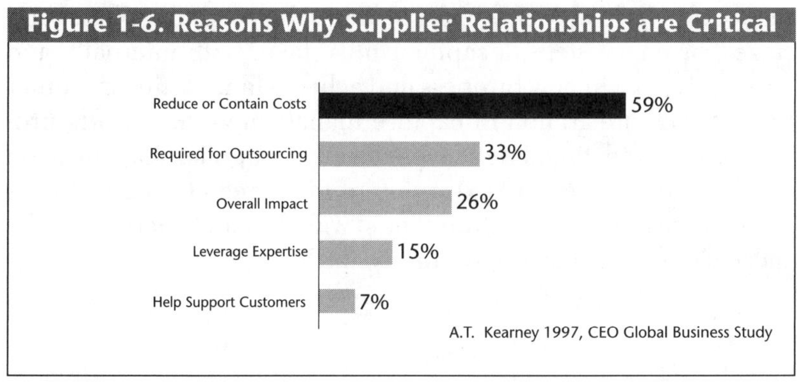

Finally, according to the A.T. Kearney 1997 CEO Global Business Study, when CEOs surveyed were asked to enumerate the key features of a successful partnership with customers, again and again executives mentioned trust. “Trust; that’s all there is,” declared a top ranking U.K. executive. “Trust, honesty, and deliveries made on time,” declared a Canadian leader. “Trust and mutual understanding,” exclaimed a top U.S. Executive. “Trust, joint understanding … and evaluation of performance,” stated an Australian business leader.

Summary

We began this chapter with a discussion of the challenges suppliers face in today’s business environment. Next, we discussed how suppliers can create value for their partners by offering, negotiating and delivering Best Value Deals. Realizing that offering and creating value for customers drives increased customer loyalty. We then analyzed the economics of customer loyalty demonstrating that loyal customers significantly and positively increase revenues and profitability for suppliers. While nearly everyone intuitively realizes the importance of having a good dedicated partner, customer loyalty, many people have not truly grasped its link to increased revenue, increased profits and the concept of net present value of their customer base. Finally, we discussed the common value challenges suppliers typically encounter. A supplier’s ability or inability to overcome these value challenges and missteps, is indeed critical to achieving long-term business success.

In the next chapter, we will introduce a proven Capture Management Life-Cycle model, which illustrates the necessary phases and stages, or dance steps, a supplier must take, both internally and externally, to win new business and achieve long-lasting customer loyalty. The integration of capture management teamwork, processes, tools and discipline at every level of a supplier’s organization combined with the joint execution of the agreed to project plans by both the customer and supplier(s) will ultimately determine the success of the business opportunity.

Questions to Consider

1. List the major challenges your organization faces to improve your bid win rate.

2. What actions can your organization take to improve your market share?

3. Does your organization work closely with your customers to establish joint performance metrics (i.e. on-time delivery, on-time payments, etc.) to analyze and track performance?

4. Does your organization survey and measure loyalty at various levels of your customer's organization?

5. What action is your organization currently taking to win more business?

chapter

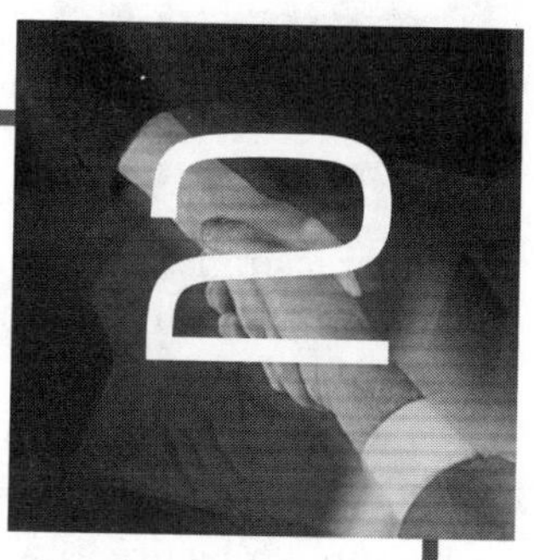

The Capture Management Life-Cycle

Introduction

Increasingly, the dance required to win strategic new business has become complex, lengthy and dynamic. With the widespread application of sophisticated technology in nearly every industry and the investment community pressure to maximize returns, commercial customers have increasingly become more sophisticated in their source selection practices. This same availability of technology has also reduced the barriers to market entry in many industries such that new competitors arise on an almost daily basis. Traditional companies are finding they must cut costs at every turn to compete with newer, smaller and more nimble competitors. All these trends converge to make it essential that every company, regardless of size or industry, has a structured approach to prioritize and focus scarce resources to maximize the win rate of new business.

The Capture Management Life-Cycle is just such a structured approach. It can be used in the commercial and government marketplace for domestic, international or global opportunities. It can be used to respond in a "reactive mode" to a customer solicitation, such as a Request For Information (RFI), Requests For Quotation (RFQ) or Request For Proposal (RFP). It can equally be used in a "pro-active mode" to generate an unsolicited offer to a customer.

Whether you work in a small start-up company or a global corporation, we are all part of a virtual workplace that is no longer bordered by geography or time zone. Traditional face-to-face communication and interaction has been largely replaced by teleconference, email, intranets and the web. The Capture Management Life-Cycle provides a framework that is geography and time zone independent. It can be used effectively in single-location companies where everyone is "under one roof" as well as global corporations where employees will never meet each other in-person and may not even have a live conversation.

Commercial customers are driven by a profit motivation and procure products and services to either increase revenues or reduce expenses. Although not driven by a profit motivation, government customers are focused on delivery of a specific program or service at the minimum cost. Even if you have the best technology or service in the world, you will not win new business unless you can show customers how to apply your technology or services to increase revenues or reduce expenses. To beat your competitors, you need to show how you can do it cheaper, faster or better.

The foundation of the Capture Management Life-Cycle is the focus on the customer's business problems or objectives. Simply stated, this process is all about winning new business by creating mutually beneficial offers which solve the customer's business problems or objectives and meet your corporate requirements for profitability and risk. When you focus on the customer's business problems or objectives, you are looking at your bid from the customer's perspective. Not only will it drive you to bid the best solution you have to offer, it will also allow you to identify alternatives which are superior to those envisioned by your customer. Bids that achieve this balance are holistic and address the multiple dimensions of a solution which are technical, delivery, pricing and contractual.

Capture Management Life-Cycle

The Capture Management Life-Cycle, as depicted in Figure 2-1, is separated into three phases and ten stages. These are the Pre-Bid Phase, Bid-Phase and Post-Bid Phase. The Pre-Bid Phase is the up front period prior to development of the customer bid during which all preparatory work is done. The Bid Phase is the period during which the customer proposal is developed. The Post-Bid Phase is the period after the bid has been submitted to the customer.

Figure 2-1. The Capture Management Life-Cycle

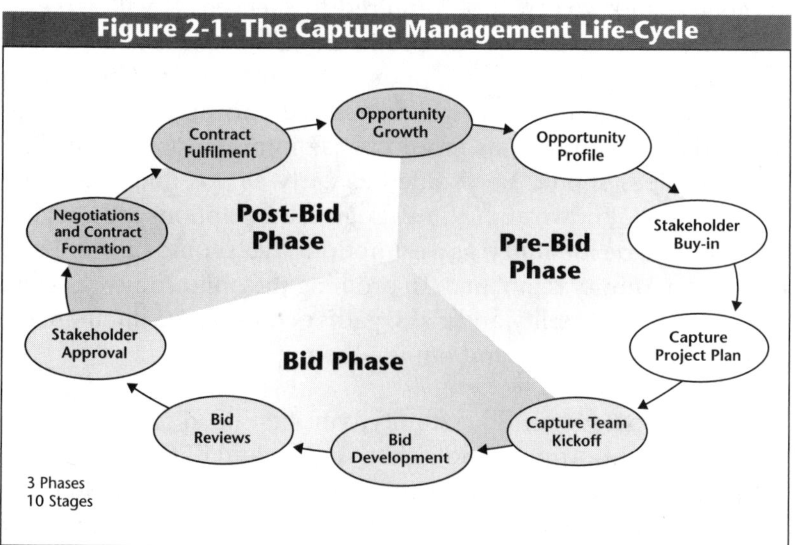

For strategic offers where the customer opts to start with an RFI, you may move through the process and then cycle-back and repeat phases when the customer issues an RFP. You may once again cycle-back and repeat phases if the customer down-selects to a short list of suppliers and then provides updated requirements upon which to base your final offer. This same pattern of cycling-back and repeating phases may also occur when generating an unsolicited offer to a customer that involves increasing layers of detail.

Pre-Bid Phase

The Pre-Bid Phase lays the foundation for success. The Pre-Bid Phase focuses on understanding the opportunity, getting support in your company to win and deliver the opportunity, and developing a plan to win. You should have completed all the stages and steps contained in the Pre-Bid Phase prior to the release of a solicitation from your customer. If this is not the case, you are playing catch-up with your competitors and may have already lost the opportunity.

The first stage of the Pre-Bid Phase is to develop an Opportunity Profile, which is covered in Chapter 3. The purpose of the Opportunity Profile is to evaluate and describe the opportunity in terms of what it means to your customer, what it means to your company, and what will be required to succeed. It will serve as the basis for decisions in your company about prioritization and allocation of resources. The Opportunity Profile should be viewed as a living document that will be refined and updated over the life of the opportunity, as more precise information is available. Opportunities should be profiled as early as possible with what information is known at the time. Logical assumptions are fine, but these should be identified as assumptions that should be validated as the opportunity is pursued. In profiling the opportunity you will qualify the opportunity and risks, gather competitive intelligence, develop a win strategy and outline the opportunity.

Before you pursue an opportunity, you first need to analyze the elements of opportunity and risk to understand if it is worthwhile (i.e., the potential benefits outweigh the potential costs). No company has infinite resources, so it is essential that your company employ a standardized methodology for all sales personnel to assess and prioritize opportunities. Having developed an understanding of the opportunity, you next will want to understand your competitors. You will want to identify each competitor or competitive team, what they plan to offer, and how they and their solution are viewed by your customer.

To be effective, you need to develop a "win strategy." To do this, you need to answer two simple questions from the customer's perspective: 1) "why us" and 2) "why not our competitor." Part of this win strategy will also include a Customer Positioning and Contact Plan with specifics on who, when and how to convey this message to the key executives and decision makers in the customer's organization. The win strategy will also serve as the basis to develop the proposal win theme.

Finally, you will outline the opportunity. While the specifics will vary based on the products and services your company provides, the basic type of information in an Opportunity Profile will include information on the customer's business problem or objective, potential solutions, potential competitors, likely risks and the win strategy for your company to win the business. In order to standardize and simplify this process, you should develop a common set of information to be collected for every opportunity to use as a guide for your sales representatives.

The second stage of the Pre-Bid Phase is to obtain Stakeholder Buy-In, which is covered in Chapter 3. Stakeholders are the individuals who control the resources needed to pursue the opportunity or deliver the solution to the customer. The purpose of Stakeholder Buy-In is to review the information gathered in the Opportunity Profile with the key constituents in your company to make a "Bid / No Bid" decision and get support to move forward. To be effective, a "Bid" decision must be predicated on all stakeholders being in alignment with the win strategy, getting a commitment to assign resources, and ensuring there is support to escalate problems and resolve roadblocks.

Even if you have a "top down" mandate from an executive in your company to pursue an opportunity, you still need to get Stakeholder Buy-In on the strategy and what is required to win. As such, you want to include stakeholders from all key organizations in your company, especially those who are likely to have objections or issues. Objections and issues need to be dealt with if you are going to be successful, so it's better to get an early start on resolving them. Typically, stakeholders will include representatives in your company from technical, delivery, financial and contractual support groups. To identify the right level of stakeholders, look at factors such the scope of the opportunity, the resource commitment required and the issues that require resolution.

You should review the opportunity with all the Stakeholders at the same time rather than individually by conducing a Stakeholder Opportunity Review. This ensures a common delivery of "the facts," and allows everyone to hear the same questions, answers and debate. Due to schedule conflicts, some Stakeholders may need to authorize a delegate to represent them at the review. You also want to formally poll Stakeholders to confirm their support or voice any reservations and document their responses. A "roll call" format has the combined benefit of bonding the Stakeholders together as a team, and ensuring there are no "silent objectors."

On opportunities with a long life-cycle, you need to plan periodic Status Reviews with the Stakeholders to keep them apprised of the status of the opportunity. Depending upon the scope of the opportunity and significance of any changes, Stakeholder Status Reviews may require reassembling the Stakeholders for a formal review or may only require a written Stakeholder Status Report

The third stage in the Pre-Bid Phase is to develop the Capture Project Plan, which is discussed at length in Chapter 4. The purpose of the Capture Project Plan is to document a game plan of "who" needs to do "what," "when," "where," "how often" and "how much" to win. In order to do this efficiently and effectively, you need a small core team of individuals who represent the key groups in your company that provide technical, delivery, financial and contractual support.

The Capture Project Plan will identify the deliverables, work tasks, timeline and resources required to pursue and win the opportunity. The plan should draw upon data from similar projects and strive to be a fair estimate of the resource commitment required. The plan should highlight any resource gaps or shortages and required dates for resolution. At this point in the life-cycle of the opportunity, there will likely be open issues or concerns that have yet to be resolved. These should be documented in an initial Risk Plan for mitigation during the Bid Phase. Examples of these include: technical/product gaps, service/delivery gaps, financial gaps, contractual gaps and competitive gaps.

The Capture Project Plan should also include how the team will be structured and communicate. For projects involving large teams, this is critical for ensuring task completion, collecting status and communicating changes to the team. You should establish team leaders and possibly even sub-team leaders with accountability for multiple team members and work tasks. While the team structure needs to be based on the specifics of your opportunity, a typical approach is to have separate Technical, Delivery, Pricing and Contractual teams. You should also develop plans for how to address common communication issues such as Status Meetings, sharing information, Change Requests and Jeopardy-Escalations.

Bid Phase

Having obtained support from the stakeholders and developed a Capture Project Plan, you can now move forward to assemble the capture team and pursue the bid. The objective of the Bid Phase is to develop an on-time bid that solves the customer's business problem and meets your company's requirements for profitability and risk. For simplicity, one can think of the Bid Phase as beginning with receipt of the customer solicitation and ending with submission of the proposal to the customer.

The first stage in the Bid Phase is to assemble and hold a Capture Team Kickoff, which is covered in Chapter 5. The purpose of the Capture Team Kickoff is to assemble the resources required to pursue the bid, review the outputs of the Pre-Bid Phase, and get them organized and energized to win the bid. You should complete this as soon as practical after the Stakeholder Buy-In and Capture Project Plan are completed. The kickoff should not be predicated on receipt of the customer's solicitation. Once the customer solicitation is received, the clock will be ticking, so you want to pre-assemble the team and review the game plan.

The Capture Team Kickoff should include all of the individuals involved in developing the bid for the customer. This will include individuals with accountability for technical/product support, product/service delivery support, financial support, and contractual support. Depending upon the dispersion of the team, this meeting may be face-to-face or a teleconference. The most important objective is to include all team members in the kickoff in some fashion, so everyone understands the game plan.

During the kickoff you should review the same information that was the basis for Stakeholder Opportunity Review. You should review and validate the details of the Capture Project Plan to ensure everyone understands the deliverables, their work task assignments, team structures and due dates, and make any changes that are needed to the plan. You should also review the communications plans developed along with the methodology and systems the team will use to develop and review the proposal during the Bid Development and Bid Review stages. Examples of topics to review at the Capture Team Kickoff include:

- Review of the opportunity
- Review of deliverables, work tasks, resource assigned and timelines
- Review of information sharing and distribution plans
- Review of change control and alert-jeopardy-escalation plans
- Review of methodology and/or systems used for proposal development including version control and bid reviews

The second stage of the Bid Phase is Bid Development, which is covered in Chapter 5. This stage begins with execution of the capture project plan and includes all work activities required to design and price the product and service solution and accurately articulate this in a proposal for the customer that accentuates the points of the win strategy. Before one can articulate the offer in a proposal for the customer, one must understand the specifics of what to offer and the price. The first work activity for the Capture Team is to develop the solution and record it in a Solution Architecture document that shows the key products and services and how they combine to solve the customer's business problem. The Solution Architecture document serves as the basis for work to begin in parallel on writing the customer proposal and designing the products and services required to provide a price for the bid. This document can also be used quite effectively to control and communicate changes that may need to be made in the offer as it is constructed.

As you develop the solution in more detail, you should take steps to ensure it is holistically compliant with the customer's technical, delivery, financial and contractual requirements. You also need to ensure the design is consistent with the description in the proposal and the pricing developed. Finally, you need to develop a delivery plan which addresses the fundamentals of who, what, when, where and how the solution will be delivered .

As you develop the solution, you will likely find gaps or potential adverse situations which could occur. These are risks that need to be addressed. For each of these risk, you need to develop a Risk Mitigation Plan using one or more strategies designed to avoid, transfer, share or reserve the risk. These plans will become an important part of the review with Stakeholders later to obtain their authority to bid.

As the solution takes shape, you will develop one or more business cases. Ideally, you will develop a customer business case showing the costs and benefits of the solution in the customer's financial terms. At a minimum, you need to develop an internal business case on the profitability of the opportunity for review with the Stakeholders in order to obtain their authority to bid.

Finally, you need to develop the proposal or customer deliverable(s). Although the actual format will vary, major components of a customer proposal typically include: a) Executive Summary, b) Technical Response, c) Delivery Response, d) Pricing Response and e) Contractual Response.

The Executive Summary provides an overview of the offer and is targeted to executive decision makers in the customer's organization. The win strategy and solution architecture serve as the skeleton for the Executive Summary, which is augmented with key details from the Technical Response, Delivery Response, Pricing Response and Contractual Response.

The Technical Response describes the products and services being offered and explains how they solve the customer's business problem. The Delivery Response describes the specifics of "how," "when" and "who" will deliver and support the offer and may include such items as an Implementation Plan, Delivery Schedule, Transition Plan, Maintenance Plan or Support Plan. Even if the

Delivery Response is not delivered to the customer, a well thought out and realistic Implementation Plan should be developed for internal purposes to understand how the project will be delivered. Depending upon the scope and complexity of what is being offered, it may be appropriate to operationally view the Technical and Delivery Response as a single deliverable for proposal development and review purposes.

The Pricing Response describes how the offer is priced and price terms. The Contractual Response describes the terms and conditions under which the offer is being made and typically includes such topics as internal commitments, warranty, payment terms and liabilities. If financing is being offered to the customer, this would typically be described in the Pricing Response, but may alternatively appear in the Contractual Response. Depending upon the scope and complexity of what is being offered, it may be appropriate to operationally view the Pricing and Contractual Responses as a single deliverable for proposal development and review purposes.

The third stage of the Bid Phase is to conduct Bid Reviews, which are covered in Chapter 5. The type and number of Bid Reviews is based on the scope and complexity of the opportunity and the time available. Bid Reviews can be classified into two types: a) internally focused review and b) externally focused review.

An internally focused review, typically referred to as a Pink Team Review, is usually conducted by members of the Capture Team reading what others on the team have written. The chief focus of an internal Pink Team review is to ensure the proposal is complete and accurate. Depending upon the complexity and scope of the offer and the time available, there may be multiple Pink Team Reviews. Due to specialization of resources, there will frequently be different review team members for the major sections of the proposal (e.g., Executive Summary, Technical, Delivery, Pricing and Contractual).

Externally focused reviews, typically referred to as a Red Team Review, are conducted by individuals who are not members of the Capture Team. These “unbiased” and “impartial” individuals will read what has been written from the customer’s perspective. The chief focus of an external Red Team review is to ensure the proposal makes sense and addresses specified customer requirements. Depending upon the scope and complexity of the offer and time available, there may be multiple Red Team reviews. Due to specialization of resources and complexity of the proposal, there will frequently be different review team members for the major sections of the proposal (e.g., Executive Summary, Technical, Delivery, Pricing, Contractual).

It is recommended that you document all reviews and the completeness of the bid. This not only provides a record of the review, it also creates a sense of formality that will motivate the reviewers to take the sessions more seriously. This documentation can take many forms, but typically consists of an Offer Certification by team leaders or reviewers that the bid is compliant with all technical, delivery, financial and contractual requirements. Areas of non-compliance need to be identified as either exceptions that will be highlighted to the customer or risks your company is assuming in the bid.

The fourth stage of the Bid Phase is to obtain Stakeholder Approval, which is covered in Chapter 5. The purpose of this stage is to reassemble the same Stakeholders from the Pre-Bid Phase Stakeholder Buy-In and go through a review of any changes in the opportunity profile, the solution, the risks and the business case to solicit their approval to submit the bid to the customer.

During the Stakeholder Approval, you should review key information from the Stakeholder Opportunity Review and any Stakeholder Status Reviews. You need to gauge the level of review required based on factors such as: the scope of the opportunity, time since the Stakeholder Opportunity Review or last Stakeholder Status Review and any changes in individual Stakeholders. Additional key information that should be reviewed includes:

- Changes in Opportunity Profile
- Solution Developed
- Risk Mitigation Plans
- Business case on profitability of the offer

Similar to the Stakeholder Opportunity Review, you should conduct this review with all the stakeholders, or authorized delegates, at one time. You should also hold a "roll call" confirming their approval. Depending upon the scope of the opportunity, and your corporate Schedule of Authorizations or Approvals, you may also need to obtain approval of senior executives in your company (i.e., CEO or President) or potentially even the Board of Directors.

Post-Bid Phase

Having submitted your bid to the customer, now the real dancing begins. The Post-Bid Phase starts once the proposal is submitted to the customer and includes all the key actions required to close the sale, deliver the solution, look for process improvements and identify follow-on opportunities.

The first stage of the Post-Bid Phase is Negotiations and Contract Formation, which is covered in Chapter 6. The Post-Bid Phase actually represents a series of activities that can occur in sequence or in parallel with the customer. The purpose of the Negotiations and Contract Formation stage is to ensure the customer understands your bid and how it is superior to your competitors, as well as, conduct negotiations and develop the contract.

For most strategic bids, you will have an opportunity to provide an oral presentation of your bid to a select group of customers. If the customer does not offer this opportunity, you should request permission to provide such a presentation. This will give you a chance to review the bid and reinforce the win strategy with the key influencers and decision makers. Depending upon the scope of the bid, this may involve multiple presentations to multiple audiences. In fact, presentations frequently mirror the general structure of the proposal with one presentation for executive customer representatives, one for technical and delivery customer representatives, and one for financial and contractual customer representatives.

As your customer reviews your proposal, and those of your competitors, they will usually have questions. These will vary from simple yes/no questions designed to confirm some minor items, to open ended questions with what appear to be new requirements. Although you may be asked to respond verbally with an answer, you will typically also be asked to document your answer in writing. Depending upon the scope of the opportunity and the questions, developing answers may begin to look like preparing a supplemental proposal. If this is the case, you should use the same steps and activities described in the Bid Phase to manage your Questions & Answer (Q&A) response.

If the customer has issued a Request For Information (RFI), this will typically be followed by a Request For Proposal (RFP) to only those providers who are deemed "qualified" on the basis of the RFI. Further, after an RFP cycle, most customers will narrow the source selection down to a short list of providers with whom they will attempt to negotiate a final price along with terms and conditions. Most customers find they can maximize their negotiating position by narrowing the field to a short list of technically acceptable providers with whom they will then attempt to negotiate terms, conditions and prices. For strategic opportunities, it is not uncommon to see an updated Request For Proposal to this short list of providers with an updated set of requirements. Regardless of whether you are moving from RFI to RFP, or "sharpening your pencil" to develop a better price or an updated proposal, you may find yourself needing to cycle-back to repeat phases and steps from earlier in the Capture Management Life-Cycle.

The second major stage of the Post-Bid Phase is Contract Fulfillment, which is covered in Chapter 7. Contract Fulfillment includes the smooth and complete transition to the organizations and individuals within your company who are accountable to deliver the solution, as well as, the activities of effective administration of the contract and management of changes.

If you have followed the Capture Management Life-Cycle during the Pre-Bid and Bid Phases by involving individuals from the delivery organizations within your company on the Capture Team this transition should be rather straightforward. Creation and maintenance of bid documentation in an organized and accessible format is essential to making this handoff complete. If both activities have occurred, you will find this transition can be achieved at a single meeting to review and explain the bid and relevant documentation.

The purpose of contract fulfillment is to ensure all appropriate products, services, and/or solutions are successfully delivered on-time, ensure all contract terms and conditions are met by both parties, and ensure proper management of changes, timely payments and timely contract closeout. The three biggest supplier impacts during contract fulfillment are loss of customer loyalty, loss of revenues and reduced profit margins as a result of failures to deliver on-time, failures to effectively administer the contract, and failures to effectively manage growth opportunities. When properly managed, contract fulfillment activities result in increased revenues, higher profit margins and higher levels of customer satisfaction.

The third stage in the Post-Bid Phase is Opportunity Growth, which is covered in Chapter 8. Opportunity Growth, is a collection of actions which may occur in sequence or in parallel and include collecting and documenting Lessons Learned, conducting a Win/ Loss Review, soliciting feedback from the customer on delivery performance and identifying future bids opportunities.

The essential purpose of Lessons Learned is to identify ways to be more efficient. Lessons Learned are typically gathered from individuals within your company who were members of the Capture Team, but can also be garnered from your customer. Perhaps the biggest challenge with Lessons Learned is to document and share these so your organization actually learns from past experience and does not repeat the same mistakes over and over again. In order to do so you will need a structured methodology that regularly evaluates this feedback and implements process improvements.

In contrast, the essential purpose of a Win/Loss Review is to identify how to be more effective. In order to be meaningful, a Win/Loss Review must involve direct feedback from your customer on why you were either selected or not selected. Attempts to conduct a Win/Loss Review with only individuals in your company, no matter how well intentioned, will at best be based on second hand information and at worst be skewed by internal politics and individual biases.

As part of delivering the solution, you should routinely solicit feedback from the customer on delivery performance. Not only will this kind of feedback provide insight on what "to do" and "not to do," to be more responsive to your customer, it frequently provides a forum for your customer to identify additional business problems and objectives. These additional problems and objectives become opportunities for future bids. In the course of delivering the solution, you will also learn more about your customer and their problems. This insight needs to be leveraged into additional new business opportunities, the requirements of which, are heavily influenced to maximize your competitive position and disadvantage your competitors.

Summary

This chapter presented an introduction to the Capture Management Life-Cycle by explaining each of the three phases and the ten stages. Figure 2-2 provides a summary in table form of the three phases, ten stages, and key steps within each of these. In subsequent chapters, we will explore the inputs, tools, techniques, outputs and tips to maximize the effectiveness and efficiency of each phase, stage and step of the Capture Management Life-Cycle.

Following the detailed discussion of the entire Capture Management Life-Cycle, Chapter 9 reviews the numerous commercially available information systems and automated tools to help facilitate capture management, as well as, such critical issues as security and version control. Chapter 10 discusses the opportunities and challenges suppliers face when going global - selling products, services and/or solutions internationally.

Figure 2-2. The Capture Management Life-Cycle (Phases & Stages)

Pre-Bid Phase	Bid Phase	Post-Bid Phase
Opportunity Profile Stage ■ Qualify Opportunity and Risks ■ Gather Competitive Intelligence ■ Develop Win Strategy ■ Outline Opportunity **Stakeholder Buy-in Stage** ■ Conduct Bid/No Bid Review ■ Obtain Strategy Alignment ■ Get Resource Commitment ■ Ensure Escalation Support **Capture Project Plan Stage** ■ Identify Deliverables ■ Identify Work Tasks ■ Identify Timeline ■ Identify Resources ■ Develop Communication Plans	**Capture Team Kickoff Stage** ■ Review Bid ■ Validate Capture Project Plan ■ Review Communication Plans ■ Review Proposal Development Plans **Bid Development Stage** ■ Execute Capture Project Plan ■ Develop Solution ■ Develop Risk Mitigation Plans ■ Develop Business Case(s) ■ Develop Proposal **Bid Reviews Stage** ■ Conduct Pink Team Reviews ■ Conduct Red Team Reviews ■ Obtain Offer Certifications **Stakeholder Approval Stage** ■ Review Changes, Solution, Risks ■ Review Business Case ■ Obtain Authority To Bid	**Negotiations and Contract Formation Stage** ■ Conduct Oral Presentations ■ Plan Negotiations ■ Conduct Negotiations ■ Develop Contract **Contract Fulfillment Stage** ■ Manage Project ■ Administer Contract ■ Manage Changes ■ Closeout Contract **Opportunity Growth Stage** ■ Conduct Bid Win/Loss Review ■ Manage Customer Expectations ■ Gather Customer Feedback ■ Document Lessons Learned ■ Build Trust

Questions to Consider

1. How well does your organization manage the process of capturing new business (i.e., profile opportunities, obtain stakeholder buy-in, develop capture plans, kickoff capture teams, develop bids, review bids, obtain stakeholder approval, negotiate and form contracts, fulfill contracts and grow opportunities)?

2. How effectively does your organization complete these activities? What is your win rate? Do you achieve your business plans? Have you entered into bad deals?

3. Does your organization have documented processes and/or standardized tools & techniques to capture new business?

4. What actions has your company taken to improve/develop the capture management skills of sales managers, capture/proposal managers, program managers and contract managers?

5. How well does your organization document and share your capture management lessons learned?

chapter

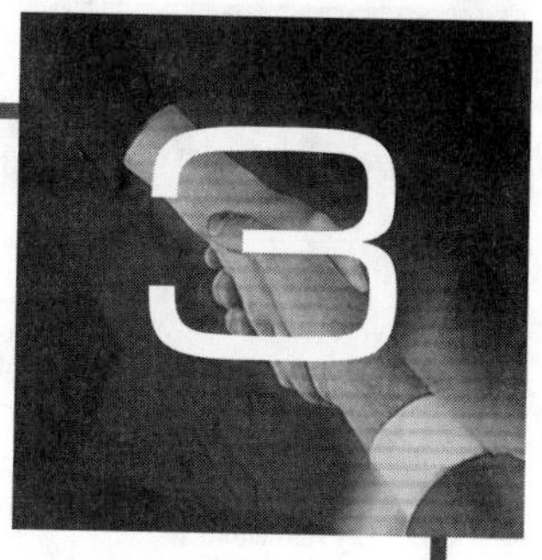

Pre-Bid Phase: Opportunity Profile & Stakeholder Buy-In

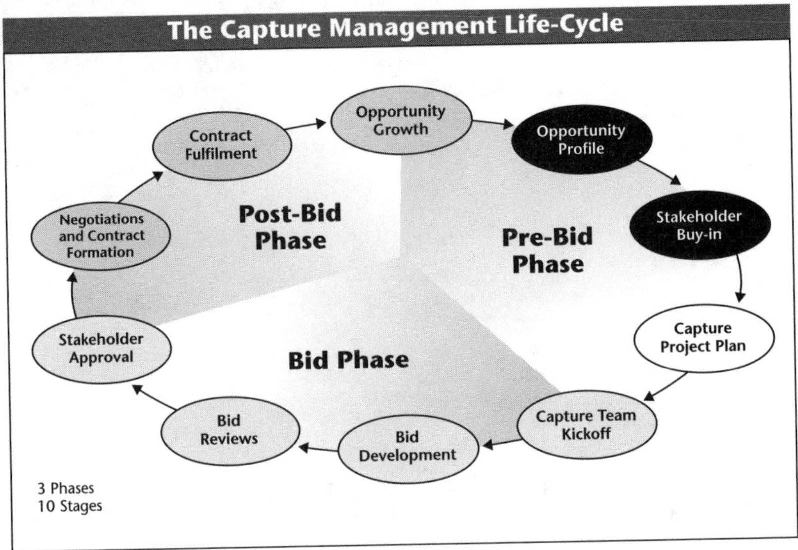

Introduction

The first two stages of the Pre-Bid Phase are Opportunity Profile & Stakeholder Buy-In. These have been combined as they are very interrelated and you may find on very large opportunities you will cycle back and forth between these stages several times to successfully accomplish both.

Opportunity Profile Stage

Opportunity Profile: The objectives of the Opportunity Profile stage are: 1) qualify the opportunity and risks, 2) gather competitive intelligence, 3) develop a Win Strategy and 4) outline the opportunity. Each of these objectives translates into a step in the Opportunity Profile stage. While these are presented as steps, it is not necessary to follow them sequentially, as it may be more practical and beneficial for you to complete them in a different order.

You should attempt to complete each step before proceeding to the Stakeholder Buy-In stage; however, you should not delay due to missing information. As time passes you will acquire more and better information, so attempt to complete each step with what you know at the time. It is appropriate to make assumptions and reasonable speculations in lieu of missing information; however, be sure such items are documented so they can be replaced later with facts as they become available.

The following graphic (Figure 3-1) summarizes the Inputs, Tools & Techniques and Outputs covered in this chapter concerning the Opportunity Profile stage of the Pre-Bid Phase.

Figure 3-1. Pre-Bid Phase: Opportunity Profile Stage

Input

- Knowledge of your customer
- Knowledge of your company
- Knowledge of your competitors

Tools & Techniques

- Qualify Opportunity & Risk
  - Opportunity-Risk Assessment Grid
  - ORA Grid with Bid-No Bid Line
  - Elements of Opportunity
  - Elements of Risk
  - Opportunity Quantification Tool
  - Risk Quantification Tool
- Gather Competitive Intelligence
  - Competitor Profile
  - Sources of Competitive intelligence
- Develop Win Strategy
  - Sweet Spot–Sour Spot Analysis
  - Win Theme & Strategy Form
  - Customer Positioning Plan
  - Customer Contact Plan
- Outline the Opportunity
  - Stakeholder Presentation Outline

Output

- Qualified Opportunity
- Competitor Profile
- Win Strategy
- Outline of Offer - Stakeholder Review Presentation

Inputs

As with all processes and approaches, the value of making a great beginning cannot be understated. The three foundations or inputs of knowledge, see Figure 3-2, for success in the Capture Management Life-Cycle are:

- *Knowledge of your customer*
- *Knowledge of your competitors*
- *Knowledge of your company*

The degree to which you master each of these will greatly impact your ability to spot potential opportunities and get a jump on your competitors.

Figure 3-2. The Three Inputs of Knowledge

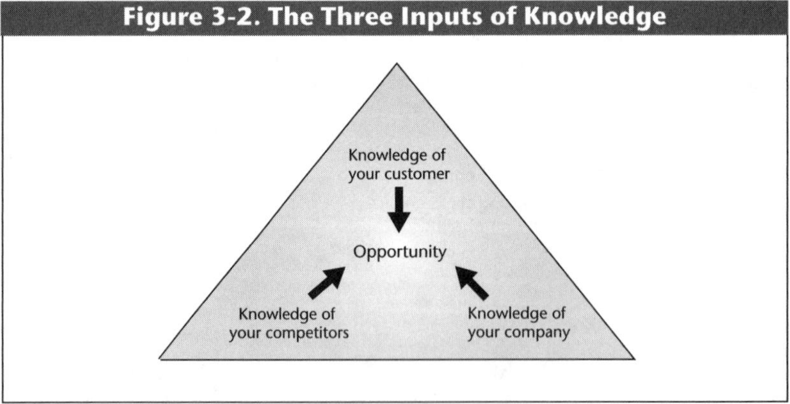

Tools and Techniques

Quantify the Opportunity and Risks

The first step of the Opportunity Profile stage is to Qualify the Opportunity and Risks. Webster's defines opportunity as "a set of circumstances providing a chance or possibility." Webster's defines risk as "the possibility of danger, injury or loss." In other words, elements of opportunity are those characteristics which increase the probability of success and elements of risk are those characteristics which have the potential to negatively impact the result.

- *Opportunity–Risk Assessment Grid:* There will often be more opportunities than you have resources to pursue, so you must prioritize and direct resources to those opportunities which have the highest probability of success and payback versus those which do not. Since you will need to compare opportunities to make choices, it is necessary to develop a methodology to assess and compare specific opportunities. This can be done using an x-y coordinate grid, see Figure 3-3, which plots opportunity on the "y-axis" and risk on the "x-axis." The grid has further been subdivided into quadrants in order to characterize different types of opportunities.

Quadrant A contains those opportunities which have a "high opportunity" value and are also "low risk". Quadrant A opportunities should be the highest priority as they have the highest probability of success with the best potential payback. In contrast, Quadrant D contains those opportunities which have "low opportunity" value yet have "high risk." Quadrant D opportunities are likely to be projects you should avoid and do not want to waste resources on pursuing as they have a low probability of success and a low potential payback.

Figure 3-3. Opportunity—Risk Assessment Grid

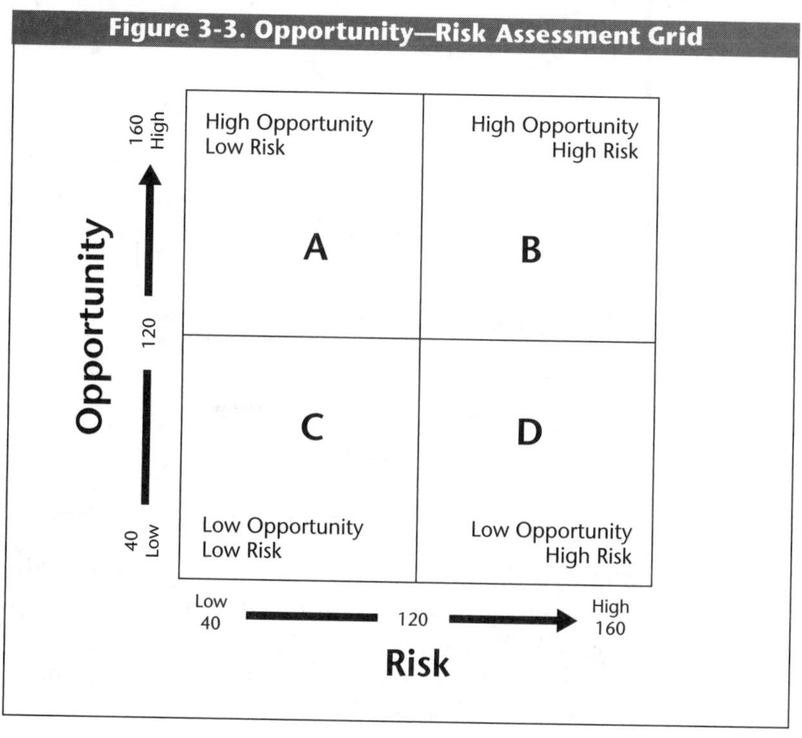

- *ORA Grid with Bid-No Bid Line:* Quadrant B opportunities have a "low opportunity" value but are also "low risk," while Quadrant C opportunities are "high opportunity" value but also have "high risk." Opportunities in quadrants B and C should be considered marginal. You should focus on pursing those opportunities which fall into the upper left had corner of each of quadrant, while avoiding those which fall into the lower right hand corner. A "bid line" can be added to the grid, as shown below in Figure 3-4. Exactly where this line is placed on the grid depends chiefly upon your company's resources and willingness to accept risk.

Figure 3-4. Opportunity—Risk Assessment Grid

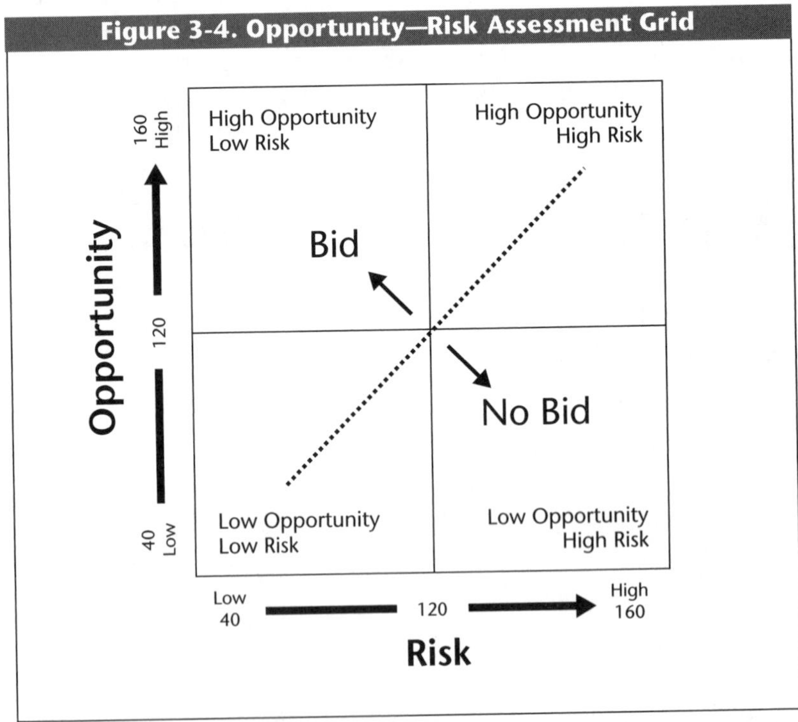

In order to plot specific opportunities, we need to look at the elements or characteristics which are typically used to assess opportunity and risk. While the specifics might vary from company to company, the elements of opportunity and risk are common. These are shown below in Table 3-1.

Table 3-1

Elements of Opportunity	Elements of Risk
Corporate Direction Match	Customer Commitment
Competitive Environment	Corporate Competence
Revenue Value	External Obstacles
Potential Profitability	Opportunity Engagement
In-House Content	Solution Life-Cycle Match
Future Business Potential	Period of Performance
Resources to Bid	Delivery Schedule
Probability to Success	Resource Coordination
Collateral Benefit	Non-Performance Penalties
Overall Strategic Value	Overall Feasibility

- *Elements of Opportunity*
  - *Corporate Direction Match*: refers to how consistent the opportunity is with your core business or corporate direction for new business. Companies have a much higher probability of winning and being successful during delivery when the opportunity is consistent with their core business and strategic direction. One way to make this assessment is to honestly ask yourself how perfect an example this opportunity is of the kind of new business your company is seeking.
  - *Competitive Environment*: refers to whether you or one of your competitors is perceived by the customer as the solution leader and is favored as the solution supplier. Opportunities where the customer perceives your company as the leader and is the favored supplier (for reasons other than price) are highly desirable. Customer's may have this perception due to technology, reputation, past experience, industry commitment, and so on. Of course, the customer may perceive your competitor as the leader for the same reasons.
  - *Revenue Value*: refers to the dollar value of the opportunity. The intent is to distinguish "small" from "large" revenue opportunities. Obviously, this needs to be assessed in the context of the size of your company and the typical size and currency of new opportunities. Since exact pricing has yet to be developed, develop your best estimate and focus only on near-term revenues, such as those likely to be generated in the first year of contract delivery.

- *Potential Profitability*: refers to the likely margins on the business given the competitive environment and what it will take to win. Most companies have guidelines on profitability of new opportunities, which should serve as the basis to assess how "rich" or "poor" the margins are likely to be. Be sure to estimate this based on the near-term margins and do not include margins on future business.
- *In-House Content*: refers to the percentage of the products or services which will be provided by your company. Frequently, opportunities require some outside supplier product or service; however, ideally all or the vast majority of the products and services are from within your company. You will always have a higher probability of success with what you know best which are products and services from your own company.
- *Future Business Potential*: refers to the degree to which this opportunity will impact additional business beyond the scope of the specific opportunity. For example, the opportunity may be a means to enter a new account or protect an existing account. Consider the degree to which specific identifiable future business is dependent upon winning and successfully delivering this business.
- *Resources to Bid*: refers to the amount of resources required to bid and the impact pursuit of this opportunity will have on other opportunities being pursued. Opportunities do not exist in a vacuum and all companies have resource constraints, so one needs to consider the "opportunity cost" of not pursuing or jeopardizing other opportunities. Conversely, you may have resources or assets which are idle that you wish to keep engaged and active to positively impact resource or asset utilization.
- *Probability of Success*: refers to the likelihood that you will win the business versus one of your competitors.
- *Collateral Benefit*: refers to the degree to which pursuit of this opportunity will improve the existing skill level or develop new skills which will benefit other opportunities or future business. Since additional work typically improves existing skill levels, consider the degree to which this opportunity will exceed the norm or have a wide-scale impact on a large population.
- *Overall Strategic Value*: refers to the overall need to win the opportunity as assessed by the sales manager or key account manager. This should be based upon consideration

of all of the opportunity elements, along with any other tangible or intangible aspects of the opportunity that are considered relevant.

- *Elements of Risk*
  - *Customer Commitment*: refers to the degree to which the customer has demonstrated a solid commitment to implement the solution offered in the opportunity. Typically this type of commitment is demonstrated through either budgeting for the implementation in a current or future business plan or identifying and assigning resources to support the implementation.
  - *Corporate Competence*: refers to your company's past experience or core competencies to deliver the solution required in the opportunity. The more past experience your company has in projects exactly like this one, the lower the risk. Conversely, if this type of project has never been successfully completed by any company in the past, then there is a tremendous risk with this opportunity.
  - *External Obstacles*: refers to the degree to which roadblocks exist that are beyond the control of either your customer or your company. A good example of this would be if your customer were a regulated utility that must obtain approval from a state or federal authority before they can implement the opportunity. Another example might be if your customer has yet to secure the capital needed to fund the implementation during a period when capital is tightly constrained.
  - *Opportunity Engagement*: refers to the degree to which your company or your competitors were involved in establishing the customer's requirements. If you did not help your customer develop their requirements, chances are one of your competitor's did. The more involved your were in establishing the requirements the more strengths your products and services will have and the more weaknesses your competitor's products and services will have.
  - *Solution Life-Cycle Match*: refers to the degree to which your solution involves the use of existing mature products versus new products or leading edge technology. If your solution involves mature products available today, your risk of the solution not working is very low. On the other hand, if your solution involves many new products which have yet

to be released or are based on leading edge technology, you have a risk of encountering development delays or the products not working as planned.

- *Period of Performance*: refers to the length of the contract. The longer the contract the greater the chance of significant changes. Personnel, customer environment and business climate are a few examples of changes which can introduce risk impacting the project.
- *Delivery Schedule*: refers to when delivery is required and who controls the schedule. The ideal situation is if the schedule is flexible and can be set by your company thus ensuring you have adequate time to be successful. Conversely, if your customer has already fixed the delivery schedule and identified penalties for missing schedules, you will be assuming a risk associated with missing deliveries. Keep in mind that while delivery schedules are typically an issue when too short, there can be situations where the delivery schedule is so far in the future that you may have risks ensuring the products you plan to deliver will still be in manufacture.
- *Resource Coordination*: refers to the number of internal groups in your company or external suppliers that must be engaged to deliver the solution. The larger the number of internal groups required, the more coordination required to ensure successful delivery and the higher the risk of having a disconnect and delivery problem. Coordination of outside suppliers introduces even more risk as you typically have more control over internal groups than external suppliers to resolve problems.
- *Non-Performance Penalties*: refers to the degree to which your customer has specified penalties for failure to deliver as promised. If your customer has not specified penalties or you can negotiate them with the customer, then you can minimize the risks. If your customer has specified monetary or other penalties which are non-negotiable, then your risk is increased.
- *Overall Feasibility*: refers to the degree of feasibility of the project as assessed by a knowledgeable representative of the group in your company accountable to deliver the solution. A major factor to consider in assessing feasibility is past experience with the customer on fulfilling their obligations or addressing unforeseen problems equitably. If the project is extremely complex and the customer has a poor track record of supporting complex projects there is a high risk of failure.

Opportunity—Risk Assessment Tool

If we take each of the above elements of opportunity, we can use a four-point scale to assess each element, as shown below in Form 3-1. Because all elements do not have equal import, we must also multiply this raw 1-to-4 score by a weight to develop a weighted score. These weighted scores can then be totaled to derive a Total Weighted Opportunity Score which can be plotted on the Opportunity axis of the Opportunity-Risk Assessment Grid.

Form 3-1. Opportunity Quantification Tool

Opportunity Element	Score				Weight	Weighted Score
	1	2	3	4		
Corporate Direction Match	Counter to core business and corporate direction	Neutral to core business and corporate direction	Partially aligned to core business and corporate direction	Fully aligned to core business and corporate direction	6	
Competitive Environment	Competitor is clear leader and is favored by customer	Customer favors the competitor and is neutral to your company	No clear leader and customer has no supplier preference	Your company is clear leader and is favored by customer	5	
Revenue Value	Geater than $500K	Between $500K and $2.5M	Between $2.5M and $5M	Over $5M	4	
Potential Profitability	Profitabilty is Negative or Break Even	Profitability is between 0-50% of corporate requirements	Profitability is between 50-100% of corporate requirements	Profitability is over 100% of corporate requirements	4	
In-House Content	Less than 50% of content is from your company	Between 50-75% of content is from your company	Between 75-90% of content is from your company	Over 90% of content is from your company	4	
Future Business Potential	Little or no connection to future business	Possible link to future business	Likely link to future business	Assured or mandatory link to future business	3	
Resources to Bid	Will significantly drain resources working on other opportunities	Will drain some resources working on other opportunities	Will have little or no impact on resources working on other opportunities	Will use resources currently underutilized	3	
Probability of Success	Probability of success is near zero	Probability of success is less than 50%	Probabilty of success is over 50%	Success is almost certain	3	
Collateral Benefit	Little or no benefit to other projects or new company skills	Some benefit to either other projects or new company skills	Some benefit to both other projects and new company skills	Significant benefit to other projects or new company skills	3	
Overall Strategic Value	It is of low importance that your company win this business	It is somewhat important that your company win this business	It is of high importance that your company win this business	It is critical that your company win this business	5	
Total Weighted Opportunity Score						

Case Study—IBM (Global Services)

IBM has a long and well deserved reputation for being very proactive with their customers. The company has for many years taken great pride in its ability to understand customers business needs and develop products, services and/or solutions to satisfy those needs. IBM also has a well established business practice of evaluating both business opportunities and risks. Account executives and project managers conduct a thorough opportunity and risk assessment for each deal.

To help mitigate business risks, IBM seeks to not only understand their customer's business situation, but to influence the customer's selection process by which they purchase products and/or services. At IBM Global Services they have an old saying "No Blind-Bids." In other words, IBM always wants to know the customer's needs, the risks and the opportunities before a solicitation document (i.e., Invitation To Bid, Request for Proposal, etc.) is ever issued by a customer. At IBM opportunity and risk assessment is a proven best practice and an essential part of their business processes.

Case Study—Boeing (Military Aircraft)

As companies become more successful in dealing with challenges, risk management becomes a structured process that is performed continuously throughout the business life-cycle. Such is the case at Boeing Military Aircraft, where designing, manufacturing and delivering aircraft can take years and require a multi-billion dollar investment. Typically, Boeing evaluates the following risk categories and develops detailed risk mitigation strategies and actions to improve their business case by reducing or eliminating potential negative aspects.

Risk Categories at Boeing, include:

- *Financial:* Up-front funding and payback period based upon number of planes sold.
- *Market:* Forecasting customer's expectations on cost, configuration and amenities based on 30 to 40 year life of a plane.
- *Technical:* Must forecast technology and its impact on cost, safety, reliability and maintainability.
- *Production:* Supply-Chain Management of a large number of subcontractors without impacting cost, schedule, quality or safety.

If we use the same methodology for risk, as is shown on Form 3-2, we can similarly develop Total Weighted Risk Score which can then be plotted on the Risk axis of the Opportunity-Risk Assessment Grid.

Form 3-2. Risk Quantification Tool

Risk Element	Score				Weight	Weighted Score
	1	2	3	4		
Customer Commitment	Customer has assigned budget and personnel	Customer has assigned budget but not personnel	Customer has assigned personnel but not budget	Customer has not assigned personnel or budget	6	
Corporate Competence	Complete replication of past projects done by your company	More than 50% replication of past projects done by your company	Less than 50% replication of past projects done by your company	No replication of past projects done by your company	5	
External Obstacles	No obstacles exist which are outside control of customer	Some obstacles - customer is actively working to address each	Some obstacles - customer has plan to address each	Significant obstacles, customer has no plan developed to address each	4	
Opportunity Engagement	Your company developed requirements for the customer	Your company guided customer in devleopment of requirements	Your company provided comments after requirements were developed	Your company had no involvement in developing requirements	4	
Solution Life-Cycle Match	All requirements can be met by mature, released products	Less than 30% of products will be pre-released or new products	Between 30-70% of products will be pre-released or new products	over 70% of products will be pre-released or new products	4	
Period of Performance	Contract is for less than 6 months	Contract is between 6 months and 1 year	Contract is between 1 year and 3 years	Contract is over 3 years	3	
Delivery Schedule	Delivery schedule is flexible and will be set by your company	Delivery schedule to be negotiated by customer and your company	Delivery schedule is fixed, but no penalties for missed dates	Delivery schedule is fixed and penalties exist for missed dates	3	
Resource Coordination	Need to coordinate less than 5 groups in your company	Need to coordinate 5 or more groups in your company	Need to coordinate company groups and up to 2 outside suppliers	Need to coordinate company groups and 3 or more outside suppliers	3	
Non-Performance Penalties	No penalties for non-performance	Penalties to be negotiated between customer and your company	Fixed monetary penalties for non-performance with a limit	Fixed monetary penalties for non-performance with no limit	3	
Overall Feasibility / Risk	Project is feasible and risks are manageable	Project is feasible but risks require mitigation	Project has some elements which are questionable but risks can be mitigated	Project has questionable feasibility and very high risks	5	
Total Weighted Risk Score						

You can adapt and modify the Opportunity and Risk Quantification Tools, Forms 3-1 and 3-2, based on the particulars of our business and past experience. The key to effective Opportunity and Risk Qualification is to ensure you have a consistent assessment methodology so opportunities can be compared and prioritized. Use of such tools is invaluable for improving your sales representatives' productivity by directing them away from quadrant D opportunities (i.e., low opportunity -high risk) and focusing their energies on quadrant A opportunities (i.e., high opportunity low risk) and the high-end quadrant B and C opportunities (i.e., low opportunity-low risk and high opportunity-high risk above the bid line).

Gather Competitive Intelligence

Having done an initial qualification of the opportunity and risks, the next step in the Opportunity Profile stage is to Gather Competitive Intelligence. Basic information to be collected includes: 1) who are the competitors or competitive teams, 2) what is the solution you believe they will bid, 3) what are the strengths of the competitor or their solution and 4) what are the weaknesses of the competitor or their solution.

- *Competitor Profile:* This information should be documented for future use and review using a template such as the one below, Form 3-3.

Form 3-3. Competitor Profile

Rank	Competitor or Competing Team	Solution Being Bid	Strengths of Competitor and Solution	Weaknesses of Competitor and Solution
1				
2				
3				
4				
5				

- *Sources of Competitive Intelligence:* The term "Competitive Intelligence" refers to information on competitors or competitive teams that is specific to the opportunity. This is in contrast to "Market Intelligence," which is general information on your competitors or competitive teams operating in the marketplace or industry. While Market Intelligence should not be discarded as an input, the real value comes from understanding what can and should be collected from a variety of sources. This not only increases the amount of intelligence gathered, but will serve to validate information by confirming it from multiple sources. Care should be taken, however, to ensure that any and all competitive intelligence is gathered legally and ethically. For example, in addition to understanding your company's rules on soliciting information, it is equally important to understand your customer's rules regarding discussions with customer personnel and access to customer information that is part of the source selection process.

Table 3-2 shows typical sources of competitive intelligence:

Table 3-2. Sources of Competitive Intelligence
■ Public press releases
■ Public websites
■ Public brochures
■ Public advertisements
■ Articles in trade publications
■ Past bids by your company to this customer
■ Past bids by your company to similar customers
■ Customer list of companies requesting solicitation*
■ Customer conversations*
■ Customer events and meetings*
■ Trade or Industry Associations
■ Competitive research or analysis companies

* Which do not violate your company's or competitor's rules on disclosure

Develop a Win Strategy

- *Win Strategy:* Having gathered Competitive Intelligence, the next step is to Develop a Win Strategy. A Win Strategy is a collection of messages or points designed to guide the customer's perception of you, your solution and your competitors.

- *Sweet Spot-Sour Spot Analysis:* Perhaps one of the best ways to graphically depict the elements of a win strategy is to use the concept of "Sweet Spot" and "Sour Spot" as presented by David G. Pugh, PhD. of the Lore International Institute in his article "A Bidder's Dozen: Golden Rules For Winning Work." The "Sweet Spot – Sour Spot" model, shown below in Figure 3-5, depicts the relationship of your company's strengths and weaknesses to the customer's needs and the strengths and weaknesses of your competitors. The "Sweet Spot" is where your company's strengths meet the customer's needs and coincide with your competitor's weaknesses. Conversely, the "Sour Spot" is where your competitor's strengths meet the customer's needs and coincide with your company's weaknesses.

  The objective of a Win Strategy is to maximize the importance of your "Sweet Spot" to your customer and simultaneously minimize the importance of your "Sour Spot." This requires considerable time and effort, as your competitors will likely be trying to do the exact opposite. Win Strategies which maximize the "Sweet Spot" are messages or points that highlight your strengths and amplify or "ghost" your competitor's weaknesses. Win Strategies which minimize your "Sour Spot" are messages or points which mitigate your weaknesses and neutralize your competitor's strengths.

Figure 3-5. Sweet Spot—Sour Spot Analysis

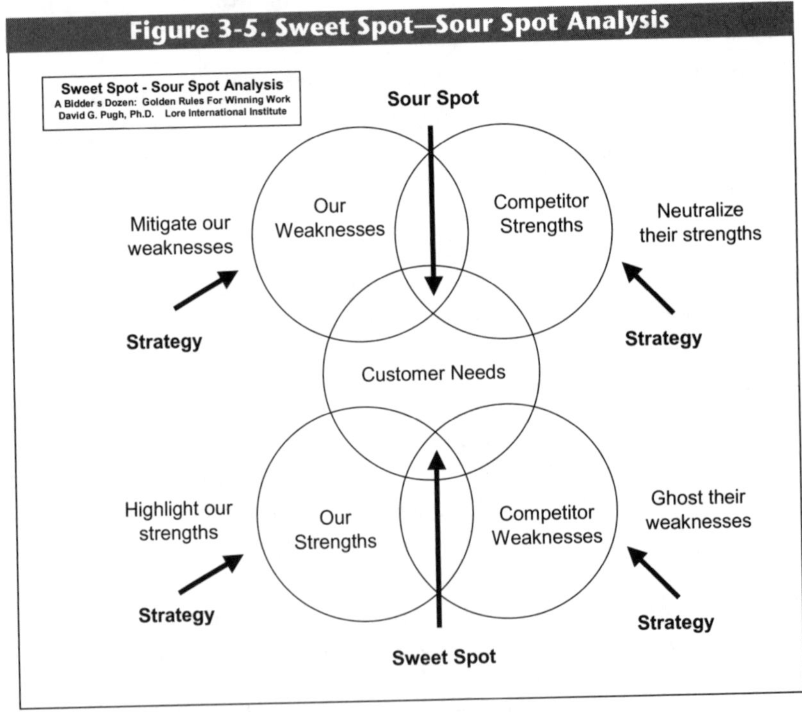

Changing customer perceptions requires repetitive communication of a consistent message to numerous individuals in the customer organization. The most effective strategies are those which can be translated into straightforward "themes" or "phrases" which differentiate you from your competitor. These "themes" or "phrases" can then be delivered to your customer in sales calls, executive contacts, proposals, presentations, advertisements and all forms of communication over a period of time, thus changing perceptions.

Your strategies should also focus on the points which are the most significant to your customer in-terms of impact on their business problem or objective. The proverbial "80-20 Rule" is a good guide to use to determine significance. Typically, 20% of the requirements account for 80% of the value, and conversely, the remaining 80% only account for 20% of the value. Ideally, you will want to position your "Sweet Spot" as being part of the 20% which creates 80% of the value, and your "Sour Spot" as being part of the other 80% which only has minimal impact (i.e., 20%).

One successful technique to develop win strategies is to gather a core team of individuals and hold a Strategy Session. During this session you should attempt to board and map the "Sweet Spot" and "Sour Spot" and develop strategies to address each. You want to keep this group small, but try to include a knowledgeable individual from each of the following areas:

- Sales or marketing
- Manufacturing or supply chain
- Engineering or technical support
- Program management or product/service delivery
- Contracting or legal
- Finance or business management

- *Win Theme and Strategies Form:* You will want to succinctly capture your Win Theme and Win Strategies for review with the Stakeholders and later as a guide for the Capture Team. Form 3-4 is an example of a Win Theme and Strategy form which can be used for this purpose.

Form 3-4.Win Themes and Strategies
Win themes:
Strategies to maximize our strengths:
Strategies to minimize our weaknesses:
Strategies to neutralize competitor's strengths:
Strategies to ghost competitor's weaknesses:

Customer Positioning Plan: As part of executing your Win Strategy you should proactively communicate your messages to the customer through various channels, in addition to your formal response or proposal. A key channel for communication is the relationship and regular contact between key customers and individuals in your company, referred to as Customer Positioning. As part of enhancing the impact of Customer Positioning, you should seize opportunities for potential customer contact by identifying major events or planned meetings and orchestrating the participation and messages to be communicated by key individuals from your company. You should also develop documented plans to address each of these.

Form 3-5, *Customer Positioning Planner,* can be used to match key customers with the appropriate contact in your company to develop relationships. The planner allows you to show the name, title, and role of each key customer along with a primary and secondary contact from your company and the type and frequency of contact. Types of contact include phone calls, personal meetings, dinner or entertainment, and frequency of contact includes weekly, bi-weekly, monthly and as-needed. You should match "like-for-like." For example, you would likely want to match the CEO of your company as the primary contact with the CEO of your customer's company with your President as the secondary contact. This will allow you and the executives in your company to establish a regular schedule of contact with your key customers.

Form 3-5. Customer Positioning Planner

Customer Position	Customer Name	Role		Primary Contact	Secondary Contact	Frequency of Contact *			
		Decision Maker	Influencer			Phone Call	Personal Meeting	Dinner	Entertainment

* Weekly, Bi-Weekly, Monthly, As-Needed

- *Customer Contact Plan*–In addition, the Customer Contact Planner, Form 3-6 below, can be used to manage contacts between key customers and individuals in your company at major events or planned meetings. This planner provides space to identify the event, date, purpose of the event, specific objective(s) you want to achieve, customer participants and participants from your company. Examples of events you may want to manage include: trade shows, sporting events, briefings, seminars, etc. This will allow you and the executives in your company to keep track of major events they need to plan to participate in to effectively establish and build relationships with key customers.

Form 3-6. Customer Contact Planner

Customer:			Prepared by:		Date:
Date	Event	Purpose	Objective(s)	Customer Participants	Your Company Participants

Outline the Opportunity

Having Developed a Win Strategy, the next step is to Outline the Opportunity and develop material to review with stakeholders to solicit their buy-in to pursue the opportunity. While you should customize this to your company and your business, below is an outline of the basic information you will want to document into some type of presentation for review.

- *Outline of Offer for Stakeholder Opportunity Review:* The format and size of the presentation will vary depending upon such factors as the scope of the opportunity, the number and level of the stakeholders, and the resource commitment required. Whether you opt to standardize on viewgraphs or in a written narrative format, the important thing is to document the opportunity in a form that can be shared and updated as the opportunity is pursued and more information is obtained. If using viewgraphs, be sure to match the size of the presentation to the opportunity. Presentations on smaller opportunities should be kept to one slide per category, while larger projects may require one or more slides per subject to provide an adequate review.

- *Introduction:* all Stakeholder Opportunity Reviews should start with a clear declaration and review of the Purpose, Agenda, Limit and Participants. This will ensure that everyone understands why they are there (i.e., the purpose), the topics to be covered (i.e., the agenda), how much time is allotted for the meeting (i.e., the limit), and most importantly, who is in the meeting and their role (i.e., the participants). An easy way to remember this is to memorize the saying "be a PAL to Participants," where "P" is purpose, "A" is agenda and "L" is limit.

  The Purpose of the stakeholder review, illustrated in Table 3-2 below, is typically to: a) review the opportunity, b) make a bid / no bid decision, c) solicit resource commitment and 4) establish escalation support. The Agenda lists the topics covered, in sequence, along with the presenters who will cover each topic. The Limit is the time allotted to the meeting. The Participants are the stakeholders, listed by name, title and functional responsibility.

  Unless all of the stakeholders and everyone who will work on the opportunity knows your customer thoroughly, you should prepare a Customer Profile. While stakeholders may have a general familiarity with your customer, you should ensure that all the stakeholders have a common appreciation for the customer's business so they can truly evaluate the opportunity and risks. Additionally, the customer profile can also be used as a reference document to introduce others to the opportunity.
- *Customer Profile*: should briefly cover three subjects: 1) Customer Business, 2) Your Presence and 3) Competitor Presence. Customer Business refers to demographics of your customer's enterprise and would include such information as mission statement, market strategy, target markets, market share, annual revenues, number of employees and/or locations and geography. Your Presence refers to your existing business with the customer, which is typically expressed in-terms of the quantities or values of past products and services purchased and the percentage of the customer's past purchases spent with your company. Competitor Presence refers to the existing business your customer has with competitors and is expressed in similar terms.
- *Opportunity Profile:* should briefly cover six subjects: 1) Problem, 2) Solution, 3) Contract, 4) Basic Scope, 5) Optional Scope and

6) Key Dates. Problem refers to the business problem your customer is trying to solve or the objective they are trying to achieve, which should be articulated as concisely and directly as possible. Solution refers to how you will potentially solve the customer's business problem including the major products and services you will use from your company and any outside products and services required. Contract refers to the anticipated type and term or length of the contract which is anticipated. Basic scope refers to the minimum or obligated geography or locations involved and the estimated value and/or quantities of major products and services. Optional scope refers to geography, locations, products or services, which the customer may or may not purchase. Key Dates refers to major milestones such as bid response date, anticipated contract signing date, first delivery date and end of contract date.

- *Competitor Profile:* should briefly cover: 1) Competitors, 2) Solutions, 3) Strengths and 4) Weaknesses. Competitors refers to the specific competitors or competitive teams, by name, pursuing this specific opportunity. Solution refers to the solution you anticipate each competitor or competitive team will offer to solve the customer's business problem. Strengths and Weaknesses refer to the specific strengths and weaknesses of the competitor or their solution. This information should have been captured and documented on the Competitor Profile form presented earlier.
- *Win Strategy:* should briefly cover: 1) Theme, 2) Sweet Spot, 3) Sour Spot and 4) Positioning Plan. Theme refers to the overarching message(s) to be conveyed to the customer in all communications of "how and why" you can solve the customer's problem. Sweet Spot and Sour Spot refers to the specific messages designed to maximize your Sweet Spot and minimize your Sour Spot to support your win strategy. Positioning Plan refers to the specific plans developed to communicate these messages to your customer, including such tactics as executive visits, briefings, tours, etc.
- *Issues/Concerns:* should briefly cover: 1) Product/Service gaps, 2) Availability gaps, 3) Resource gaps and 4) Contract issues. Product/Service gaps refers to any major gap between your product/service and the customer's requirements. Availability gaps refers to either the need to commit to requirements which your company has identified as a future capability but has yet to be funded for development

or the need to deliver a product or service prior to the currently planned release schedule. Resource gaps refer to shortages or mis-matches in availability, skill set or funding for required resources for either the response or the delivery. Contract issues refers to terms, conditions or liabilities which are outside the norm for your company for an opportunity of this type.

- *Response Requirements*: should briefly cover: 1) Timeline, 2) People Resources and 3) Other Resources. Timeline refers to the key milestones and dates required to develop an offer and prepare a deliverable document for the customer, whether it be in response to a customer solicitation or a proactive proposal. People Resources refers to the quantity and skill set of individuals required to develop the response. Other Resources refers to non-personnel resources required to develop the response and may include such items as lab equipment, travel and living expenses, proposal production costs and/or outside consulting costs. Together the People Resources and Other Resources represent the "resource commitment" you are asking the stakeholders to spend to pursue the opportunity.
- *Bid / No Bid Decision*: should briefly cover: 1) Stakeholder Commitment and 2) Action Items. Stakeholder Commitment refers to soliciting a clear commitment from the stakeholders that they: a) fully support development of the response, b) agree to promptly assign resources, c) agree to be a point of escalation to help resolve roadblocks and d) agree to meet again to review and approve the response prior to customer submittal. These above categories and subjects are summarized below in Table 3-3.

Case Study—NCR (Professional Services)

More than 10 years ago, NCR Professional Services formalized their Bid/No Bid Decision Making process by including a tool which enabled them to assess both the opportunities and risks pertaining to a possible deal in a more objective and quantifiable manner. NCR calls their Bid/No Bid decisionmaking support tool the "Project Opportunity and Risk Assessment" (PORA). PORA allows NCR to identify opportunities and risks, assess probability, assess monetary impact and determine the expected monetary value associated with the overall business scenario in a timely, cost effective and automated manner.

Table 3-3. Outline for Stakeholder Opportunity Review

Category	Subject	Suggested Topics or Contents
Introduction	Purpose	Purpose is typically to: 1) review opportunity, 2) make bid/no bid decision, 3) solicit resource commitment and 4) establish escalation support.
	Agenda	Agenda is typically the topics covered, in sequence, with presenters.
	Limit	Identify time allotted for meeting.
	Participants	List of stakeholders with name, title and functional responsibility.
Customer Profile	Customer Business	Customer mission and market strategy, size of their business (e.g. market share, annual revenues, customers, employees, locations, etc.).
	Your Presence	Existing business with customer (e.g. products/services, value, units, etc.).
	Competitor Presence	Competitor's business with customer (e.g. products/services, value, units, etc.).
Opportunity Profile	Problem	Concise explanation of the customer's business problems and/or objectives.
	Solution	Concise explanation of your potential solution identifying major products/services and any outside products/services required.
	Contract	Anticipated type and term of contract.
	Basic Scope	Primary geography/locations involved, major products/services with estimated volume in dollars and/or units over life of contract.
	Optional scope	Optional geography/locations involved, major products/services with estimated volume in dollars and units over life of contract.
	Key Dates	Bid response date, contract signing date, first delivery date, end of contract date.
Competitor Profile	Competitors	Competitor's or competing teams in order from toughest to weakest.
	Solution	Potential solution(s) bidding against.
	Strengths	Strengths of competitor and solution.
	Weaknesses	Weakness of competitor and solution.
Win Strategy	Theme	Theme with basic "message" on how/why you will solve problem the best.
	Sweet Spot	Strategy to maximize strengths.
	Sour Spot	Strategy to neutralize competitor's strengths.
	Positioning Plan	Matrix matching your executives with key customers and actions required.
Issues/ Concerns	Product/Service	Gaps in product/service with requirements, development funding and time required, mismatch of delivery interval with product/service availability.
	Resources	Gap in availability, skill set or funding for required resources for response or delivery.
	Contract	Terms, conditions or liabilities outside norm for your firm for this kind of business.

Table 3-3 Cont'd. Outline for Stakeholder Opportunity Review

Response Requirements	Timeline	Timeline showing key milestones in development of response.
	People Resources	Chart showing resources required by function or skill set to develop response.
	Other Resources	List of non-people resources required to develop response, such as: lab equipment, travel and living, proposal production costs, outside consultants, etc.
Bid/No Bid Decision	Stakeholder Commitment	Ensure stakeholder's understand they are committing to: 1) fully support development of bid response, 2) promptly assign resources, 3) resolve roadblocks and 4) meet again to review and approve response prior to submittal.
	Action Items	Matrix showing action items identified and assigned during stakeholder meeting.

Outputs

At the completion of the Opportunity Profile Stage you should have:

- *A Qualified Opportunity*
- *Competitor Profile*
- *Win Strategy*
- *Outline of Offer for Stakeholder Opportunity Review*

Stakeholder Buy-In Stage

Having completed the Opportunity Profile stage, the next stage of the Capture Management Life-Cycle is to solicit Stakeholder Buy-In. All of the inputs, tools/techniques and outputs of the Stakeholder Buy-In stage are reflected below in Figure 3-6. The objectives or desired outputs of the Stakeholder Buy-In stage are: 1) Bid/No Bid Decision, 2) Strategy Alignment, 3) Resource Commitment and 4) Escalation Support.

Inputs

If you successfully completed all the steps described in the Opportunity Profile Stage, you will have created all the inputs required for the Stakeholder Buy-In Stage. These are:

- *A Qualified Opportunity*
- *Competitor Profile*
- *Win Strategy*
- *Outline of Offer for Stakeholder Opportunity Review*

If you do not have all these inputs, refer to the appropriate step in the Opportunity Profile stage to create the missing item(s).

Tools & Techniques

- *Stakeholder Opportunity Review:* Countless opportunities are lost and resources wasted by failing to properly solicit and secure Stakeholder By-In. This is especially true for larger companies, and in industries where technology and supply channels change rapidly and frequently. Each of these factors means changes in the fundamental relationship between your company, your customer and your competitors. One can not assume support based on a set of "fixed rules." Rather, one must solicit and positively confirm support since there is a set of "dynamic rules" which are constantly changing, thus allowing you to stay one step ahead of the competition.

The most frequently asked questions regarding Stakeholders are: "who are stakeholders" and "how do I identify them?" According to Kevin Forsberg, Ph.D. and Hall Mooz, in the best seller "Visualizing Project Management," a stakeholder is "any individual, group or organization that can affect, or be affected by, the project." Operationally, stakeholders are individuals who can make commitments on behalf of key groups or organizations in your company. For most opportunities, you should include representatives from the following groups organizations:

- Sales or marketing
- Manufacturing or supply chain
- Engineering or technical support
- Program management or product/service delivery
- Contracting or legal
- Finance or business management
- If product/service or availability issues, include a representative from Product Management or Research & Development

Another frequently asked question is "what level are stakeholders?" It is essential to ensure you have stakeholders authorized to make commitments. However, you need to match the level to the size of the commitment required. While you don't want to waste the time of executives to review opportunities that could be approved by subordinates, you do want to ensure you have a commitment from someone with proper authority. Most companies have a "Schedule of Authorizations" or "Schedule of Approvals" which identifies the type and dollar value of commitment that can be made by individuals at various levels, which is an excellent guide for ascertaining the "right level" stakeholder. If due to schedule availability, you opt to not include stakeholder(s) who need to approve the final bid, you will have to account for this additional approval step in your Capture Project Plan work tasks and timeline.

- *Tips for an Effective Opportunity Stakeholder Review:* A common mistake made, especially by large companies, is to minimize the number of stakeholders whose support is solicited. Frequently this is done to avoid or "go around" individuals who are known as being negative or difficult. Be careful in opting to exclude stakeholders. The individuals who have the biggest objections or concerns are exactly the people you need to get aligned with the solution and strategy. If you don't get these stakeholders "on board with the plan," you will likely encounter problems during the Bid Phase.

Another common mistake is for a sales representative to attempt to gain support from the CEO, President or a senior executive in their company and use this as "unconditional authority" to pursue an opportunity. While this approach is certainly easier and less time consuming on the sales representative, it is also a recipe for disaster. Despite a decree from a senior executive in your company identifying the opportunity as a "must win," you still need to solicit stakeholder support to obtain alignment on strategy, get resources committed, and establish escalation support to resolve problems. On a related note, over time you should find that you have fewer and fewer "No Bids." This is generally a sign that your sales representatives have become better at qualifying opportunities and discarding those which are poor.

Like all group meetings, there is art to effectively managing a Stakeholder Review, especially if it involves senior executives in your company. Form 3-7 provides a checklist of tips to improve the effectiveness of your Stakeholder Opportunity Review.

Form 3-7. Checklist of Tips for an Effective Stakeholder Opportunity Review

Prior to the meeting:

- ❑ Pick a time for the meeting which maximizes stakeholder participation and provide adequate notification
- ❑ Confirm stakeholder participation and have stakeholders who cannot attend identify an authorized delegate
- ❑ Minimize the inclusion of individuals other than the stakeholders or presenters at the review
- ❑ Ensure presenters understand their material, the agenda and the time each has been allotted.

If the review will be via conference call:

- ❑ Distribute presentation materials in-advance of the meeting
- ❑ Take role of participants as they "beep in" to ensure there are no unauthorized participants
- ❑ If possible use a unique bridge number for the review to reduce risk of uninvited participants
- ❑ Have participants put all speakerphones on "mute" to reduce background noise
- ❑ Have participants on cell or cordless phones with excessive noise drop-off and call-back on a different phone

During the meeting:

- ❑ Introduce yourself as the individual running the review
- ❑ Review the Purpose, Agenda and Limit for the review
- ❑ Introduce the stakeholders being sure to identify their role/accountability
- ❑ Keep track of time and "prod" presenters to move along if they are taking too long
- ❑ Do not try to solve problems on the call, identify them as action items and assign a owner to resolve each item
- ❑ Allow for adequate discussion, but do not permit endless debating or "grandstanding"
- ❑ Explain to stakeholders what you are asking them to commit to with their vote
- ❑ Perform a "roll call" of stakeholders where each stakeholder must vote "yes" or "no"
- ❑ If a stakeholder votes "no," have them explain why and make the issue an action item so they can vote "yes"

After the meeting:

- ❑ Update and redistribute the presentation with any material changes made during the review
- ❑ Document stakeholder participation and commitment as part of the updated presentation
- ❑ Share the updated presentation with those working on the opportunity to show stakeholder commitment

Outputs

At the completion of the Stakeholder Opportunity Review you want to have successfully obtained the following outputs -

Bid/No Bid Decision

The first objective, the Bid/No Bid Decision, refers to presenting the facts to the stakeholders so they understand the opportunity and the risks and make a reasoned decision to pursue the opportunity (bid) or to not pursue the opportunity (no bid). This should be done in as unbiased and objective manner as possible. The future of your company depends upon consistently making the best decisions on how to prioritize opportunities and commit scarce resources. Don't try to "white-wash" problems and don't try to over-sell the opportunity. Not only will you lose personal credibility over time, you will potentially cause your company to waste resources that could have been spent on a better opportunity.

Alignment on Strategy

The second objective, Alignment on Strategy, refers to ensuring all the stakeholders not only understand and agree to pursue the opportunity, but more importantly, are in alignment on the solution proposed and the win strategy. Alignment is defined by Webster's as "being in correct relative position to something else." This "alignment" is critical to ensuring everyone on the team is headed in the right direction, is conveying the correct message internally and to customers, and is not unintentionally creating problems or wasting resources on activities which are inconsistently with the win strategy.

Resource Commitment

The third objective, Resource Commitment, refers to ensuring all the stakeholders agree to provide the people and non-personnel resources needed to pursue the opportunity. Because many opportunities will operate on a fixed and short timeline, this commitment also means the resources will be provided when they are needed. It is always better to identify and highlight resource problems as early as possible in the process so there is time to develop a solution.

Escalation Support

The fourth objective, Escalation Support, refers to soliciting agreement from stakeholders that they will actively help resolve roadblocks. This item is frequently overlooked and taken as a "given," leading to undue problems and stress during the Bid Phase. There will most assuredly be problems during the Bid Phase and you will need to act quickly, so now is the best time to establish a rapport and expectation with the stakeholders that you are likely to call upon them for help.

Stakeholder Opportunity Review Package

The Stakeholder Opportunity Review Package should be updated after the session with any material changes which occurred during the presentation, as well as, recording Stakeholder participation on commitment. This package will serve as an excellent introduction of the opportunity to new team members and should be used at the Capture Team Kickoff during the Bid Phase for this purpose.

Capture Core Team

As part of the initial resource commitment, the Stakeholders should assign a Capture Core Team to develop the Capture Project Plan. This team should include a Capture Manager, Proposal Manager, Sales Leader, Technical Leader, Delivery Leader, Pricing Leader and Contracts Leader. The roles & responsibilities of each of these individuals is discussed in-depth in the next chapter.

Summary

Before proceeding to the Capture Project Plan stage of the Pre-Bid Phase, be sure to review the Input-Tools & Techniques-Output charts in this chapter and assess if you have successfully completed all the outputs identified. If you find gaps, go back and use the tools and techniques provided to complete the missing outputs.

Questions To Consider

1. How well does your organization qualify opportunities, gather competitive intelligence, develop win strategies, develop customer positioning plans and obtain stakeholder buy-in to pursue opportunities?

2. How effectively does your organization complete these activities? Do you walk away from poor opportunities? Do you know how to beat your competitors on factors other than price? Do you ensure stakeholder buy-in before capture resources are expended?

3. Does your organization have documented processes or tools & techniques used to qualify opportunities, gather competitive intelligence, develop win strategies, develop customer positioning plans and obtain stakeholder buy-in to pursue opportunities?

4. What actions have your organization taken to improve/develop opportunity qualification, competitive intelligence, win strategy, customer positioning planning or stakeholder buy-in skills for your sales managers, capture/proposal managers and contract managers?

5. How well does your organization document and share your opportunity qualification, competitive intelligence, win strategy, customer positioning planning and stakeholder buy-in lessons learned?

chapter

Pre-Bid Phase: Capture Project Plan

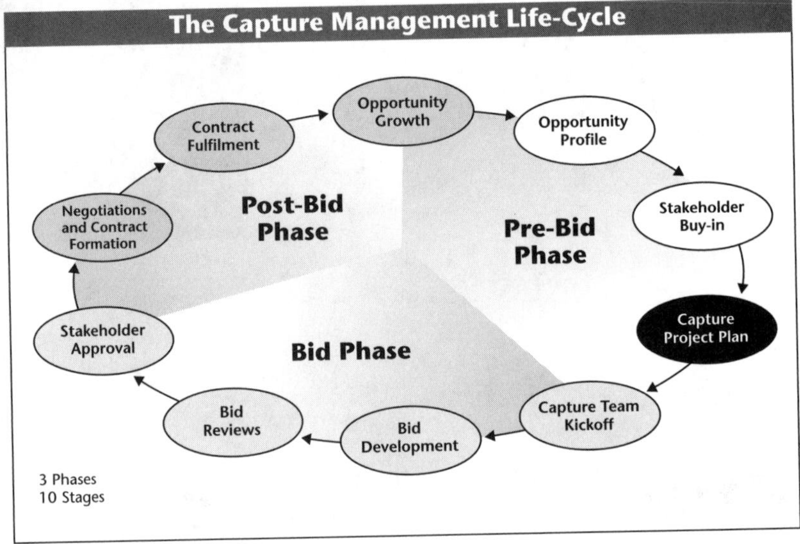

Introduction

The third stage of the Pre-Bid Phase is the Capture Project Plan. This stage is perhaps the most overlooked in the entire process and is the root of most problems. According to Kevin Forsberg, Ph.D. and Hal Mooz in Visualizing Project Management, "failure often results from fundamental confusion over precisely what is involved in managing a project successfully from inception through completion." Another more cryptic saying gets right to the point–"if you fail to plan, then you are planning to fail."

Capture Project Plan Stage

The objectives of the Capture Project Plan stage are to:

- *Identify the deliverables*
- *Identify the work tasks*
- *Identify the resources*
- *Identify the timeline*
- *Develop communication plans*

Each of these represents a step in the Capture Project Plan stage. While, in some stages, the order of the steps may be interchangeable, in this stage it is recommended that you follow the steps in the sequence presented as each step builds upon the preceding step. The following graphic (Figure 4-1) summarizes the Inputs, Tools & Techniques and Outputs covered in this chapter concerning the Capture Project Plan.

Figure 4-1. Pre-Bid Phase: Capture Project Plan Stage

Input	Tools & Techniques	Output
■ "Bid/No Bid" Decision ■ Alignment on Strategy ■ Resource Commitment ■ Escalation Support ■ Stakeholder Opportunity Review Package ■ Capture Core Team	■ Capture Core Team ❑ Capture Core Team Roles & Resp. ■ Deliverables ❑ Proposal Layout ❑ A Bidder's Dozen: Golden Rules ❑ Proposal Development Checklist ❑ Proposal Production Checklist ■ Work Tasks ❑ Work Breakdown Structure ■ Resources ❑ Organization Breakdown Structure ❑ Types of Team Structures ❑ Responsibility Assignment Matrix ❑ Opportunity Budget Plan ■ Timeline ❑ Types of Timelines ❑ Task List Schedule ■ Communication Plans ❑ Project Communication Plan ❑ Change Request Plan ❑ Alert-Jeopardy-Escalation Plan	■ Identified Deliverables ■ Identified Work Tasks ■ Identified Resources ■ Identified Timeline ■ Communication Plans

Inputs

Having successfully completed the Opportunity Profile and Stakeholder Buy-In stages, you will have produced the following outputs, described in Chapter 3, which are the inputs to the Capture Project Plan stage:

- *"Bid/No Bid" Decision*
- *Alignment on Strategy*
- *Resource Commitment*
- *Escalation Support*
- *Stakeholder Opportunity Review Package*
- *Capture Core Team*

Tools & Techniques

Capture Core Team

It is critical that you work with the Capture Core Team to create the Capture Project Plan for several reasons. First, and most obviously, it is unlikely that a single individual will be familiar with all the details of the what, who and when required. Second, a little less obvious but equally important, is that you want the team to support the plan created. It is much easier to obtain support if the individuals executing the plan are party to creating the plan. This "buy-in" for the plan starts by including the Capture Core Team in its creation.

- *Capture Core Team Roles and Responsibilities:* The Capture Core Team should be composed of the Capture Manager, Proposal Manager, Sales Leader, Technical Leader, Delivery Leader, Pricing Leader and Contractual Leader. On smaller opportunities, individuals may have multiple roles. For example you may have a combined Technical-Delivery or Pricing-Contractual Leader. Table 4-1 below summarizes the typical Roles & Responsibilities of each member of the Capture Core Team.

Tabel 4-1. Team Leader Roles & Responsibilities

Role	Responsibilities
Capture Manager	Creates Capture Plan, working with Team Leaders, including identification of deliverables, work tasks, resources and timeline
	Ensures information is communicated throughout team and between subteams
	Monitors work tasks to ensure overall timeline is met
	Manages Stakeholder Approval session and ensures company approvals are secured
	Oversees Alert-Jeopardy-Escalation Plan and ensures timely resolution of issues
	Oversees Change Control Plan and ensures approved changes are communicated to team
	Develops Risk Mitigation Plan working with Team Leaders
Proposal Manager	Acts as single point of contact regarding development of customer deliverables
	Collects inputs, edits, formats and produces finished deliverables
	Runs Pink Team and Red Team Reviews
	Oversees production, packaging and shipment of customer deliverables
Sales Leader	Acts as the single point of contact to address all customer matters
	Develops Win Themes and Strategies
	Leads completion of competitive assessment
	Translates customer business needs into technical and delivery requirements
	Serves as a surrogate for the customer to answer questions, provide assumptions and/or direction regarding missing or unclear information
	Writes Executive Summary
Technical Leader	Acts as the single point of contact to address all technical matters
	Identifies, organizes and directs technical personnel to complete technical response
	Identifies, organizes and directs technical support to design the solution
	Translates customer business needs into technical requirements for the solution
	Certifies that all components of the solution are properly reflected in the pricing
	Supports assessment of competitors solution technical strengths and weaknesses
	Identifies and recommends strategies to mitigate technical risks
Delivery Leader	Acts as the single point of contact to address all delivery matters
	Identifies, organizes and directs program management, order & billing, engineering, installation, documentation, training and OA&M personnel to complete delivery response
	Identifies, organizes and directs support resources to create a delivery plan
	Translates customer business needs into delivery requirements for the solution
	Certifies that all components of the delivery plan are properly reflected in the pricing
	Supports assessment of competitors solution delivery strengths and weaknesses
	Identifies and recommends strategies to mitigate delivery risks
Pricing Leader	Acts as single point of contact to address all pricing matters
	Identifies, organizes and directs pricing personnel to complete pricing response
	Supports business manager in development of business case
	Ensures appropriate approvals have been secured for pricing included in response
	Certifies pricing is complete and accurate
	Supports assessment of competitors solution pricing and creation of price targets
	Identifies and recommends strategies to mitigate pricing risks
Contractual Leader	Acts as single point of contact to address all contractual matters
	Identifies, organizes and directs contracts, legal and purchasing personnel to complete contractual response
	Certifies that all terms and conditions are consistent with company polices and that all contractual language has been properly approved
	Supports assessment of competitors solution contractual strengths and weaknesses
	Identifies and recommends strategies to mitigate contractual risk

Telecommunications Equipment Suppliers—Case Study

The past few years have been turbulent times for the global telecommunications industry. Once giant corporations with huge stock values, companies like *Cisco, Lucent Technologies, Motorola, Nortel Networks* and *Ericsson* have all fallen on difficult times, largely due to global economic downturns, reduction in customer capital investments, over-spending during the 1990s and numerous risky business decisions. Thus, the telecommunications equipment and service providers are facing extremely tough competition in the market for relatively fewer important big deals.

To help not only survive, but try to thrive during these challenging times in the telecom industry, companies like *Lucent Technologies* have worked hard to streamline their functional organizational structures into more integrated teams to both capture more business and improve execution of customer projects. Clearly, defining roles and responsibilities is vital to cost-effectively and efficiently winning more business and successfully delivering products, services and/or solutions on-time.

Like *Lucent, Motorola* and *Nortel Networks* have worked very hard during the past two years to streamline their functional silos into more closely aligned integrated project teams. Each company is striving to get closer to their respective customers to ensure they understand both what the customers need and what they can afford at this time of heavily reduced capital expenditures.

The major U.S. telecommunications service providers, (i.e., *Verizon, BellSouth, SBC* and *Qwest*) and the major U.S. wireless service providers, (i.e., *AT&T Wireless, Sprint, Cingular, Nextel, US Cellular, MetroPCS, Alltel* and others) have nearly all focused their capital investments on trying to get the most capacity out of their current equipment, thereby keeping their balance sheets as positive as possible. Clearly, the telecom equipment/service providers must continue to focus their reduced number of talented people on the needs of their customers in an integrated and cost-effective manner to survive this challenging period in their industry. Thus, capture management is critical to the future of the telecom suppliers.

Deliverables

The first step in creating the Capture Project Plan is to define the goal, which in this case consists of the deliverables which will be assembled to create a response or proposal for your customer. If your customer has created a solicitation document such as a Request For Information (RFI) or Request for Proposal (RFP) then the proposal layout or deliverables will likely be defined for you. If there is no customer solicitation document, or if it does not provide sufficient detail, then you will need to create one with the Capture Core Team. In addition to the customer deliverables, there will also be internal deliverables which need to be created to produce the customer deliverables.

- *Proposal Layout:* Typically, a proposal will include the following sections: 1) Executive Summary, 2) Technical Response, 3) Delivery Response, 4) Pricing Response and 5) Contractual Response. On smaller opportunities, you may see these sections combined. For example, it is common to combine Technical-Delivery and Pricing-Contractual responses. On some opportunities you may not see all sections required. For example, an RFI to "test the waters" on future technology may require only a Technical Response. Similarly, in multi-step procurements, which are common with the U.S. Government, you may prepare your Technical and Delivery response during step one and your Pricing and Contractual response during step two.

  Regardless of the sections required, the proposal layout should contain sufficient detail to provide direction to the team on the specific topics which will be described in each section of the response so the customer has a clear understanding of the solution offered. There are several techniques which can be used to create a proposal layout. If the format for the response will be a text document, the most common technique is to create an outline in the form of a "table of contents" listing each of the major topics and subtopics. If the format for the response will be a presentation (e.g., PowerPoint), the most common technique is to create an outline in the form of a "story board" which identifies the key messages and graphics used to reinforce the messages. Be sure the Win Themes and Strategies developed in the Opportunity Profile stage are integrated throughout the proposal layout.

  Form 4-1 below can be used to create the Proposal Layout. Note that it also includes columns to identify the owner of each section, support resources assigned and solicitation reference if you are working from a customer solicitation. While you may not have all the detailed writing assignments at this time, you will need to identify the owner of each section prior to the Capture Team Kickoff stage of the Bid Phase.

Form 4-1. Proposal Layout With Volume & Section Owner Assignments

Section	Owner	Support Resource	Solicitation Reference
Cover Letter	Sales Leader		
Executive Summary	Sales Leader		
Technical Response	Technical Leader		
Problem or Objective			
Solution			
Benefits			
Commitment to Quality			
Delivery Response	Delivery Leader		
Delivery Plan			
Delivery Services			
Delivery Schedule			
OA&M Plan			
Documentation			
Training			
Past Experience			
Pricing Response	Pricing Leader		
Customer Business Case			
Pricing and Incentives			
Contractual Response	Contractual Leader		
Terms & Conditions			
Letter of Intent			

When creating a Proposal Layout, always view it from the perspective of the reader or evaluator. You must gauge your response to the skill and experience level of the customers who will be reading each section. For example, are the customers reading the Technical Response engineers with extensive in-depth experience or business managers with little or no technical acumen? For some sections, it may be a mix of readers, in which case you should decide upon the target reader so the response is not too overwhelming or simplistic. If portions of a section will be read by different customers, you may want to consider writing each portion to a different target reader.

- *A Bidder's Dozen: Golden Rules:* The key to creating an effective proposal layout is having the right mindset it takes to win. David G. Pugh, Ph.D. of the Lore International Institute developed "A Bidder's Dozen: Golden Rules of Winning Work," Table 4-2, which succinctly captures the elements of the mindset needed to win more business.

Table 4-2. A Bidders Dozen: Golden Rules of Winning Work

1. First and foremost, a proposal is a sales document.
2. A proposal should not be an isolated event.
3. If you do not have an effective strategy or take the time to develop one, lower your price.
4. Customers do not buy what it is; they buy what it does for them. They buy benefits, not features.
5. In a proposal, you do not just sell here and there. You sell all the way through.
6. Virtual planning is virtually useless.
7. The audience, not the author, drives the design.
8. Ease of evaluation is a very real factor of success.
9. In the early phases of evaluation, they are not looking for the winner. They are looking for losers.
10. In most cases, proposals do not win contracts, but they can lose them in a heartbeat.
11. When writing a proposal, writing is the last thing you should do.
12. Win or lose, always debrief with the customer. If you have to choose, debrief after a win.
Source: A Bidder's Dozen: Golden Rules for Winning Work, David G. Pugh, Ph.D. - Lore International Institute

- *Proposal Development Checklist:* In addition to the Proposal Layout, you should define the process that will be used to develop the proposal and production requirements. The following two checklists, Forms 4-2 and 4-3, provide a set of questions to answer regarding the development and production of the proposal. Some of these questions may be answered by company policy or practices; others are response specific. You do not need to answer all of these questions at this time. However, you should assign owners to develop the answers for each prior to the Capture Team Kickoff stage of the Bid Phase.

Form 4-2. Proposal Development Checklist

		✔
Mechanics	What software applications and versions are to be used for each type of response (e.g., text, spreadsheet, graphics, drawings, etc.) ?	
	Is there a specific file naming convention to be followed ?	
	Is there a specific response format (e.g., start all responses with a solid bar followed by "Company 'x' Response:" in bold, followed by the response in unbolded italics, followed by another solid bar) ?	
	Will a response template be provided to writers ? If so, when and by whom ?	
	How and when should writers submit their responses and to whom ?	
	How does the writer make a change after they have submitted their response ?	
Style	Should responses by single, 1.5 or double spaced ?	
	What font type and size should be used for plain text responses ?	
	What font type and size should be used for title pages, chapters headings, section headings ?	
	What font type and size should be used in tables or spreadsheets ?	
	What font type and size should be used in graphics or drawings ?	
	What type bullets should be used ? How far should they be indented?	
	What margin limits must be followed to account for headers and footers inserted during editing ?	
Reviews	How will responses be shared and made available for review ?	
	Will changes be made during reviews or do writers submit changes after the reviews ?	
	How and when should writers submit their changes and to whom ?	
	Should writers resubmit the entire response or just the changes ?	
	How will version control be maintained ?	

■ *Proposal Production Checklist*

Form 4-3. Proposal Production Checklist

		✔
Hardcopy	How many copies are required of each volume ?	
	What type binders or covers will be used ?	
	What type tabs or section dividers (e.g., numbered, lettered, custom) will be used ?	
	What type paper (e.g., weight, texture, color) will be used ?	
	Are pre-printed materials to be included (e.g., brochures, reports, etc.) ?	
Electronic	How many diskettes or compact discs copies are required of each volume ?	
	Should the entire response be included on each CD or just selected volumes ?	
	What type labels or covers will be used for each diskette or compact disc ?	
	Will source files be delivered to the customer or postscript image files (e.g., Adobe *.pdf) ?	
	Are electronic copies available of pre-printed materials (e.g., brochures, reports, etc.) ?	
Delivery	Will the response need to be sent electronically to the customer (if so, by whom) ?	
	When is the electronic version due (date and time zone) ?	
	When are the hardcopy, diskette and/or compact disc copies due (date and time zone) ?	
	How will the hardcopy, diskette and/or compact disc copies be delivered (and by whom) ?	
	What is the contingency plan if there are production or delivery problems ?	

Internal deliverables – Equally important to the creation of the Proposal Layout, is to define the internal deliverables which need to be created to produce the proposal. While these will vary with the specific opportunity, typical internal deliverables include –

- ❑ Solution design – required to generate the pricing response and business case
- ❑ Solution delivery plan – required to understand costs and risks associated with the delivery solution
- ❑ Business case – required to understand potential profitability
- ❑ Approval documents – required to obtain signatures approving offer

Reference information – Key components of information which add more detail and context to the Proposal Layout and Internal Deliverables include the Customer Profile, Opportunity Profile, Competitor Profile, Win Strategy and Issues/Concerns. This information should have been created during the Opportunity Profile stage and be contained in the Stakeholder Opportunity Review Package.

Work Tasks

■ *Work Breakdown Structure (WBS):* The second step to creating the Capture Project Plan is to define the work tasks which will be required to produce the deliverables identified - the Work Breakdown Structure (WBS). It is called a WBS because it is a breakdown of the work organized into a logical structure. A WBS is often referred to as a decomposition of the work, since it is usually created by "decomposing" or "breaking down" a deliverable into the various tasks required to produce it. The logical structure in the WBS represents how the tasks fit together to produce deliverables. This logical structure is applied to the work tasks through the use of a hierarchical numeric coding scheme.

Table 4-3 is an example of a WBS to create a generic response for a customer.

Table 4-3. Tabular Work Breakdown Structure

	Work Tasks
1	Schedule Capture Team Kickoff
2	Hold Capture Team Kickoff
3	Define Solution
4	Assign Section Owners
4.1	Executive Summary
4.2	Technical / Delivery Response
4.2.1	Section 1
4.2.n	Section n
4.3	Pricing / Contractual Response
5	Design Solution
5.1	Product / Service A
5.2	Product / Service B
5.3	Product / Service C
6	Price Designs and Collect Costs
6.1	Product / Service A
6.2	Product / Service B
6.3	Product / Service C
7	Develop Draft Responses
7.1	Executive Summary
7.2	Technical / Delivery Response
7.2.1	Section 1
7.2.n	Section n
7.3	Pricing / Contractual Response
8	Pink Team Review
8.1	Executive Summary
8.2	Technical / Delivery Response
8.3	Pricing / Contractual Response
9	Develop Final Responses
9.1	Executive Summary
9.2	Technical / Delivery Response
9.2.1	Section 1
9.2.n	Section n
9.3	Pricing / Contractual Response
10	Red Team Review
10.1	Executive Summary
10.2	Technical / Delivery Response
10.3	Pricing / Contractual Response
11	Develop Business Case
12	Stakeholder Approval Session
13	Produce Responses
13.1	Edit and Format Responses
13.2	Print Responses
13.3	Assemble Binders
13.4	Produce CDs
13.5	Package Binders and CDs
14	Submit Responses
14.1	Send Responses to Customer
14.2	Confirm Receipt by Customer

The sample WBS shown has three levels of detail. Notice that the highest level tasks, or Level One Tasks, are coded as numbers 1 through 14. We can break down Level One Tasks into more detail to create Level Two Tasks, which are coded with the Level One number followed by a "." and a sequential number. For example, we can breakdown Task 7: Develop Draft Responses into the Task 7.1 Executive Summary, Task 7.2 Technical/Delivery Response, and 7.3 Pricing/ Contractual Response. Similarly, we can breakdown Level Two Tasks into more detail to create Level Three Tasks, which are coded with the Level Two number followed by "." and a sequential number (e.g., 4.2.1, 4.2.2). For example, we can breakdown Task 7.2 Technical/Delivery

Response into sections, such as 7.2.1 Section One, Section 7.2.2 Section Two, through 7.2.n Section n (where n represents highest numbered section). Some tasks will require more detail to complete than others, and some tasks may have no lower level tasks at all, so the hierarchy need not and will not be symmetric or have equal levels of detail in all areas.

It is key to remember that a WBS reflects the level of detail and organization of how the Capture Manager and Core Team want to manage the work. A delicate balance must be struck between having "too much" versus "too little" detail in the WBS. For example, the WBS required for a large, complex opportunity would be unnecessarily cumbersome if used on a smaller opportunity. Conversely, a WBS created for a small opportunity would not provide sufficient direction or control to manage a large, complex opportunity. In other words, "one size does not fit all," so a generic WBS may be a good starting point. However, you should tailor the WBS to the specific opportunity your are pursuing.

Resources

The third step in creating the Capture Project Plan is to identify the resources required to complete the work tasks. Resources include the people, travel and living, office space, office supplies and production costs required to complete the work tasks. Depending upon how your company controls the allocation of resources and the amount of resources required to pursue the opportunity, you may or may not need to identify the budget for all of these items. Regardless of whether you have to budget for an item, never lose sight of the fact that your company does not have infinite resources, use them judiciously so as not to jeopardize the pursuit of other opportunities.

- *Organization Breakdown Structures:* Similar to how the work tasks were defined in the Work Breakdown Structure (WBS), you need to define the people who will be part of the team in an Organization Breakdown Structure (OBS). An OBS represents how the individual team members are grouped into teams to complete the work tasks. This is extremely critical, especially on large and complex opportunities which have several dozen, and frequently a hundred or more, people assigned to the team. The best way to manage a large team is to establish Team Leaders who have accountability for the completion of specific deliverables or a group of outputs. This allows you to rely upon the Team Leader to manage the individuals and provide status on the completion of work.

- *Types of Team Structures:* The teams should be structured based upon the deliverables to be developed and the amount of interaction and sharing of information between the teams. It is essential to understand the level of inter-team dependency so you do not find yourself with missed deliverables due to a "responsibility gap."Webster's defines "responsibility" as "the state of being in control and having to give satisfaction," whereas, "accountability" is defined as "the state of being answerable or bound to give an explanation." In other words, an individual can have "accountability" to ensure delivery of an output without having the "responsibility" to produce the output. It is critical to understand these two concepts as they will help you effectively delegate control over outputs, especially on large complex projects.

Let's look at a few examples of how to apply these concepts in different team structures given the amount of inter-dependency between team members. For simplicity, this example involves a six person team composed of a capture manager and five individual team members who need to create a generic five section response.

In the first example (Figure 4-2), no information needs to be exchanged between team members and a single team member controls all the inputs to create a single section. This structure can be called an Isomorphic Team Structure. The adjective Isomorphic comes from the Greek *iso,* which means equal or same, and *morph,* which means form or shape. In this structure each team member is "responsible" for producing a section. While this structure is simple and easy to manage, and allows for sections to be developed independently, the downside is that the sections will be independent and may not fit together into an integrated package.

Figure 4-2. Isomorphic Team Structure

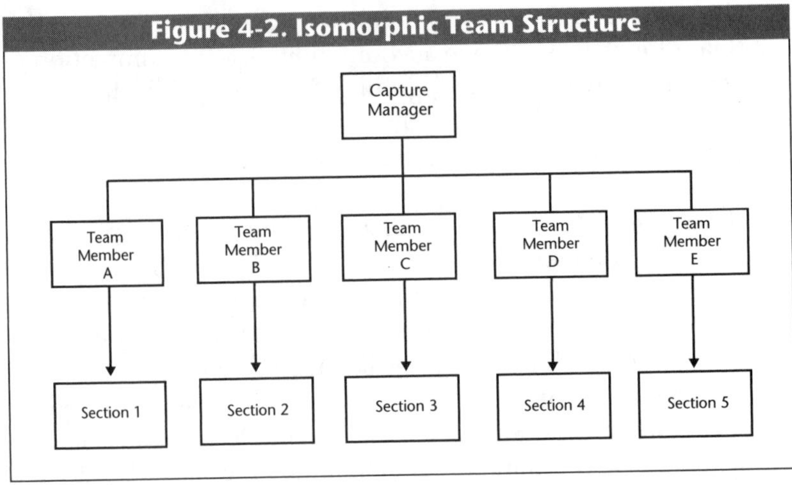

In the second example (Figure 4-3), information must be exchanged between team members; no single team member should control all the inputs to create a section. This structure can be called a Specialist Team Structure, in that each team member is a specialist in a particular area and contributes inputs to each section. In this structure each team member is "responsible" for the outputs they create; however, the only individual "responsible" to produce each integrated section is the Capture Manager. While, this structure applies the best expertise to development of each part of the response, it is very complex to manage, and will quickly overwhelm the Capture Manager on a large complex opportunity.

Figure 4-3. Specialist Team Structure

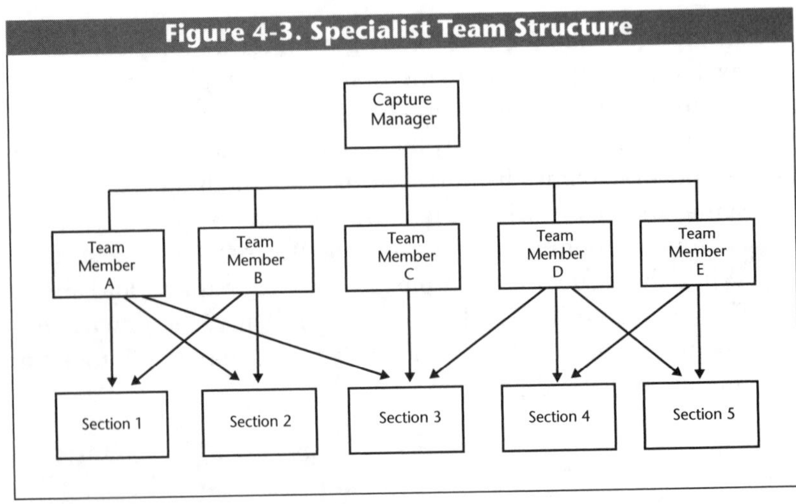

In the third example (Figure 4-4), information must be exchanged just as in the second example, although in this structure, team members are tasked differently. Like the Specialist Team Structure, individuals are "responsible" for their outputs; but each team member is also held "accountable" for delivery of one section. This structure builds on the best of the Isomorphic and Specialist Team structures by using the best expertise to be "responsible" for inputs, while simplifying the management by tasking individuals to be "accountable" for the delivery of an integrated output. This approach is also effective on large and complex responses where no Team Leader can be "responsible" for all the inputs, but should be "accountable" for a deliverable.

Figure 4-4. Section Leader Team Structure

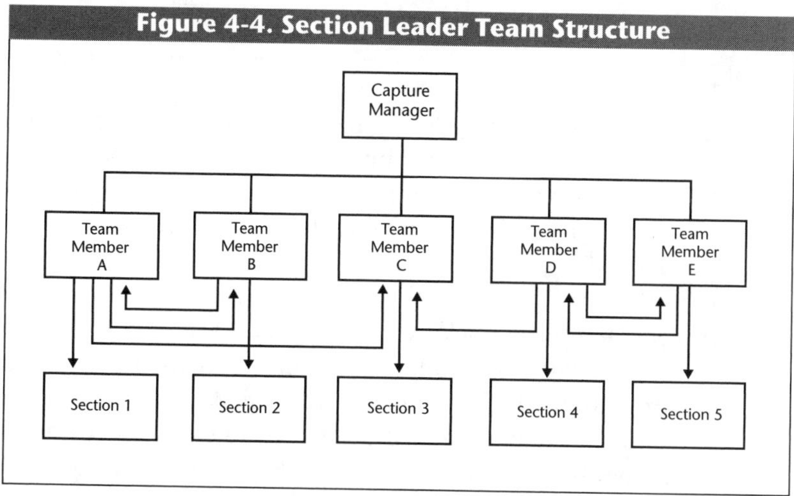

Figure 4-5 is an example of an Organization Breakdown Structure for a generic response to showing a typical Section Leader Team structure for a capture team.

Figure 4-5. Generic Response: Organization Breakdown Structure

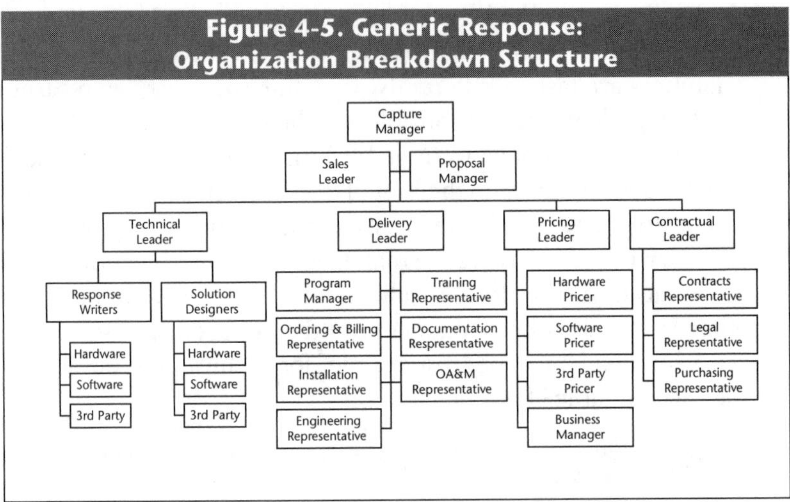

- *Responsibility Assignment Matrix (RAM):* In addition to identifying the resources and determining the best team structure, you should also quantify how much resource is required. For example, how much of an individuals' time is required (e.g., 100% for 60 days, 50% for 30 days, etc.) for a specific task. A simple way to develop this estimate is to look at the time required to complete each "work package." A "work package" is one or more inter-related activities completed by a single team member resulting in an output which is either an identified deliverable or an input to the "work package" of another team member. A simple way to identify all the work packages is through a Responsibility Assignment Matrix (RAM). A RAM plots the WBS on one axis and the OBS on another axis. The intersection boxes on the matrix represent the work packages to be completed. Figure 4-6 provides an example of the RAM to develop a generic response – note how the boxes, which represent work packages, are populated with an "x" on the grid.

Figure 4-6. Responsibility Assignment Matrix (RAM)

Generic Response — Work Breakdown Structure (WBS)	Organization Breakdown Structure (OBS)			Technical						Delivery								Pricing					Contractual			
	Captur e Manager	Sales Leader	Proposal M anager	Technical Leader	Hardware Writer	Software Writer	3rd Party Writer	Hardware Designer	Software Designer	3rd Party Designer	Delivery Leader	Program Mgmt	Order & Billing	Engineering	Installation	Documentation	Training	OA&M	Pricing Leader	Hardware Pricer	Software Pricer	3rd Party Pricer	Business Manager	Contractual Leader	Contracts	Legal	Purchasing
1 Schedule Capture Team Kickoff	x																										
2 Hold Capture Team Kickoff	x																										
3 Define Solution	x	x		x							x								x					x			
4 Define Response Layout & Assign Owners																											
4.1 Executive Summary		x																									
4.2 Technical / Delivery Response																											
4.2.1 Section 1				x			x				x																
4.2.n Section n				x			x				x																
4.3 Pricing / Contractual Response																			x			x		x			
5 Design Solution																											
5.1 Hardware								x																			
5.2 Software									x																		
5.3 3rd Party										x																	
6 Price Designs and Collect Costs																											
6.1 Hardware																				x							
6.2 Software																					x						
6.3 3rd Party																						x					
7 Develop Draft Responses																											
7.1 Executive Summary		x																									
7.2 Technical / Delivery Response																											
7.2.1 Section 1				x	x	x	x				x	x	x	x	x	x	x	x									
7.2.n Section n				x	x	x	x				x	x	x	x	x	x	x	x									
7.3 Pricing / Contractual Response																			x	x	x	x	x	x	x	x	x
8 Pink Team Review																											
8.1 Executive Summary	x	x	x	x							x								x					x			
8.2 Technical / Delivery Response	x	x	x	x	x	x	x				x	x	x	x	x	x	x	x									
8.3 Pricing / Contractual Response	x	x	x																x	x	x	x	x	x	x	x	x
9 Develop Final Responses																											
9.1 Executive Summary		x																									
9.2 Technical / Delivery Response																											
9.2.1 Section 1				x	x	x	x				x	x	x	x	x	x	x	x									
9.2.n Section n				x	x	x	x				x	x	x	x	x	x	x	x									
9.3 Pricing / Contractual Response																			x	x	x	x	x	x	x	x	x
10 Red Team Review																											
10.1 Executive Summary	x	x	x	x							x								x					x			
10.2 Technical / Delivery Response	x	x	x	x	x	x	x				x	x	x	x	x	x	x	x									
10.3 Pricing / Contractual Response	x	x	x																x	x	x	x	x	x	x	x	x
11 Develop Business Cases	x	x																					x				
12 Stakeholder Approval Session	x	x		x							x								x				x	x			
13 Produce Responses																											
13.1 Edit and Format Responses			x																								
13.2 Print Responses			x																								
13.3 Assemble Binders			x																								
13.4 Produce CDs			x																								
13.5 Package Binders and CDs			x																								
14 Submit Responses																											
14.1 Send Responses to Customer			x																								
14.2 Confirm Receipt by Customer			x																								

- *Opportunity Budget Planner:* Having developed an estimate of the time required by each team member, you should also identify the discrete or incremental non-personnel costs that will be incurred in pursuit of the opportunity. The most common of these non-personnel costs are Travel & Living, Office

Space, Office Supplies and Production Costs. Travel & Living is any incremental airfare, train, hotel, meal, rental car, taxi, mileage, parking or toll incurred by a team member. Space or facilities is any incremental office space, lab space, dedicated work room, cubicle or meeting space. Equipment or supplies is any incremental office equipment (e.g. PCs, projectors), lab equipment, office supply or material. Product costs are the incremental costs for reproduction, paper, binders, tabs, covers, compact discs, supplies and shipping of the response. Note that you should capture only the incremental costs for each category attributable to the opportunity. For example, most companies have a "loaded rate" for employees that includes regular work space and office supplies, in which case you only need to budget for the incremental expenses beyond what is included in the "loaded rate."

Form 4-4. Opportunity Budget Planner

Opportunity:		Prepared by:		Date:
Role	Level	Monthly Rate	Person Months	Total Cost
Capture Manager				
Sales Leader				
Proposal Manager				
Technical Leader				
Hardware Response Writer				
Software Response Writer				
3rd Party Response Writer				
Hardware Solution Designer				
Software Solution Designer				
3rd Party Solution Designer				
Delivery Leader				
Program Management Representative				
Order & Billing Representative				
Engineering Representative				
Installation Representative				
Documentation Representative				
Training Representative				
OA&M Representative				
Pricing Leader				
Hardware Pricer				
Software Pricer				
3rd Party Pricer				
Business Manager				
Contractual Leader				
Contracts Representative				
Legal Representative				
Purchasing Representative				
TOTAL LABOR COSTS				
Item	Budget Occurrence *	Amount per Occurrence	Number of Occurrences	**Total Cost**
Travel & Living				
Space & Facilities				
Equipment & Supplies				
Production Costs				
TOTAL NON-LABOR COSTS				
TOTAL B&P BUDGET				

Form 4-4 is an Opportunity Budget Planner based on developing a generic response which can be used to develop the overall costs associated with pursuit of an opportunity. You should keep your budgeting simple, but reasonably accurate. Items like personnel costs should be based on their loaded rates and number of person months of effort. Non-personnel items are typically costed based on "Budget Occurrence." For example, so much per trip for Travel & Living, or so much per month for Space & Facilities.

Timeline

- *Types of Timelines:* The fourth step in developing the Capture Project Plan is to identify the timeline. This is done by determining how long each task will take to complete and the order in which tasks must be completed. On large, complex projects you may have multiple timelines based on the level of detail. For example, you may have an Overall Project Timeline which shows the time to complete Level One Tasks, and Detailed Timelines for each Level One Task showing the time to complete all the subordinate Level Two and Level Three Tasks.

  There are three fundamental approaches used to develop and represent a timeline or schedule in graphical form. These are a Gantt or Bar Chart, a Milestone Chart and a PERT/CPM Chart, each of which is described below.

  A Gantt or bar chart (see Figure 4-7), shows each work task as a bar placed on a timeline with one end being the start time and the other end the stop time. Gantt or bar charts are popular because they make it easy for the reader to visualize the tasks and when they must be completed. The disadvantage is that it can be difficult to see the status of work completed and they do not show the interdependency of tasks.

Figure 4-7. Gantt or Bar Chart

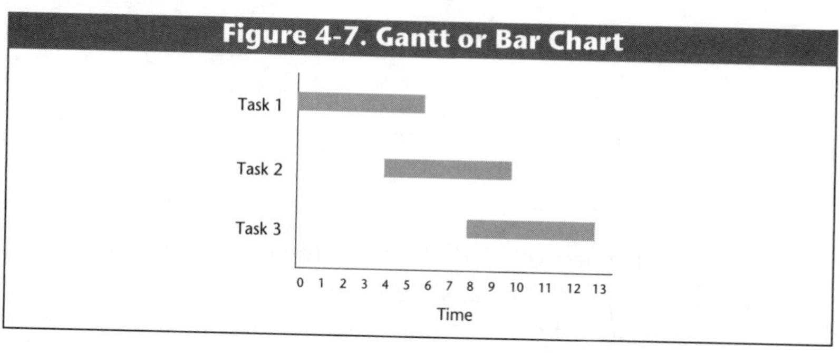

A milestone chart (see Figure 4-8), shows each task as a series of milestones. For example, you can represent the task of writing a draft response for a section using the milestones: Draft Started, Draft Reviewed and Draft Complete. Milestone charts are also popular because they make it easy to see the status of work completion. The disadvantage is they do not show the interdependency of tasks.

Figure 4-8. Milestone Chart

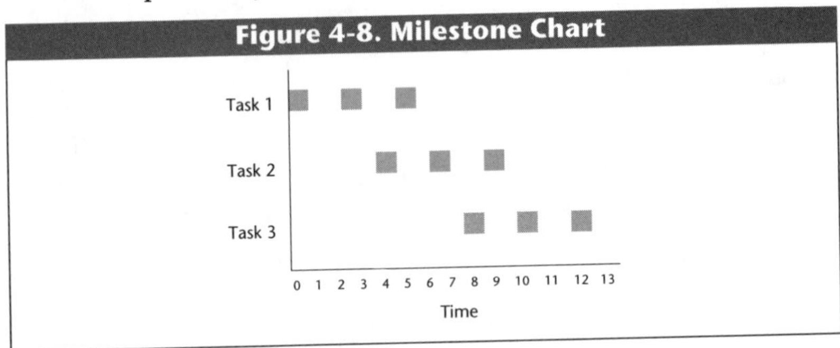

A PERT/CPM chart (see Figure 4-9), shows tasks on a flow chart using lines or arrows to depict the interdependencies. PERT or Program Evaluation and Review Technique was developed for the US Navy's Polaris missile program in the late 1950's, while CPM or Critical Path Method was developed around the same time by Dupont. Although, there are subtle differences between PERT and CPM, both are based on similar looking flow charts, so it has become common to see the terms used interchangeably. The prime advantage of PERT/CPM Charts is they show the impact of delays or improvements in the completion of specific work tasks on the overall project.

Figure 4-9. PERT/CPM Chart

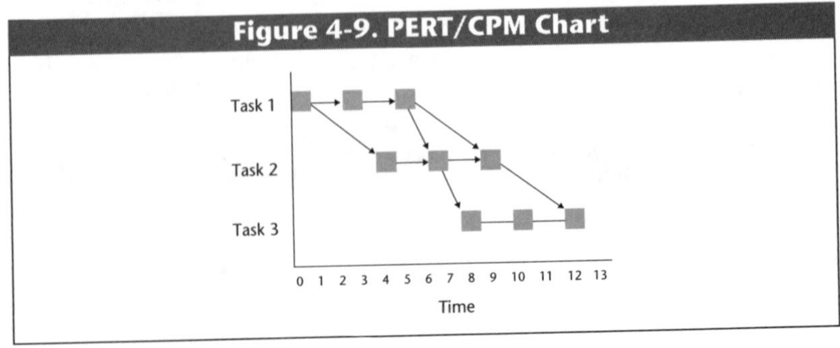

An essential aspect of PERT/CPM is the concept of the Critical Path. The Critical Path is simply the longest path through the flowchart. Using the PERT/CPM Chart for a generic response (see Figure 4-10), where the time to complete each tasks is shown below each box, the Critical Path is shown by the heavy arrowed line. The sequence 1-2-3-4.2-7.2-8.2-9.2-9.1-10.1-13-14 is the longest path through the PERT/CPM chart and is, therefore, the shortest time during which all the tasks can be completed (i.e., 17 days).

The tasks on the critical path must be completed on schedule or the end date for the project will slip. Conversely, if tasks on the critical path can be completed ahead of date, the project may be completed early. While attention should be paid to the timely completion of all tasks, the delayed completion of tasks which are not on the critical path may have no impact on the end date. Note that as the time to complete tasks becomes longer or shorter, the Critical Path through the PERT/CPM Chart will shift. There can even be multiple Critical Paths if multiple paths take the same amount of time.

Figure 4-10. PERT/CMP Chart: Generic Response

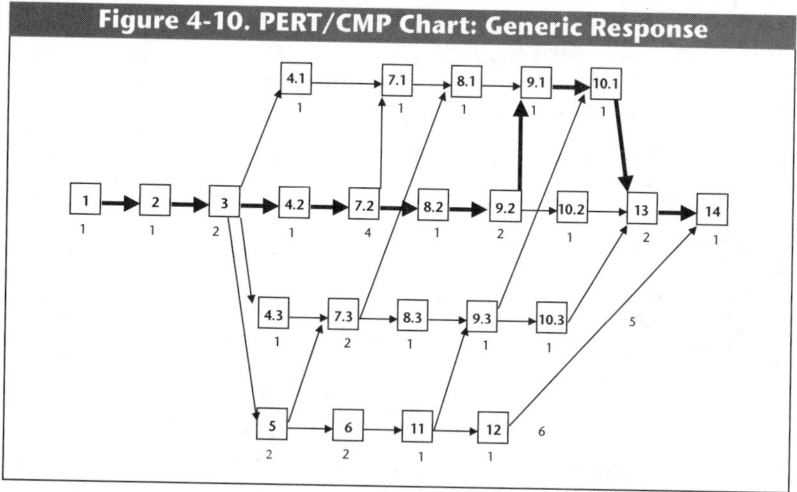

- *Task List Schedule:* It is essential to remember that you want to gauge the timeline approach used to the size and complexity of the project. For example, if you have an experienced team with lots of interdependencies between team members and a very short period of time, you may want to focus visibility chiefly on who is accountable to complete tasks and the status of their completion. A simple method to create this visibility is the use of a Task List Schedule, which presents the tasks along with their owner and both the Baseline and Current Working View completion dates. An example of the Task List Schedule (Form 4-5) for a generic response is shown on the next page.

Form 4-5. Generic Response: Task List Schedule

Work Task	Owner	Baseline Due Date	Current Working View Due Date
1 Schedule Capture Team Kickoff			
2 Hold Capture Team Kickoff			
3 Define Solution			
4 Define Response Layout & Assign Owners			
4.1 Executive Summary			
4.2 Technical / Delivery Response			
4.2.1 Section 1			
4.2.n Section n			
4.3 Pricing / Contractual Response			
5 Design Solution			
5.1 Product / Service A			
5.2 Product / Service B			
5.3 Product / Service C			
6 Price Designs and Collect Costs			
6.1 Product / Service A			
6.2 Product / Service B			
6.3 Product / Service C			
7 Develop Draft Responses			
7.1 Executive Summary			
7.2 Technical / Delivery Response			
7.2.1 Section 1			
7.2.n Section n			
7.3 Pricing / Contractual Response			
8 Pink Team Review			
8.1 Executive Summary			
8.2 Technical / Delivery Response			
8.3 Pricing / Contractual Response			
9 Develop Final Responses			
9.1 Executive Summary			
9.2 Technical / Delivery Response			
9.2.1 Section 1			
9.2.n Section n			
9.3 Pricing / Contractual Response			
10 Red Team Review			
10.1 Executive Summary			
10.2 Technical / Delivery Response			
10.3 Pricing / Contractual Response			
11 Develop Business Case			
12 Stakeholder Approval Session			
13 Produce Responses			
13.1 Edit and Format Responses			
13.2 Print Responses			
13.3 Assemble Binders			
13.4 Produce CDs			
13.5 Package Binders and CDs			

The frequent criticism of PERT/CPM schedules is that they can be physically large and difficult to read. The Task List Schedule is a method of presenting selected pieces of information from a PERT/CPM schedule in a condensed format. The Baseline date is the date established at the start of the project. The Current Working View date is today's view of the date. It is essential to have both views in order to assess if you are ahead, on-track or behind schedule. A simple color coding can be overlaid on the dates to show "on or ahead of schedule" in green, "behind but not jeopardizing completion" in yellow and "jeopardizing completion" in red. This simple format is especially useful in showing status to stakeholders as it pinpoints problem areas.

Communication Plans

The fourth step in developing the Capture Project Plan is to develop communication plans. For most projects, you should develop three plans: 1) Project Communications Plan, 2) Change Request Plan and 3) Alert-Jeopardy-Escalation Plan. It is essential to develop these plans at the start of the opportunity as you want to proactively decide how you will address key events during pursuit of the opportunity.

- *Project Communication Plan:* The Project Communication Plan states how you intend to communicate with the team and stakeholders over the life of the opportunity. With the proliferation of communications technology, it is ironic that the root cause of most of the problems on project teams is still poor communication. As projects become larger and more complex the number of team members increases. With the addition of each new team member, the channels of communication increases dramatically, as shown in Figure 4-11 below. Communication should be taken seriously, it requires advance planning and thought to be done effectively.

Figure 4-11. Communicatiions Channels

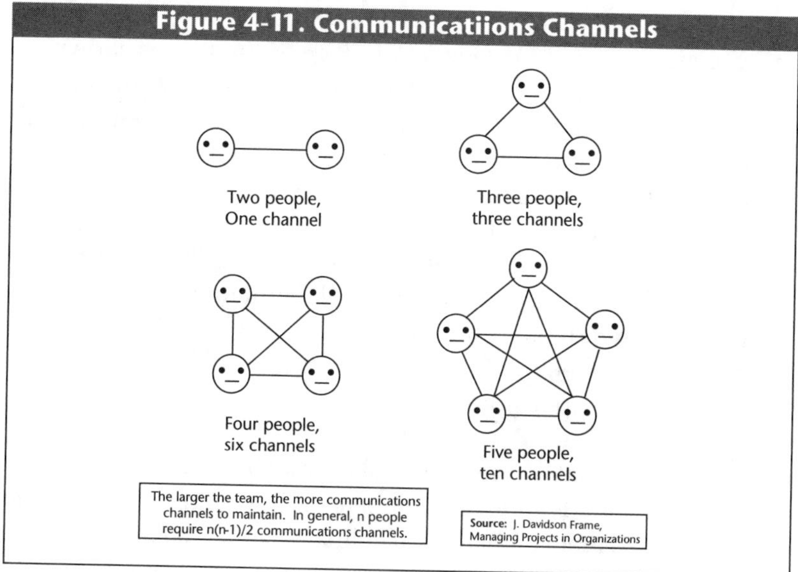

A common debate in the flow of information are the approaches of "pushing" versus "pulling" information. "Pushing" information means that you send individuals the information you think they want or should have and they use it, save it or throw it away. The advantage of "pushing" information is that information is sent automatically to individuals. The disadvantage is that they may not want or need much of what they receive. Traditional methods to "push" information include meetings, conference calls and mailing documents, while new methods range from email to pop-up message windows or advertisements. "Pulling" information means that you store the information where individuals can access and retrieve the information as they need it. The advantage of "pulling" is individuals only get the information they want, when they need it. The disadvantage is that they have to know where and how to retrieve the information. Traditional methods to "pull" information include document libraries, while new methods range from electronic bulletin boards to intranet websites.

Effective communication on a Capture Team requires a combination of "pushing" and "pulling" information. When dealing with a small team or inexperienced team members, or at the start of an opportunity, you should "push" information you know the team needs. As team members become more experienced or the team grows large, you can and will need to rely upon team members to "pull" the information as necessary.

A generic *Project Communication Plan* (Form 4-6) is shown on the following page. On the top half you will see the meetings planned to communicate to the team and on the bottom half you will see the key documents that will be used to share information with the team. For each type of meeting, it identifies the medium (i.e., face-to-face, conference bridge, intranet), meeting purpose, frequency (i.e., one-time, daily, as-needed) and participants. For each type of document, it identifies how it will be shared (i.e., hardcopy, email, intranet), the document content, frequency of updates (i.e., daily, weekly, as-needed) and who is responsible to update the document.

This consolidated view of all key meetings and documents provides a guide to team members on how information will be "pushed" to them or made available so it can be "pulled." While it will not eliminate all communication issues on the team, it certainly will eliminate the most common questions regarding the what, when, why, who and how communication will flow to the team. Chapter 9 presents a survey of Information Systems, Tools and Technology that can be used to "push" and "pull" information.

Form 4-6. Project Communication Plan

Meeting	Medium: Face-to-Face	Medium: Conf. Bridge	Medium: Intranet	Purpose	Frequency of Meeting: One-Time	Frequency of Meeting: Daily	Frequency of Meeting: As Needed	Participants
Capture Team Kickoff				Review Opportunity, Validate Capture Project Plan, Review Communication Plans	X			Entire Team
Subteam Meetings				Complete Work Tasks			X	Subteam members
Capture Team Status Meetings				Review Status of Work Tasks, Review Changes, Identify Alert-Jeopardy-Escalation Issues		X		Required Subteam Leaders Optional: All other team members
Pink Team Review(s)				Ensure Accuracy and Completeness of Proposal	X			Proposal Manager, Sales Leader, Capture Manager, and Subteam members based on section being reviewed
Red Team Review(s)				Ensure proposal makes sense and addresses specified customer requirements	X			Proposal Manager, Sales Leader, Capture Manager, and Subteam members based on section being reviewed
Stakeholder Approval Session				Obtain authority to bid	X			Stakeholders, Capture manager, Subteam Leaders
Document	**How Shared: Hardcopy**	**How Shared: E-mail**	**How Shared: Intranet**	**Content**	**Frequency of Updates: Daily**	**Frequency of Updates: Weekly**	**Frequency of Updates: As Needed**	**Updated by**
Stakeholder Buy-In Presentation				Customer Profile, Opportunity Profile, Competitor Profile, Win Strategy Issues/Concerns, Response Requirements, Bid-No Bid Decision			x	Capture Manager
Customer Solicitation Documents				Describe as appropriate			x	Proposal Manager
Proposal Layout				Overall layout of response, response win themes			x	Proposal Manager
Work Breakdown Structure				Work tasks			x	Capture Manager
Point-by-point Assignments				Detailed response assignments			x	Subteam Leaders
Team Organization Chart				Team structure			x	Capture Manager
Team Contact List				Team member name, phone, email			x	Capture Manager
Milestone List Timeline				Milestones, owners, due dates, completion status	x			Capture Manager
Project Communication Plan				How will communicate			x	Capture Manager
Change Control Plan				Process to identify and communicate changes with form			x	Capture Manager
Alert-Jeopardy-Escalation Plan				Process to identify and resolve issues along with form			x	Capture Manager
Action Item Register				Action Items, owners, status	x			Capture Manager
Status Reports						x		Capture Manager

- *Change Request Plan:* Inevitably there will be changes that occur during pursuit of the opportunity, so you should develop a *Change Request Plan* to understand how you want to manage change. Perhaps the most important point to learn regarding change is that you will not, and more importantly, do not need to, eliminate change. Rather, what you need to do is have an established plan of how you will manage change. Some changes will originate from your customer, whereas others will come internally from team members who find a "better idea," "better information" or realized an "error" in something. Some changes will have little or no impact, some will be to your benefit, and others will be to your detriment.

  There are three fundamental elements to a *Change Request Plan:* 1) how and who identifies or requests changes, 2) how and who identifies the impact of the change and 3) how and who decides if the change is approved. On the following pages are a generic *Change Request Form* and *Change Request Flow,* which provide an example of a Change Request Plan.

Using the *Change Request Form,* Form 4-7, an individual team member can identify or request a change by completing the top section. Following the *Change Request Flow,* see Figure 4-12, they would forward this to the Capture Manager. The Capture Manager would assign a tracking number and then forward the form to the appropriate team member, most likely one of the Team Leaders, to evaluate the impact of the change. The evaluator would complete the next section of the form showing: the impact if the change is approved, the impact if the change is not approved, a recommendation to "approve" or "do not approve" and an identification of the areas impacted by the approval or disapproval. The form is then forwarded on to the Sales Leader and Team Leader of each area impacted to concur with the recommendation. It is wise to always include the Sales Leader in this concurrence as they may have insights from the customer regarding the importance of the change that others do not.

Form 4-7. Change Request Form

Section to be filled by individual requesting the change

Opportunity:	Tracking #:
Requested by:	Date:
Description of requested change:	
Reason for requested change:	

Section to be filled by individual evaluating the change

Evaluated by:
Impact if change request approved:
Impact if change request not approved:

Action Recommended	☐ Approve	☐ Do Not Approve	Action Impacted	☐ Technical	☐ Pricing	☐ Delivery	☐ Contractual

Concurrence of team leaders impacted by change

Team Leader	Concur Yes	Concur No	Date	Initials	If no concurrence, provide reason
Technical					
Delivery					
Pricing					
Contractual					
Sales					

Section to be filled by capture manager

Action Taken	☐ Approve	☐ Not Approved	Reason (if deviates from recommendations
Signature:		Date:	

Figure 4-12. Change Request Flow

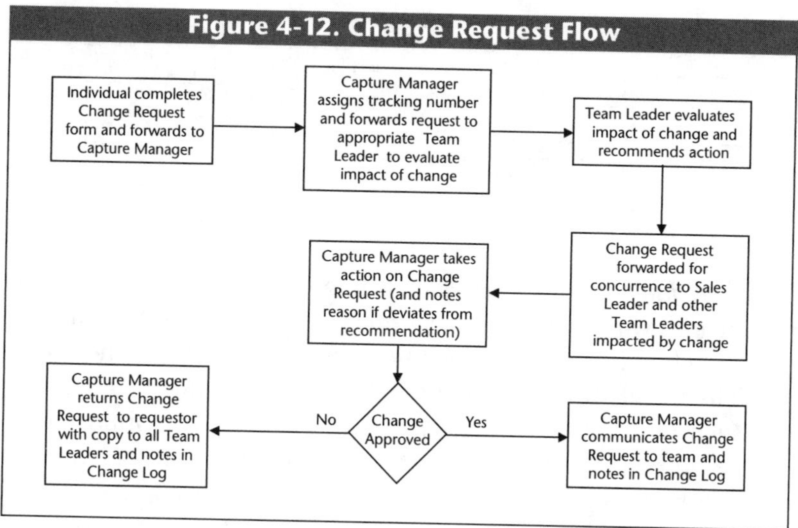

Having either concurred or explained why they disagree with the recommendation, the Change Request Form is returned to the Capture Manager who makes a final decision on the change along with their explanation if they deviate from the recommendation. If approved, the Capture Manager communicates the change to the team so it can be implemented, and notes its approval on the Change Request Log. If not approved, the Capture Manager returns the form to the requestor with a copy to all Team Leaders, and notes the disapproval on the Change Request Log.

Form 4-8 is an example of a Change Request Log. A Change Request Log should capture the key information regarding the change request such as: Tracking Number, Date Opened, Brief Description, Evaluated By, Date Sent, Disposition and Date Closed. This will allow you to track the status of all active change requests, who is evaluating them and the date sent for evaluation. It will also allow you to track the disposition of change requests and the date closed. On larger projects you may have numerous change requests in process simultaneously, so a log will help both the Capture Manager and all team members understand the status of changes.

Form 4-8. Change Request Log

Tracking Number	Date Opened	Brief Description	Evaluated By	Date Sent	Dispostion		Date Closed
					Approved	Disapproved	

- *Alert-Jeopardy-Escalation Plan:* While it would be ideal to assume that all work will go along exactly as planned and completed on schedule with no disruptions, this is unrealistic and naïve. There will always be unforeseen events or changes which have such an impact that they jeopardize the overall opportunity. Additionally, no company has unlimited resources, so there will be conflicts over resources with other opportunities and projects. As such, you need to develop a plan for how you will address issues when they arise.

  The key is to have an early warning system to spot issues before they become problems. To do this, you can use the concepts of "Alert," "Jeopardy" and "Escalation." An "Alert" is an issue that will jeopardize the overall project if not resolved. However, there is time for a member of the team to attempt resolution without management intervention. "Jeopardy" refers to an issue that will jeopardize the overall project if not resolve and requires management intervention for resolution. An "Escalation" is an issue jeopardizing the overall project and requires immediate stakeholder or executive level intervention for resolution.

  The ability to effectively resolve issues, while maintaining good working relations with team members, is to have an "early warning system" in-place along with frequent communication with Team Leaders and team members regarding issues. An "Alert," "Jeopardy" or "Escalation" should never come as a surprise to a Team Leader or a team member. In fact, the Team Leader or team member should be the person identifying the need for an "Alert," "Jeopardy" or "Escalation."

Form 4-9. Alert-Jeopardy-Escalation Form

Alert ☐	Jeopardy ☐	Escalation ☐
Date Identified:	Date Escalated:	Tracking Number:
DateResolved:	Times Escalated:	
From:	Phone:	Email:
To:	Phone:	Email:
Description of issue:		
Actions taken to resolve		
Impact of issue:		
Recommended resolution:		
Action plan and owner:		
Resolution:		

Form 4-9 presents an example of a Alert-Jeopardy-Escalation Form and Figure 4-13 presents an Alert-Jeopardy-Escalation Flow demonstrating how to use to the form to resolve issues. Using the Alert-Jeopardy-Escalation Form, you can capture a brief description of the issues, prior actions taken to attempt to resolve the issue, impact of the issue and recommended resolution. As the same information is needed for each scenario, keep it simple by using the same form for an Alert, Jeopardy and Escalation. There is also a place to capture the date the issue was identified, the date resolved, date escalated, number of times escalated, tracking number, who completed the form along with their phone and email and who the form is being sent to for action. There is a block for the recipient to identify their action plan for resolution, along with a block to note the final resolution of the issue.

Figure 4-13. Alert-Jeopardy-Escalation Plan Flow

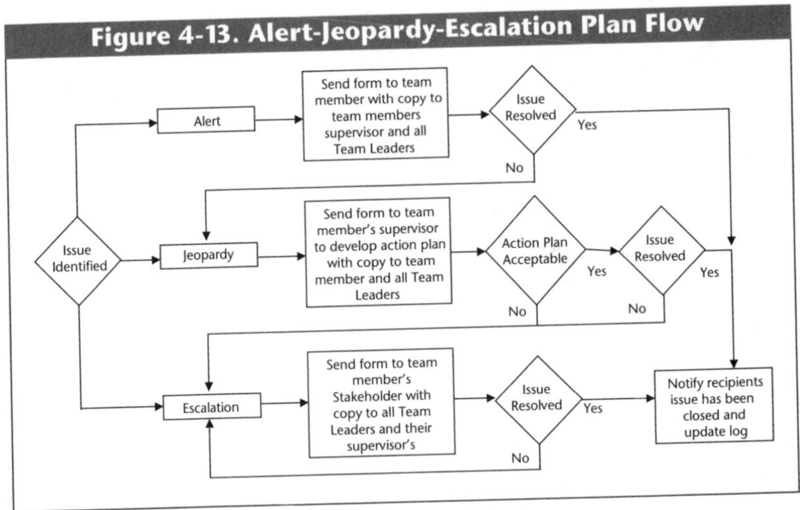

Using the Alert-Jeopardy-Escalation Flow, send an "Alert" to team member with a copy to their supervisor along with a copy to all Team Leaders. This allows the team member to continue working the issue and "save face" with their supervisor, while ensuring their supervisor and the Team Leaders are aware there is a potential problem. In most organizations, issues can be resolved while still an Alert, because no one wants them to become a Jeopardy. If the issue is not resolved it should become a "Jeopardy."

Using the same flow, a "Jeopardy" is sent to the team members supervisor requesting an action plan for resolution within a specified period of time, usually 24 to 48 hours, along with a copy to their supervisor as well as the team member and all the Team Leaders. This distribution engages the supervisor, while also "pre-alerting" their supervisor of an issue that may be escalated. You should copy the team member, because they will likely be engaged by their supervisor for more details. Similarly, you should copy the Team Leaders so they are aware of the situation. If the action plan is acceptable, then monitor it to closure. If the action plan is not acceptable or is not successfully addressed, the issue should become an "Escalation."

Using the same flow, an "Escalation" is sent to the appropriate stakeholder or executive for immediate attention. Due to the severity of an "Escalation" you should not only copy the Team Leaders, but their supervisors as well.

All notifications should be tracked using some type of log, such as the one shown below in Form 4-10. You should assign each issue a tracking number, and track the date opened, a brief description, severity type (i.e., alert, jeopardy, escalation), who the owner is for resolution, the date severity changed (i.e., if unresolved) and date closed.

Form 4-10. Alert-Jeopardy-Escalation Log

Tracking Number	Date Opened	Brief Description	Severity Level			Resolution Owner	Date Severity Changed	Date Closed
			Alert	Jeopardy	Escalation			

Outputs

Having completed the four steps of the Capture Project Plan stage, you will have developed the following outputs which compose the Capture Project Plan:

- *Identified Deliverables*
- *Identification of Work Tasks*
- *Identified Resources*
- *Identified Timeline*
- *Communications Plans*

Summary

Before proceeding to the Bid Phase, be sure to review the Input-Tools & Techniques-Output chart at the beginning of this chapter and assess if you have successfully completed all the outputs identified. If you find gaps, go back and use the tools and techniques provided in this chapter, as well as, Chapter 3 – Pre-Bid Phase: Opportunity Profile & Stakeholder Buy-In Stages, to complete the missing outputs.

Questions to Consider

1. How well does your organization develop capture project plans?

2. How effectively does your organization complete these activities? Are capture teams well organized? Are capture team well managed? Are capture resources used efficiently?

3. Does your organization have documented processes or tools & techniques used to develop capture project plans?

4. What actions has your organization taken to improve/develop capture project planning skills for your sales managers, capture/ proposal managers and contract managers?

5. How well does your organization document and share your capture project planning lessons learned?

chapter

Bid Phase: Capture Team Kickoff, Bid Development, Bid Reviews and Stakeholder Approval

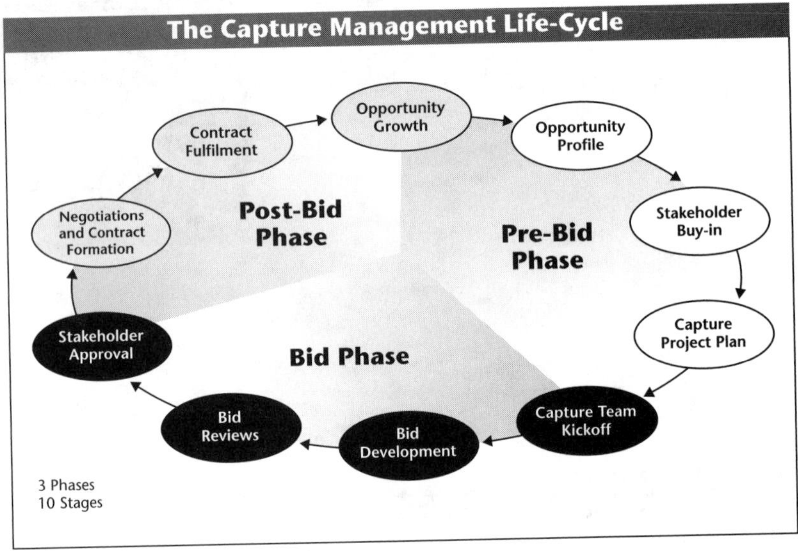

Introduction

The Bid Phase is composed of four stages which are Capture Team Kickoff, Bid Development, Bid Reviews and Stakeholder Approval. The four stages should be completed in the sequence presented as each stage builds upon the preceding stage. Similarly, the Bid Phase builds upon the Pre-Bid Phase, so be sure you have completed all outputs described in Chapters 3 and 4.

Capture Team Kickoff Stage

Objectives of the Capture Team Kickoff stage are to assemble and engage the Capture Team and ensure they understand the:

- *Opportunity*
- *Capture Project Plan*
- *Communications Plans*
- *Proposal Development Plans*
- *Action Items and Next Steps*

The following graphic, Figure 5-1, shows the Inputs, Tools & Techniques and Outputs of the Capture Team Kickoff stage.

Figure 5-1. Bid Phase: Capture Team Kickoff Stage

Input	Tools & Techniques	Output
▪ Identified Deliverables ▪ Identified Work Tasks ▪ Identified Resources ▪ Identified Timeline ▪ Communication	▪ Initial Actions ❑ Capture Team Kick-off Agenda ❑ Checklist of Tips for an Effective Capture Team Kick-off ❑ Kick-off Follow-Up Actions ▪ Review Opportunity ▪ Validate Capture Project Plan ▪ Review Communication Plans ▪ Review Proposal Development Plans	▪ Engaged Capture Team ▪ Validated Capture Project Plan ▪ Agreed to Communications Plans ▪ Documented Proposal Development Plans ▪ Identified Action Items with Owners and Due Dates

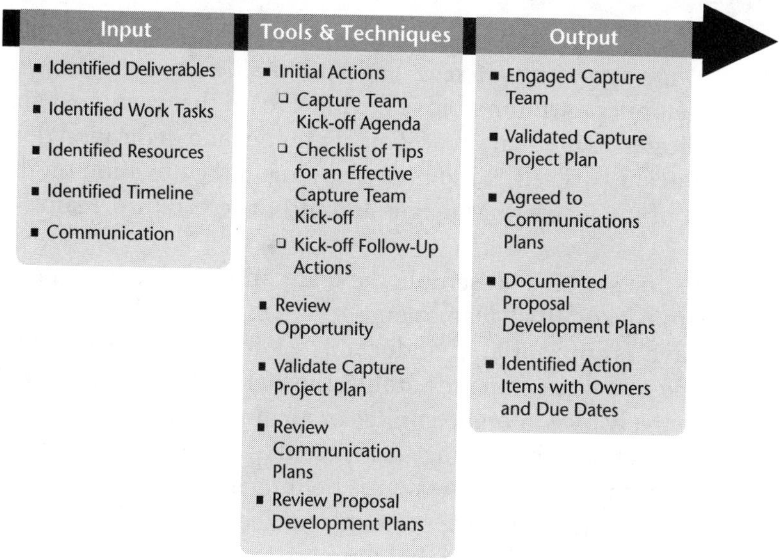

Inputs

Having successfully completed the Pre-Bid Phase, you should have developed the following inputs to the Capture Team Kickoff stage:

- *Identified Deliverables*
- *Identified Work Tasks*
- *Identified Resources*
- *Identified Timeline*
- *Communications Plans*

If you are missing any of these inputs, you need to return and complete the steps outlined in Chapter 3 – Pre-Bid Phase: Capture Project Plan and, if necessary, Chapter 2 – Opportunity Kickoff and Stakeholder Buy-In.

Tools & Techniques

Initial Actions

- *Capture Team Kickoff Agenda:* Perhaps the single biggest factor in developing a winning bid is having a team that is aligned and dedicated to the same goal. This alignment and dedication does not occur by itself, it requires planning and cultivation on the part of the Capture Manager and the Core Capture Team.

  The first step is to assemble the team and conduct a Capture Team Kickoff. If all team members are in the same location, or if travel is appropriate, conduct this session face-to-face. While a face-to-face session is desirable, the kickoff can be conducted effectively by conference bridge or an intranet sharing application, such as NetMeeting. It is essential to maximize participation, so even if the session is held face-to-face, you should use a conference bridge or an intranet sharing application for anyone who can not be there in person.

  The following Capture Team Kickoff Agenda, Form 5-1, presents the recommended topics, sequence and presenters for the session. Note that for most topics on the agenda there is a reference document which was developed during the Pre-Bid Phase so there should be no special presentation materials required for the session.

Form 5-1. Capture Team Kickoff Agenda

Agenda Topics	Reference Documents	Discussion Leader
Introduction Purpose, Agenda, Limit Introduce Team Members		Capture Manager
Review Opportunity Customer Profile Opportunity Profile Competitor Profile Win Theme & Strategies Issues/Concerns	■ Stakeholder Opportunity Review Package	
Validate Capture Plan Work Tasks Resources Timeline Communication Plans	■ Work Breakdown Structure (WBS) ■ Organization Breakdown Structure (OBS) ■ Responsibility Assignment Matrix (RAM) ■ Team Leader Roles & Responsibilities ■ Task List Schedule ■ Customer Positioning & Contact Plans ■ Project Communication Plan ■ Change Request Plan ■ Alert-Jeopardy-Escalation Plan	Capture Manager
Review Proposal Development Plans Development Process Production Requirements Layout & Assignments Proposal Reviews	■ Proposal Development Checklist ■ Proposal Production Checklist ■ Proposal Layout with Assignments ■ Pink Team & Red Team Checklists	Proposal Manager
Action Items and Next Steps Action Items Meeting Schedule	■ Action Item Register	Capture Manager

As with all meetings, you should start by reviewing the purpose, agenda and limit for the meeting and introduce all participants. You want the Sales Leader to review the customer, opportunity, competitors and issues/concerns. Use the Stakeholder Opportunity Review as the presentation materials. This will eliminate the need for a separate presentation, and serve to communicate to the team Stakeholder support for the opportunity.

The next topic should be validation of the capture project plan, including a review of the deliverables, work tasks, resources, team structure, timeline and communications plans. The objective during this portion of the session is to get feedback on the plans, so prepare yourself for criticism and don't take any of the feedback personally. It is recommended that the Capture Manager lead this discussion as it will serve to establish their role as leader of the capture team. It also provides the opportunity for the Sales Leader to endorse this role at the close of their presentation.

The next topic should be a review of the proposal development plans by the Proposal Manager. This should include a review of the Proposal Development Process, Proposal Production Requirements and Proposal Layout with Volume & Section Assignments, all of which should have been developed during the Capture Project Plan stage. If any Section Assignments have not been made, you can complete this during the kickoff session, by assigning them as action items to the Volume Owners, or completing them at the next team meeting. If there are still open questions concerning either Proposal Development or Proposal Production, assign them as action items with an owner and due date. You may also opt to review the objective and format for Proposal Reviews at a later team meeting to save time.

The last topic on the agenda should be to review any action items developed during the session, and establishing a schedule for team meetings.

- *Checklist of Tips for an Effective Capture Team Kickoff:* Form 5-2 contains a checklist of several tips on how you plan, inform, conduct and follow-up, which can improve the effectiveness of the Capture Team Kickoff.

Form 5-2. Checklist of Tips for an Effective Capture Team Kickoff

Prior to the meeting:

- ❑ Pick a time for the meeting which maximizes participation and provide adequate notification
- ❑ Confirm team leader participation and have team leaders who cannot attend identify an authorized delegate
- ❑ Use means to maximize the inclusion of all team members (e.g., conference bridges, intranet bridge)
- ❑ Ensure presenters understand their material, the agenda and the time each has been allotted

If the meeting will be via conference call:

- ❑ Distribute presentation materials in advance of the meeting
- ❑ Take role of participants as they "beep in" to keep a log of all participants
- ❑ Use a unique bridge number for the opportunity to reduce conflicts with other teams
- ❑ Have participants put all speakerphones on "mute" to reduce background noise
- ❑ Have participants on cell or cordless phones with excessive noise drop-off and call-back on a different phone

During the meeting:

- ❑ Start the meeting on time and direct late comers to contact you or their Team Leader on what they missed
- ❑ Be sure to project a positive and supportive attitude and tone to encourage teamwork and trust
- ❑ Introduce yourself as the Capture Manager for the opportunity to explain your role
- ❑ Review the Purpose, Agenda and Limit for the Capture Team Kickoff
- ❑ Introduce the team leaders being sure to identify their role and responsibility
- ❑ Encourage team members to direct issues or questions after the meeting to their Team Leader
- ❑ Keep track of time and "prod" presenters to move along if they are taking too long
- ❑ Do not try to solve problems on the call, identify them as action items and assign an owner to resolve
- ❑ Encourage discussion and Q&A, but do not permit endless debating or "grandstanding"
- ❑ DO NOT take feedback personally - accept it and look for how to make the plans better

After the meeting:

- ❑ Distribute minutes along with the Action Item Register and a list of participants
- ❑ Update and redistribute any materials which changed as a result of the meeting
- ❑ Publish meeting schedule and conference bridge information

Follow-up Actions

- *Review Opportunity*
- *Validate Capture Project Plan*
- *Review Communications Plans*
- *Review Proposal Development Plans*

Outputs

At the end of the Capture Team Kickoff stage, you should have a Capture Team assembled and aligned on a plan of attack and moving forward to develop a winning bid. Specifically, you should have accomplished the following during the Capture Team Kickoff: 1) Engaged Capture Team, 2) Validated Capture Project Plan, 3) Agreed to the Communications Plans, 4) Documented Proposal Development Plans and 5) Identified Action Items along with owners and due dates.

Bid Development Stage

The primary objective of the Bid Development stage is to execute the Capture Project Plan, including:

- *Develop the Customer Solution*
- *Develop Risk Mitigation Plans*
- *Develop Business Case(s)*
- *Develop the Proposal*

The following graphic, Figure 5-2, shows the Inputs, Tools & Techniques and Outputs of the Bid Development stage.

Figure 5-2. Bid Phase: Bid Development Stage

Input	Tools & Techniques	Output
▪ Engaged Capture Team ▪ Validated Capture Project Plan ▪ Agreed to Communication Plans ▪ Documented Proposal Development Plans ▪ Identified Action Items with Owners and Due Dates	▪ Execute the Capture Project Plan ❑ Capture Team Status Meetings ❑ Action Item Register Stakeholder Status Report ❑ Stakeholder Status Review Outline ▪ Develop Solution ❑ Solution Architecture ❑ Compliance Matrix ❑ Solution Linkage Matrix ❑ Delivery Plan ▪ Develop Risk Mitigation Plans ❑ Sources of Risk ❑ Ways of Mitigating Risks ❑ Risk Mitigation Plan ❑ Risk Mitigation Plan Log ▪ Develop Business Case ❑ Business Case Scenarios ❑ Business Case Models ❑ Product/Service Profile ❑ Customer Business Case ❑ Common Business Case Terms ▪ Develop Proposal ❑ Attributes of Winning Proposals	▪ Customer Solution ▪ Risk Mitigation Plans ▪ Business Cases ▪ Customer Proposal

Inputs

The inputs for the Bid Development stage are: (1) Engaged Capture Team, (2) Validated Capture Project Plan, (3) Agreed to Communication Plans, (4) Documented Proposal Development Plans and (5) Identified Action Items with Owners and Dues Dates.

Having completed the Capture Team Kickoff, the capture team should be fully engaged and actively working to complete tasks under the direction of their respective team leader.

Tools & Techniques

Execute Capture Project Plan

- *Capture Team Status Meetings:* While each subteam (i.e., Technical, Delivery, Pricing, Contractual) will meet on their own to complete work tasks and resolve open items, you should establish a schedule of regular status meetings with the entire team. Regular status meetings are essential to ensuring the team is aligned and on-track by collecting status on work tasks and action items, as well as providing a forum to exchange information with the team.

  The frequency of the regular status meetings should be gauged to the length of the bid development stage and how close you are to completion. As a rule of thumb, meet daily during the last 3-4 weeks, two to three times per week when 4-10 weeks from completion, and once per week if 10 weeks or more from completion. You should meet more frequently if you have a large team that is not well aligned or a large complex opportunity with lots of open items or changes.

  The key with regular status meetings is to keep them focused and brief. Status meetings are not working meetings or forums to resolve open items, they are a forum to share information and collect status on work completed. The more frequently you meet, the shorter the meetings should be as there is less to report since the last meeting. Daily meetings should strive to be no more than 30 minutes, whereas, once per week meetings should not be more than 60 minutes.

  Form 5-3 is a sample agenda for Regular Status Meetings which shows the recommended topics, sequence, time, reference documents and discussion leader. Start the meeting by doing a roll-call of participants, followed by a poll for new agenda items and any team announcements. Have each core team member provide a brief update on work tasks focusing on work started, work completed, problems they need help with and issues that should become new action items. This should be followed by a review of the Action Item Register to collect status on open items, after which you can discuss new agenda items the team identified. Finally, close with reminders regarding upcoming events and a reminder regarding the next status meeting.

Form 5-3. Capture Team Status Meeting Agenda

Time	Agenda Topics	Reference Documents	Discussion Leader
3-6 min	Introduction Roll call of participants Poll team for new agenda items Team announcements	Team List	Capture Manager
15-30 min	Core Team Updates Technical Leader Delivery Leader Pricing Leader Contractual Leader Sales Leader Proposal Manager	Task List Timeline	Core Team Member
10-20 min	Review of Action Item Register	Action Item Register	Capture Manager
tbd	New Agenda Items (if any)	to be determined	to be determined
2-4 min	Closing Reminders on upcoming events Reminder on next meeting		Capture Manager

- *Action Item Register:* One of the biggest challenges during bid development is to effectively and efficiently resolve open items. Open items may be the result of new information, a change, an unforeseen event, a work task which is running behind schedule or an unanswered question identified in the capture project plan. There is an old expression "bad news does not get better with age," and the same is true of open items–the longer they remain unresolved, the bigger the potential negative impact. The key to resolving open items is identify them early as action items for resolution.
  - *Action Items:* There are four parts which compose a solid action item and increase the probability of resolution. The first part is a clear and concise definition of the open item which is the issue or problem. The second part is a clear and concise definition of the expected outcome or result. The third part is an owner, identified by name, who agrees to resolve the action item. The fourth part is a due date by which the action item must be resolved.
  - *Action Item Register:* For each action item, document the issue, required action, owner and due date on an Action Item Register, see Form 5-4. Note the action item as having an "open" status, which will later change to "closed" once resolved. Each action item should be assigned a unique tracking number for easy reference, and the status should be noted as either "open" or "closed." Action items should also be assigned a severity level such as "high," "medium" or "low" impact, so they can be prioritized for resolution and escalation if not resolved.

Form 5-4. Action Item Register

STATUS	NO.	ISSUE	ACTION REQUIRED	OWNER	DUE DATE	SEVERITY	PROGRESS

During each status meeting review the Action Item Register to ascertain progress toward closure of each item. Each owner should report on the actions they have taken and a prognosis on resolution. Make sure owners understand that if items do not get resolved by the due date, or there is no prognosis of resolution by the owner, it will result in an Alert-Jeopardy-Escalation being issued. This will serve as an incentive for owners to resolve open items, and ensure there are no surprises later if an Alert-Jeopardy-Escalation is used.

- *Alert-Jeopardy-Escalation:* Alert-Jeopardy-Escalation is a means to raise the visibility of an issue and ask for help when an open item has not been resolved. In fact, there will be some open items which can only be closed by an Escalation, in which case, issue an Escalation early to provide stakeholders time to take action. By identifying action items and regularly reviewing the Action Item Register, you and the team can identify the need for an Alert-Jeopardy-Escalation in a timely manner, thus maximizing the time available and increasing the probability for resolution.
- *Customer Questions or Missing Information:* You will frequently need to ask your customer questions or find more information to develop your bid. Be sure you ask questions as early as possible so it does not delay work tasks or lead to last minute changes. Do not delay a work task on the critical path due to a question or missing information, rather make an assumption with input from the Sales Leader and appropriate team members and document it in your response. If you are working on a competitive solicitation where questions are shared with all bidders, review your

questions carefully to ensure they do not telegraph your strategy or weaknesses to your competitors.

- ❑ *Change Requests:* There is a saying true in life and especially true in pursuit of opportunities, which is "the only constant is change." While change is inevitable, ensure the team understands that changes should not be incorporated into work tasks until a change request is approved. The inclusion of unapproved changes can easily result in mismatches during handoffs, jeopardizing the integrity of the solution and likely resulting in the need for re-work. Do not delay work tasks on the critical path due to potential or pending change requests, rather engage the core team leaders and decide on a course of action.

- *Stakeholders Status Report:* An important aspect of ensuring continued stakeholder support is to keep them informed on progress. This can be done informally through a broadcast voice mail or a regular email sent to all stakeholders, which is fine for smaller opportunities of a short duration. On large, complex or long duration opportunities, you should use a more formal means to report progress, such as a Stakeholder Status Report or a Stakeholder Status Review.

  Form 5-5 is an example of a status report which can be used on a regular basis to update stakeholders' on progress. Note that it has blanks to identify the capture manager, due date of response, customer, opportunity tracking number, opportunity name, date of this report, date of last report and date of next report. It also provides a space to provide an assessment regarding the solution, proposal and budget using a simple "Red," "Yellow" or "Green" indicator. This provides a means to advise Stakeholders if things are on-track (i.e., green), somewhat off-track (i.e., yellow) or completely off-track (i.e., red). There are also blanks to briefly highlight work tasks completed since the last report, work tasks due before the next report and any outstanding jeopardies or escalations.

Form 5-5. Stakeholder Status Report

Capture Manager:									Due Date:			
Customer:									Tracking #:			
Opportunity:												
Report Date:				Last Report:					Next Report:			
Solution Assessment	Red	Yellow	Green	Proposal Assessment	Red	Yellow	Green		Budget Assessment	Red	Yellow	Green
Work tasks completed since last report												
Work tasks due before next report												

- *Stakeholder Status Review Outline:* If there is a lengthy time between the Stakeholder Opportunity Review and Stakeholder Approval Review you may want to hold a Stakeholder Status Review. The purpose of the review should be to update stakeholders on the status of work completed and remaining, changes in the custo opportunity, competitors or win strategy, and issues including jeopardies and escalations and potential issues. Form 5-6 is a recommended outline for a stakeholder status review showing the topics and sequence of material to review.

Form 5-6. Stakeholder Status Review Outline

Category	Subject	Suggested Topics or Contents
Introduction	Purpose	Purpose is typically to: 1) Review Status, 2) Review Changes, 3) Review Issues
	Agenda	Agenda is typically the topics covered, in sequence, with presentors
	Limit	Identify time alloted for meeting
	Participants	List of stakeholders with name, title, and functional responsibility
Status	Work Completed	Update on response timeline showing status of work completed
	Work Remaining	Update on response timeline showing status of work remaining
Changes	Customer Profile	Update on changes in customer business, your presence or competitor presence
	Opportunity Update	Update on changes in problem, solution, contract, basic scope, optional scope or key dates
	Competitor Update	Update on changes in competitors, solutions, strengths or weakenesses
	Win Strategy Update	Update on changes in win theme, sweet spot, sour spot or positioning plan
Issues	Jeopardies	Review of Jeopardies and Escalations
	Potential Issues	Review potential problem areas or areas of concern
Closing	Next Review	Set date for next review or stakeholder meeting
	Action Items	Review of Action Items created during review

Develop the Solution

As the capture team develops the solution, including a solution design, solution pricing and delivery plan, it is critical that the team remain tightly linked to ensure holistic compliance of the solution. Holistic compliance means that the technical, delivery, pricing and contractual aspects of the solution are consistent and linked with each other (see Figure 5-3) to: 1) solve the customer's problem or objective and 2) satisfy company requirements for profitability and risk.

Figure 5-3. Holistic Compliance

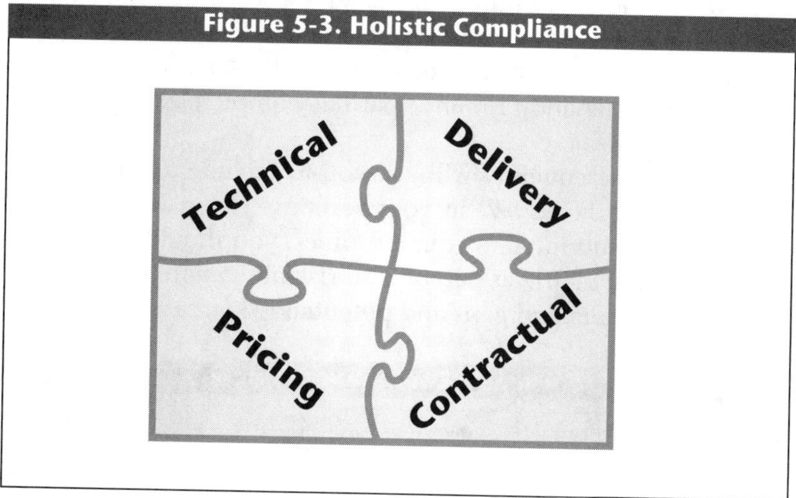

- *Solution Architecture:* Typically, you will be on a short time frame when responding to customer solicitations, hence it is necessary for work activities to occur concurrently. You should find a way to communicate the solution to the team in a summary form. One technique which is effective at achieving both ends, is to create a Solution Architecture document.

  A Solution Architecture document is typically composed of one or more pictures or diagrams which show the solution, usually with a "before" and "after" view. This is augmented by a list of the products (e.g., hardware, software, version, release) and services which compose the solution. This document can serve as the basis for the detailed design and pricing to occur concurrently with development of the technical/delivery response. Additionally, this documentation can be used as an introduction for new team members, as well as to review the solution later during the Stakeholder Approval stage.

- *Compliance Matrix:* When responding to customer solicitations, it is not uncommon to have customer requirements which you cannot fully meet and potentially even some you cannot meet at all. This is chiefly due to the fact that most customer's solicit input from multiple suppliers and create a solicitation document taking the best from each. A common technique used to identify where you have gaps in your ability to meet customer requirements is through the use of a compliance matrix, as shown below. A compliance matrix lists all the solicitation reference and functional requirements, along with an indication of whether your compliance is "full," "partial" or "none" and an explanation for any "partial" compliance.

Customers frequently will ask you to include a Compliance Matrix (see Form 5-7) in your response. Even if it is not required for submittal to your customer, you should complete a compliance matrix as part of your risk mitigation plan in order to help understand gaps and potential risk areas.

Form 5-7. Compliance Matrix

Solicitation Reference	Functional Requirement	Compliance			Explanation
		Full	Partial	None	

- *Solution Linkage Matrix:* Another common problem is ensuring linkage of the solution's design, description and pricing. This can easily occur when you have different team members performing each role and there are many changes. A Solution Linkage Matrix, such as the one shown in Form 5-8, is a simple tool which can help ensure the solution designed matches the solution described and the solution priced. Start by listing the solicitation references, functional requirements and your solution product or service which satisfies the requirements. Then identify the accountable team member for the design, description (i.e., response), pricing and overall linkage. Typically, the overall linkage will be provided by either the Technical or Delivery Team leader.

Form 5-8. Solution Linkage Matrix

Solicitation Reference	Functional Requirement	Solution Product/Service	Individual Accountable for Solution			
			Design	Description	Pricing	Overall Linkage

- *Delivery Plan:* As part of developing the solution, you need to develop a Delivery Plan, which answers the who, what, when, where, how and how much of delivering the solution to your customer. Typical elements to consider in a delivery plan include: program management, site inspections, engineering, ordering, manufacturing, transportation, warehousing, staging, installation, testing, acceptance, training, documentation and OA&M (Operations, Administration & Maintenance). Gauge the extent and detail of the Delivery Plan to the scope of the solution being offered and priced. For example, if the solution offered includes "minimum delivery," your Delivery Plan may only need to address ordering, manufacturing, transportation and acceptance.

Develop Risk Mitigation Plans

- *Sources of Risk:* As you develop the solution and your response, you will find there is uncertainty regarding future events which represent risks. Table 5-1 presents examples of common Sources of Risk.

Table 5-1. Sources of Risk

Technical Risks	Delivery Risks		Financial Risks
Hardware Design Errors	Material Availability	Reliability	Changes in COGS
Software Design Errors	Personnel Availability	Maintainability	Changes in SG&A Expenses
Testing / Modeling	Personnel Skills	Operations & Support Equipment Availability	Changes in Interest Rates
Integration / Interface	Safety		Changes in Exchange Rates
Safety	Security	Transportation	Pricing Errors
Requirement Changes	Environmental Impact	Training Availability	Customer Financial Stability
Fault Detection	Communication Problems	Documentation Accuracy	Supplier Financial Stability
Operating Environment	Labor Strikes	Zoning-Regulatory Approval	**Contractual Risks**
Unproven Technology	Requirement Changes	Degree of Concurrency	Terms & Conditions
System Complexity	Subcontractor Stability	Number of Critical Path Items	Supplier Contracts

- *Ways of Mitigating Risk:* Risk is mitigated through one of four fundamental strategies: 1) Avoid the risk, 2) Transfer the risk, 3) Share the risk or 4) Reserve the risk. Avoid the risk means you avoid the scenario which causes the risk, such as staying away from requirements you cannot satisfy. Transfer the risk means you shift the risk to another, such as buying hazard insurance or hiring a subcontractor under a turnkey contract. Share the risk means you spread the risk, such as having a partner or other related projects to assume some of the risk. Reserve the risk means you establish a reserve of funds to cover all or a portion of the risk, kind of like self insurance.

  Table 5-2 is a summary of various "Ways of Mitigating or Avoiding Risks" developed by John R. Schuyler, which can serve as a good generator of ideas.

Table 5-2. Ways of Mitigating or Avoiding Risk

Portfolio Risks
- Share risks by having partners
- Spread risks over time
- Participate in many ventures
- Group complementary risks into portfolios
- Seek lower-risk ventures
- Specialize and concentrate in a single, well-known area
- Increase the company's capitalization

Commodity Prices
- Hedge or fix in the futures markets
- Use long- or short-term sales (price and volume) contracts
- Tailor contracts for risk sharing
- Interest Rate and Exchange Rate
- Use swaps, floors, ceilings, collars, and other hedging instruments
- Restructure the balance sheet
- Denominate or index certain transactions in a foreign currency

Environmental Hazards
- Buy insurance
- Increase safety margins
- Develop and test an incident response program

Operational Risks
- Hire contractors under turnkey contracts
- Tailor risk-sharing contract clauses
- Use safety margins; overbuild and overspecify designs
- Have backup and redundant equipment
- Increase training
- Operate with redirect and bail-out options
- Conduct tests, pilot programs, and trials

Analysis Risks (Reducing Evaluation Error)
- Use better techniques (I.e., decision analysis)
- Seek additional information
- Monitor key and indicator variables
- Validate models
- Include evaluation practices along with project post-reviews
- Develop redundant models with alternative approaches and people
- Involve multiple disciplines, and communicate cross-discipline
- Provide better training and tools

Source: Schuyler, John R. Decision Analysis in Projects: Summary and Recommendations. *PM Network*, October 1995.

When considering a mitigation strategy, you need to understand both the probability that a event will occur as well as the impact if the event does occur. For risks with a high probability of occurrence and high impact, consider an "avoid" strategy. For risks with a low probability of occurrence and a high impact, consider a "transfer" strategy. For risks with a high probability of occurrence but a low impact, consider a "share" strategy. For risks with a low probability of occurrence and a low impact, consider a "reserve" strategy. These guidelines are summarized on the following grid, Figure 5-4.

Figure 5-4. Probability of Occurence

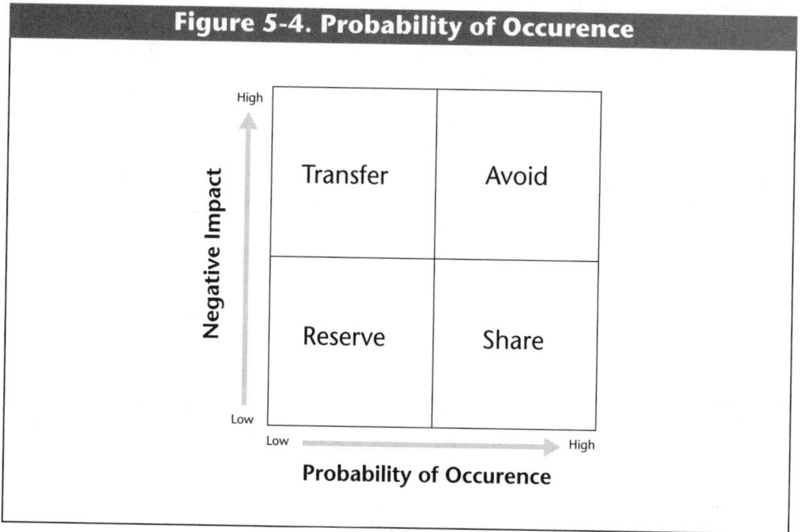

- *Risk Mitigation Plan:* For each risk identified, you should develop and document a Risk Mitigation Plan, which can be done using Form 5-9. The Risk Mitigation Plan provides a space to identify the opportunity, opportunity tracking number, risk name (i.e., what you refer to the risk as), an assigned risk number, who developed the plan, their title and the date prepared. There is a space to indicate the type of risk (i.e., technical, delivery, pricing, contractual) and a brief description of the risk along with it's probability and impact. There is a space to show the mitigation strategy used (i.e., avoid, transfer, share, reserve) along with a brief description of the specific strategy. Finally, there is a place to identify who owns implementation of the mitigation plan and their title.

Form 5-9. Risk Mitigation Plan

Opportunity:		Tracking #:	
Risk Name:		Risk #:	
Developed by:	Title:		Date:
Type Risk ☐ Technical	☐ Delivery	☐ Pricing	☐ Contractual
Briefly describe the risk it's probability and it's impact:			
Mitigation Strategy ☐ Avoid	☐ Transfer	☐ Share	☐ Reserve
Briefly describe the migitation strategy:			
Mitigation Plan Owner:		Title:	

- *Risk Mitigation Planning Log:* As you may identify a number of risks, you need a means to track them and summarize them for the stakeholders. Form 5-10 is a template of a Risk Mitigation Planning Log which can be used for this purpose. It provides a space to list each risk, the risk number, the type of risk, who is developing the mitigation, the date (once it is developed) and the strategy used.

Form 5-10. Risk Mitigation Planning Log

Risk Number	Risk Name	Type Risk				Mitigation Plan Developed By	Date	Strategy			
		Technical	Delivery	Pricing	Contractual			Avoid	Transfer	Share	Reserve

Develop Business Case

You will need to develop two business cases. One will be an internal business case showing your company's revenues and costs associated with the opportunity which will be required to secure authority to bid. The other will be a customer business case which you will include in your response to show the costs and benefits your customer will incur and realize by implementing your solution. Commercial customers purchase solutions to either generate revenues or reduce expenses, so your customer will need a business case to justify the expenditure within their company. It is to your benefit to prepare a customer business case to ensure all the benefits are identified and costs are not overstated. Another reason is to show your customer you understand the business problem and its impact on their business.

- *Business Case Scenarios:* For both business cases you will need to develop a clear set of assumptions regarding the size of the opportunity and timing of the delivery. You should develop most of what is needed as you develop the solution (i.e., design, pricing, delivery plan); however, you may need additional assumptions to produce a Worst Case, Most Likely Case and Best Case scenario. The Worst Case scenario is the minimum solution your customer will choose to implement assuming you have a winning bid. The Best Case scenario is the maximum solution your customer will choose to implement. The Most Likely Case scenario is between the two and represents how much of the solution the customer is most likely to implement. Factors to consider in each scenario include –
    - ❑ Single versus multiple supplier awards
    - ❑ Minimum or maximum purchase requirements
    - ❑ Factors which could delay or accelerate the speed of delivery
    - ❑ Factors which could shorten or extend the life of the solution
    - ❑ Factors which could increase or decrease the size of the problem

- *Business Case Models:* You can simplify the work required to create each scenario by using business case models. It is likely that your overall solution can be broken down into a model solution composed of the typical products/services delivered to solve one instance of the problem for your customer. You may find there are several size or types of problems to be solved, so several solution models may be required. Using these solution models, identify how many instances of each of the problems exist and how many solution models you expect to deliver per year under a set of assumptions for each scenario.

Table 5-3 shows how to develop these estimates using one problem which occurs 8,000 times over five years and one solution model. In the Worst Case Scenario, which might represent the minimum purchase under a multiple supplier award, you assume solving 25% of the problems each year in years one through three for a total of 1,500 solution models. In the Best Case Scenario, which might be the maximum delivery under a single award, assumes solving 50% in year 1 and increasing to solve 90% in year 5, for a total of 5,350 solution models. The Most Likely Case Scenario, which might be a modest delivery under a multiple supplier award, assumes 35% in year 1 increasing to 55% in the last three years, for a total of 3,850 solution models. You can make the model more realistic by introducing different size problems, multiple solution models or different assumptions about the number of problems under each scenario.

Table 5-3. Business Case Models

Item	Year					Total
	1	2	3	4	5	
# of Problems	1,500	2,500	2,000	1,000	1,000	8,000
Worst Case Scenario						
% of problems solved	25%	25%	25%	0%	0%	
# of solutons delivered	375.00	625.00	500.00	0	0	1,500
Most Likely Case Scenario						
% of problems solved	35%	45%	55%	55%	55%	
# of solutons delivered	525	1125	1100	550	550	3,850
Best Case Scenario						
% of problems solved	50%	60%	70%	80%	90%	
# of solutons delivered	750	1500	1400	800	900	5,350

- *Product/Service Profile:* You may find that your company does not have 100% of the solution to offer and you need to source product or service from a third party. The use of third parties introduces risk of their performance, which should be reserved by including a mark-up or margin on their products and services. The amount of third party versus in-house products and services will significantly impact profitability and price competitiveness of your solution. When you develop your solution models, determine the in-house versus third party product and service amount in each model. You can then use the units per year to populate a summary (see Form 5-11), which shows the percentage of in-house versus third party product and service for each scenario.

Form 5-11. Product/Service Profile

Product / Service	Year One	Year Two	Year Three	Total
In-House Product				
3rd Party Product				
Product Subtotal				
% In-House Product				
In-House Service				
3rd Party Service				
Service Subtotal				
% In-House Service				
In-House P & S Total				
3rd Party P & S Total				
Product & Service Total				
% In-House				
% Product				

- *Customer Business Case:* The customer business case can be developed using the same problem and solution models. For costs, use your price for each solution model times the number of models delivered. For benefits, determine the revenue increase or cost savings associated with solving each instance of each size problem and multiply by the number of problems solved. Alternatively, you may find it easier to estimate the benefits by looking at the revenue increase or cost savings associated with the aggregate number of problems solved. Look at the following factors to estimate your customer's benefits:
    - ❑ Increased revenues from new products or services
    - ❑ Increased revenues from a larger volume of products or services
    - ❑ Increased revenues from introducing products or services earlier
    - ❑ Reduced personnel or contractor costs
    - ❑ Reduced space, utilities, or support hardware/software
    - ❑ Reduced insurance, interest or cash flow requirements
    - ❑ Depreciation/amortization on capital assets

- *Common Business Case Terms:* While the business cases should be developed by someone on the Pricing Team with financial training, Table 5-4 provides definitions of the common business case terms you will encounter.

Table 5-4. Common Business Case Terms

Item	Definition
Gross Sales	Total revenues at invoice value before any discounts or allowances
Discounts, Allowances and Returns	Price discounts, returned merchandise
Net Sales	Gross Sales minus Discounts, Allowances and Returns
Variable Costs	Costs associated with production that change directly with the amount of production, e.g., the direct material or labor required to complete the build or manufacturing of a product
Fixed Costs	Operating expenses that are incurred to provide facilities and organization that are kept in readiness to do business without regard to actual volumes of production and sales. Examples of fixed costs consist of rent, property taxes, and interest expense
Cost of Goods Sold (COGS)	Direct costs of producing finished goods for sale
Gross Profit Margin	Net Sales minus Cost of Goods Sold. Also called Gross Margin, Gross Profit or Gross Loss
Gross Profit Margin % or Ratio	Gross Profit Margin $ divided by Net Sales
Contribution Margin	Net Sales minus Variable Costs. Also called called Marginal Income. It is the amount of money available to cover fixed costs and generate profits
Contribution Margin % or Ratio	Contribution Margin divided by Net Sales
Selling, General & Administrative (SG&A) Expenses	Administrative costs of running business
Depreciation	Amount of expense charged against earnings by a company to write off the cost of a plant or machine over its useful live, giving consideration to wear and tear, obsolescence, and salvage value
Amortization	Process of spreading the cost of an intangible asset over the expected useful life of the asset
Operating Expenses	SG&A plus Depreciation and Amortization
EBITDA	Earnings Before Interest, Taxes, Depreciation and Amortization, but after all product / service, sales and overhead (SG&A) costs are accounted for. Sometimes referred to as Operating Profit.
EBITDARM	Acronym for Earnings Before Interest, Taxes, Depreciation, Amortization, Rent and Management fees
Discounted Cash Flow (DCF)	Combined present value of cash flow and tangible assets minus present value of liabilities
Discount Rate	Interest rate used in calculating present value

Develop Proposal

Having developed the solution, you need to explain the solution to your customer through a well written response or proposal. You should develop several inputs to define the who, what and how of what needs to be written along with the whys in the form of messages to convey. The Proposal Layout with Volume & Section Assignments define who is responsible to write which responses. The Proposal Development Checklist defines the mechanics of how to develop your assigned sections and share them. The Win Themes and Strategies defines the overarching message to convey in the response and specific strategies to maximize your strengths, minimize your weaknesses, neutralize the competitor's strengths and ghost the competitor's weaknesses.

- *Attributes of Winning Proposals:* Before team members start writing responses, share with them the following attributes (see Table 5-5) of a proposal designed with ease of evaluation in mind developed by David G. Pugh, Ph.D. of the Lore International Institute to help them develop the right mindset.

Table 5-5. Attributes of a Proposal Designed With Ease of Evaluation In Mind

A Powerful Executive Summary	Powerful Proposal Design
Audience Designed	Double Exposure on a Single Page
1/3 Visuals, 2/3 Text, Ample White Space	Double or Message Column
Separately Bound	Themed and Captioned
Customer Focused	Emphatically written
Strategy Driven	Active Voice and Personal Pronouns
Benefits Rich (Answers Why us? And So what?)	Effective Organization
Source: A Bidder's Dozen: Golden Rules for Winning Work, David G. Pugh, Ph.D. - Lore International Institute	

Outputs

The outputs of the Bid Development stage are a well developed Customer Solution, including the design, pricing and delivery plan, Risk Mitigation Plans and Business Cases both internal and customer. You also need to develop a winning Customer Proposal, generally composed of an Executive Summary, Technical Response, Delivery Response, Pricing Response and Contractual Response.

Bid Reviews Stage

The objectives of the Bid Reviews stage are to:

- Certify the solution is sound and compliant
- Ensure proposal is accurate and complete

Below is a graphic (Figure 5-5) showing the Inputs, Tools & Techniques and Outputs of the Bid Review stage.

Figure 5-5. Bid Phase: Bid Reviews Stage

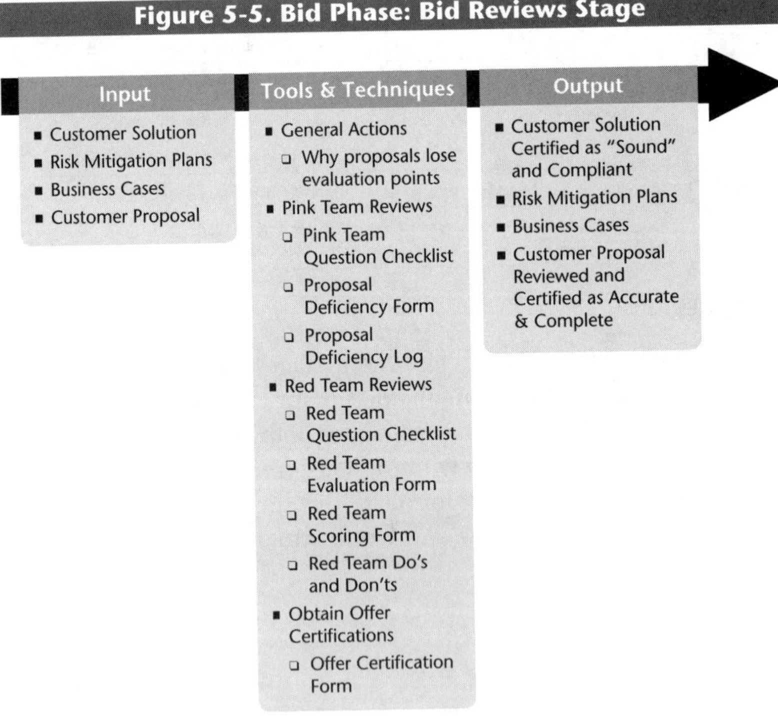

Inputs

The inputs to the Bid Reviews stage are:

- *Customer Solution, including the design, pricing and delivery plan*
- *Risk Mitigation Plans*
- *Business Cases, both internal and customer*
- *Customer Proposal*

Tools & Techniques

General Actions

- Why proposals lose evaluation points: Before describing the steps of the Bid Reviews stage, it is important to first understand why proposals lose evaluation points. You should look at your proposal very closely and watch for signs of the following pitfalls (see Table 5-6), as noted by the National Contract Management Association (NCMA).

Table 5-6. Why Proposals Lose Evaluation Points
Questionable or inadequate understanding of requirements or needs
Incomplete response to the solicitation; critical sections left out of the proposal
Noncompliance with specifications; misinterpretation of the specificications
Insufficient resources (time, funds, personnel, etc.) to accomplish the required services or tasks
Insufficient information about the resources required for satisfactory performance under the contract
Poor proposal organization; obstacles in correlating proposal content to the solicitation or requirements
Failure to show relevance of past experience to the proposed project
Unsubstaintiated or unconvincing rationale for proposed approaches or soutions
Wordiness. Mindboggling wordiness.
Repeating requirements without discussing how they will be performed
Source: Building a Contract: Solicitations/Bids and Proposals - A Team Effort National Contract Management Association

Conduct Pink Team Reviews

The first step in the Bid Reviews stage is to conduct Pink Team Reviews. The objective of Pink Team Reviews is to ensure the proposal is complete and accurate. Due to the size of the response, the timing of when it is available for review, the size of the opportunity and team and the content in each response you will likely have multiple Pink Team Reviews. For example, it is not unusual to have one Pink Team for the Technical-Delivery response, a separate Pink Team for the Pricing-Contractual response, and a third Pink Team for the Executive Summary.

The participants in the Pink Team Reviews are the individuals who wrote the responses, with the reviewers being other team members, team leaders, the Sales Leader, Proposal Manager and Capture manager. Ideally, Pink Team Reviews can be conducted face-to-face; however, they can be equally as effective with the right preparation and use of technology. On small responses with few authors, you may prefer not to conduct a "live" Pink Team Reviews session, opting instead to distribute the responses and have reviewers forward comments directly to the author by a specified deadline. This approach can also be used on larger responses as the means to conduct a Pink Team Review of the Executive Summary.

Be sure to distribute responses to the reviewers prior to the actual review session. This will allow for a shorter review session, while maintaining the quality of the review. The Pink Team Reviews should be managed by the Proposal Manager. Also, ensure reviewers understand the purpose, format, time and location for the Pink Team Reviews.

- *Pink Team Question Checklist:* Form 5-12 is a Pink Team Question Checklist, which can be used as a guide for questions to consider during Pink Team Reviews. The Pink Team Review provides general questions to consider in reviewing all responses for organization, appearance, accuracy and graphics. There are also specific questions to consider for the Executive Summary, Technical-Delivery response and the Pricing-Contractual response.

Form 5-12. Pink Team—Question Checklist

		Is the proposal complete and accurate?	✔
GENERAL	Organization	Is the proposal organized in a logical manner?	
		Does it have a clear table of contents? Is is logical?	
		Does the internal organization follow the table of contents?	
		Is the proposal a consistent document that appears to have been written by one person?	
	Appearance	How does the overall proposal look? Does it look professional?	
		Is it inviting to read? Is the proposal easy to follow?	
		Is the style consistent? Is the format consistent?	
		Is the proposal free of serious mistakes or typographical errors?	
	Accuracy	Is the solution presentation credible?	
		Are the facts correct? Is the data accurate?	
		Are the claims believable? Are the claims proven?	
		Is every claim supported? Is there an appropriate amount of supporting data?	
	Graphics	Are there enough graphics? Are there too many? Are they appropriate?	
		Are they well-designed, to truly present information and key concepts at a glance?	
		Are they creative as well as accurate?	
		Are they correctly referenced in the text?	
EXECUTIVE SUMMARY		Does it give a sense of the overall proposal?	
		Does it present the customer problem/objective and the solution?	
		Is it an effective presentation of your company ?	
		Is it sensitive to the customer's needs & requirements ?	
		Does it sufficiently and clearly convey the win theme and strategies ?	
		Was it worthwhile reading?	
TECHNICAL / DELIVERY		Is the customer problem or objective stated and analyzed?	
		Does the proposed solution solve the problem or attain the objective?	
		Is it clear? Too much detail? Not enough detail?	
		Is this the best solution? Why? Are there alternative solutions?	
		Are all customer specified questions answered?	
		Are there any conflicting responses?	
		Do the responses support the solution?	
		Are all responses satisfactory to the team and properly represent your company?	
		Is the delivery response complete and realistic?	
		Will the delivery response satisfy the customer's requirements?	
PRICING / CONTRACTUAL		Do all of the numbers add up?	
		Are the detailed pricing pages consistent with the summary pricing pages?	
		Has anything been "double counted"? Has anything been left out?	
		Is there a logical flow of information that follows an outline?	
		Are the terms and conditions explicit?	
		Are all appropriate terms and conditions included? Are any missing?	

- *Proposal Deficiency Form:* In order to ensure feedback is properly captured for the authors, you should document deficiencies using a Proposal Deficiency Form (see Form 5-13). This form provides space to identify the proposal, proposal manager, deficiency owner (i.e., the author), who identified the deficiency, volume, section, solicitation reference, page number, brief description of the deficiency and recommended action. There is also space to assign a deficiency number as well as space to capture how the deficiency was resolved and when.

Form 5-13. Proposal Deficiency Form

Proposal:	Volume:	Deficiency Number:
Proposal Manager:	Section:	
Deficiency Owner:	Solicitation Reference:	
Identified By:	Page Number:	Date Resolved:
Deficiency:		
Recommended Action:		
How Resolved:		

- *Proposal Deficiency Log:* In order to ensure all deficiencies are closed you should create a summary of the deficiencies by the volume/section which can be used as a checklist by the volume/section owner. You can also use the Proposal Deficiency Log to collect and document the deficiencies in lieu of using an individual form for each deficiency. The Proposal Deficiency Log, Form 5-14, includes space to identify the opportunity, proposal, volume/section, volume/section owner, deficiency number, solicitation reference, page number, deficiency, recommended action, deficiency owner, who identified the deficiency and date deficiency was resolved.

Form 5-14. Proposal Deficiency Log

Opportunity:				Proposal:		
Volume/Section:				Volume/Section Owner:		
Deficiency Number	Solicitation Reference	Page Number	Deficiency	Recommended Action	Deficiency Owner	Identified By

Red Team Reviews

The second step in the Bid Review stage is to conduct Red Team Reviews. The objective of Red Team Reviews is to ensure the proposal makes sense and solves the customer's business problem. If resources and time permits, you can also have reviewers evaluate and score the responses as if they were the customer. Similar to the Pink Team Review, you will likely have one Red Team for the Technical-Contractual response, one for the Pricing-Contractual and one for the Executive Summary.

The Red Team reviewers should be individuals who are familiar with the customer's requirements and the subject matter in the response, but who were not part of the response team. Peers or supervisors of the individuals who wrote the response are good candidates for Red Team reviewers. You should have reviewers who "mirror" the customers and will evaluate each section. For example, you may want to have stakeholders review the Executive Summary. In addition to the responses, be sure reviewers have access to the solicitation, win themes and strategies, and relevant reference material which will help them in their review.

- *Red Team Question Checklist:* Form 5-15 is a Red Team Question Checklist, which can be used as a guide on the questions to consider during Red Team Reviews. This checklist provides general questions to consider in reviewing all responses for organization and emphasis, win theme and strategies, compliance and responsiveness, appearance and presentation, consistency, brevity and visuals.

Form 5-15. Red Team—Question Checklist

	Does the proposal make sense and solve the customer's problem?	✔
Emphasis	Do the content and organization of the response follow the content and organization of the customer request?	
	Are all of the main ideas up front?	
	Has the content of each section been previewed at the beginning?	
	Summarized content at the end?	
	Are the paragraphs logical and easy to follow?	
	Does each paragraph have only one main idea?	
Win Theme and Strategies	Does the response effectively present the value of your company' solution?	
	Is it persuasive? Does it sell?	
	Does it follow the overall win theme ?	
	Are the win strategies reflected throughout the document?	
	Does the response emphasize your company's strengths?	
	Does the response mitigate your company's weaknesses?	
	Does the response ghost the competition's weaknesses?	
Compliance and Responsiveness	Does the solution solve the customer's problem or attain the objective?	
	Have all the customer's questions been answered?	
	Has every part of every question been answered?	
	Does the response address every customer request requirement?	
	Do the answers echo the customer's language?	
	Is the writing clear and to the point? What would make it clearer?	
	Do all the sentences make sense?	
	Are any statements vague or confusing or misleading?	
Appearance and Presentation	Is the response document professional?	
	Does it reflect the proper image of your company?	
	Do the pages have a clean, professional appearance?	
	Are all of the names and dates right?	
	Do all of the cross-references have the correct page numbers?	
	Are all of the figures numbered consecutively?	
Consistency and Brevity	Do the writing styles match? Does the response seem as though one person wrote it?	
	Were consistent terms and abbreviations used?	
	Are your numbers consistent?	
	Have extraneous words, sentences, paragraphs, visuals, facts, or data been eliminated?	
	Has all of the boilerplate been customized for this customer and their requirements?	
	Do any brochures or information sheets reflect a different format, give extraneous information,	
Visuals	Do visuals and text complement each other?	
	Are any visuals unnecessary?	
	Does the text make them redundant?	
	Are visuals appropriate for the technical level of the readers?	
	Are visuals simple, uncluttered?	
	Does each one have a clear message?	
	Do visuals stand by themselves?	
	Was each visual introduced before it appears?	
	Do the key visuals reflect the strategy?	
	Do they illustrate the major benefits for the customer emphasized in the bid?	

- *Proposal Evaluation Form:* You should document feedback from the Red Team reviewers for the authors. You can use the Proposal Deficiency Form and Proposal Deficiency Log from the Pink Team Reviews to capture specific feedback. In addition, you should have the reviewers provide an overall evaluation of each volume using the Proposal Evaluation Form shown below in Form 5-16. This form identifies the opportunity, volume and evaluator; and asks reviewer to assign a score of 1-to-5 for each category on the Red Team Question Checklist. Reviewers can then total the scores to provide an overall rating of each volume.

Form 5-16. Proposal Evaluation Form

Opportunity:						
Volume:	Evaluator:					
Evaluation Factor/Subfactor	Excellent 5	Good 4	Average 3	Poor 2	Terrible 1	Score Assigned
Organization and Emphasis	☐	☐	☐	☐	☐	
Win Themes and Strategies	☐	☐	☐	☐	☐	
Compliance and Responsiveness	☐	☐	☐	☐	☐	
Appearance and Presentation	☐	☐	☐	☐	☐	
Consistency and Brevity	☐	☐	☐	☐	☐	
Visuals	☐	☐	☐	☐	☐	
Totals						

- *Proposal Scoring Form:* If you have the specific criteria your customer will use to evaluate the response, you may opt to have the reviewers score the responses as if they were the customer using the Proposal Scoring Form (Form 5-17 below). This form identifies the opportunity, volume and evaluator. You can populate it with the factors for evaluation, maximum score, weighting (if any) and the weighted maximum score. Reviewers can then use the form to assign an evaluated score and weighted evaluated score.

Form 5-17. Proposal Scoring Form

Opportunity:					
Volume:	Evaluator:				
Evaluation Factor/Subfactor	Maximum Score	Weight	Weighted Maximum Score	Evaluated Score	Weighted Evaluated Score
Factor One					
Factor Two					
Factor Three					
Factor Four					
Factor Five					
Factor Six					
Factor Seven					
Factor Eight					
Factor Nine					
Factor Ten					
Totals					

- *Red Team Do's and Don'ts.* Table 5-7 is a compilation by David H. Herond of recommended things to do and not to do to improve the effectiveness of Red Teams.

Table 5-7. Red Team DOs and DON'Ts

Dos	Do organize and plan the proposal review process early in the proposal preparation.
	Do select the proposal review method that will do the most to increase win probability.
	Do consider using a running red team for a proposal that is to be written on a very tight schedule.
	Do consider dual red teams for major, must-win proposals.
	Do use a majority of outsiders and proposal professionals on red teams.
	Do make an early review of the proposal (sometimes called a "pink team") to ensure proper proposal structure and approach methodologies.
	Do have the proposal complete (including executive summaries, section/subsection introductions, and graphics) prior to red team review.
	Do hard edit a proposal prior to red team review.
	Do provide red team members with copies of both the solicitation and a comprehensive solicitation-to-proposal compliance matrix well before the proposal review.
	Do keep the red team members co-located during the proposal review.
	Do be specific in making comments and recommendations - general statements are usually useless.
	Do combine red team comments into a single volume.
	Do present proposal strengths and well-written areas during the red team debrief to the proposal team.
	Do remember that the proposal manager has total authority to accept or reject red team recommendations.
Don'ts	Don't select any red team member who is not fully committed to work full time on the review and to stay and participate in making recommended fixes.
	Don't use a formal red team review if the review process delay will hurt the proposal effort.
	Don't ask a red team to score a proposal against the evaluation factors unless the proposal is complete.
	Don't ask the red team to pick between multiple approaches or solutions.
	Don't present minor issues during the red team debrief —concentrate the presentation on important issues.
	Source: Focus on Basics - Using Red Teams Effectively, David H. Herond, APMP Proposal Management Journal, Fall 2000

Obtain Offer Certifications

- *Offer Certification Form:* The third step of the Bid Reviews stage is to Obtain Offer Certifications, using Form 5-18 below, before proceeding to Stakeholder Approval and submittal of the response to the customer. The purpose of Offer Certification is to have each Team Leader certify their portion of the solution is "sound" (i.e., is doable and is the appropriate solution for your company to offer), complies with all stated customer requirements and the response has been reviewed and is accurate and complete. Additionally, you should also ask the Sales Leader and Capture Manager to concur that they have reviewed the entire solution and responses and the package meets the same criteria.

Form 5-18. Offer Certification Form

Certifications			
Technical	Solution is certified as being Technically Sound and compliant with all stated customer requirements Technical Response has been reviewed and is certified as being accurate and complete		
	Signature:	Name:	
		Title:	Date:
Delivery	Solution is certified as being Delivery Sound and compliant with all stated customer requirements Delivery Response has been reviewed and is certified as being accurate and complete		
	Signature:	Name:	
		Title:	Date:
Pricing	Solution is certified as being Financial Sound and all pricing is certified as complete and accurate Pricing Response has been reviewed and is certified as being accurate and complete		
	Signature:	Name:	
		Title:	Date:
Contracts	Solution is certified as being Contractually Sound and includes all appropriate Terms & Conditions Contractual Response has been reviewed and is certified as being accurate and complete		
	Signature:	Name:	
		Title:	Date:
Concurrences			
	Solution is concurred as being compliant with all stated customer requirements Entire response has been reviewed and is concurred as being accurate and complete		
Sales Leader	Signature:	Name:	
		Title:	Date:
Capture Manager	Signature:	Name:	
		Title:	Date:

Outputs

At the completion of the Bid Review stage, you should have completed reviews and certifications to ensure: 1) the solution is certified as sound and compliant and 2) the response has been reviewed and is accurate and complete.

STAKEHOLDER APPROVAL STAGE

The objectives of the Stakeholder Approval stage are to:

- Obtain Authority to Bid
- Delivery of Customer Proposal

The graphic, Figure 5-6 below, shows the Inputs, Tools & Techniques and Outputs of the Stakeholder Approval stage.

Figure 5-6. Bid Phase: Stakeholder Approval Stage

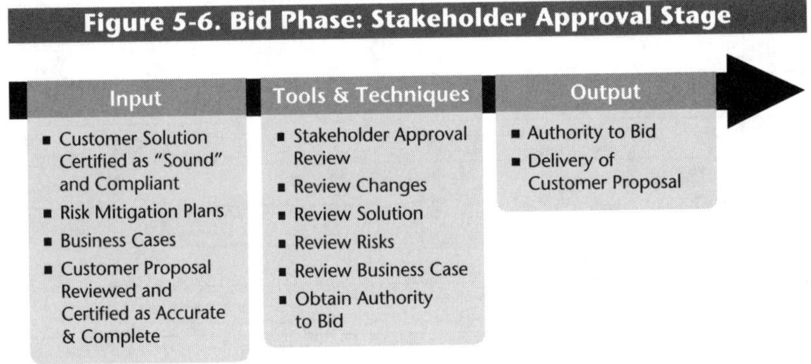

Inputs

The inputs to the Stakeholder Approval stage are:

- *Solution certified as sound and compliant*
- *Risk Mitigation Plans*
- *Business Case*
- *Proposal certified as accurate and complete*

Tools & Techniques

Stakeholder Approval Review

Earlier in the process you identified stakeholders who were part of a Stakeholder Opportunity Review, and approved development of an offer. In this last stage of the Bid Phase, you will reassemble these same stakeholders and solicit their approval to submit the bid to the customer. If you held a Stakeholder Opportunity Review and issued Stakeholder Status Reports, or held Stakeholder Status Reviews, the stakeholders will be very familiar with the opportunity and you should not have an issue with obtaining approval.

Form 5-19 is an outline of the topics to review with the stakeholders and recommended presenters. The Capture Manager should start by reviewing the purpose, agenda and limit for the session, introduce all the stakeholders, and then provide a review of the timeline. The Sales Leader should review any changes in the customer profile, opportunity profile, competitor profile or win strategy since the last stakeholder meeting. This should be followed by a review of the solution by the Technical or Delivery Leader, although this could be done by the Sales Leader if they are comfortable with the material. The Capture Manager should then review of the Risk Mitigation Plans, followed by the Pricing Leader, who should review the Business Case. Once all material is reviewed and questions answered, the Capture Manager should poll the stakeholders.

Form 5-19. Outine for Stakeholder Approval Review

Category	Subject	Suggested Topics or Contents	Presenter
Introduction	Purpose	Purpose is typically to: 1) Review Changes, 2) Review Solution, Risks and Financials, 3) Obtain Authority to Bid	Capture Manager
	Agenda	Agenda is typically the topics covered, in sequence, with presentors	
	Limit	Identify time alloted for meeting	
	Participants	List of stakeholders with name, title, and functional responsibility	
Status	Timeline update	Update on response timeline showing status	
Changes	Customer Profile Update	Update on changes in customer business, your presence, or competitor presence	Sales Leader
	Opportunity Update	Update on changes in problem, solution, contract, basic scope, optional scope or key dates	
	Competitor Update	Update on changes in competitors, solutions, strengths or weakenesses	
	Win Strategy Update	Update on changes in win theme, sweet spot, sour spot or positioning plan	
Solution	Solution	Review of solution showing before and after along with products and services offered	Technical or Delivery Leader
Risks	Risk Mitigation Plans	Review Risk Mitigation Plans	Capture Manager
Financials	Business Case	Review Business Case Assumptions, Inputs and Analysis	Pricing Leader
Authority to Bid	Stakeholder Commitment	Ensure stakeholder's understand they: 1) agree solution is Technically Sound, Delivery Sound, Financially Sound, and Contractually Sound, 2) grant Authority to Bid	Capture Manager

Refer back to the "Tips for an Effective Stakeholder Opportunity Review" in Chapter 3, as these same tips are appropriate for the Stakeholder Approval Review. Similar to the Stakeholder Opportunity Review, you should issue an update of the review package after the session to document stakeholder participation and approval along with any material changes or important points from the session.

Depending on the size of the opportunity and potential liabilities, you may need additional approval from a senior executive, such as the company President or CEO, and potentially even the Board of Directors. This is an important safeguard in companies to ensure that offers to enter into contracts with significant obligations are only done so by individuals with authority to bind the company. This information is generally identified in a Schedule of Authorizations or Approvals which should be available from the CFO or General Counsel of your company.

This approval will typically require an executive briefing document and approval package which should have been identified as a work task in the Capture Project Plan. Details on the format of this package should be available from the Pricing Leader or the CFO, business management or contracting stakeholder. These same individuals should be able to explain who should secure the approval and the time required.

Outputs

The outputs of the Stakeholder Approval stage is the Authority to Bid which grants permission for the proposal to be delivered to the customer. Stakeholder approval is documented in the updated Stakeholder Approval Review package along with the appropriate signed approval documents as required by your company's Schedule of Authorizations or Approvals.

Summary

Having successfully completed the Bid Phase, you can submit your offer to the customer and proceed to the Post-Bid Phase. Review this chapter, as well as Chapters 3 and 4 to ensure you have completed all the outputs identified as this material will be needed during the Post-Bid Phase.

By following the steps outlined in this chapter, you should have developed a solid solution to the customer's business problem which is good business for both you and your customer. More importantly, you will have done this while optimizing scarce resources, by having a well defined strategy and process to manage work tasks, manage change, minimize rework and maximize the probability of success.

Questions to Consider

1. How well does your organization kickoff capture teams, develop bids, review bids and obtain stakeholder approval to submit bids?

2. How effectively does your organization complete these activities? Are deliverables completed on time? Do deliverables reflect the quality your customers expect? Do you submit proposals which are win-win for your customer and you?

3. Does your organization have documented processes, tools and techniques used to kickoff capture teams, develop bids, review bids and obtain stakeholder approval to submit bids?

4. What actions has your organization taken to improve/develop capture team kickoff, bid development, bid review and stakeholder approval skills for your Sales managers, capture/proposal managers and contract managers?

5. How well does your organization document and share your capture team kickoff, bid development, bid review and stakeholder approval lessons learned?

chapter

Post-Bid Phase: Negotiations & Contract Formation

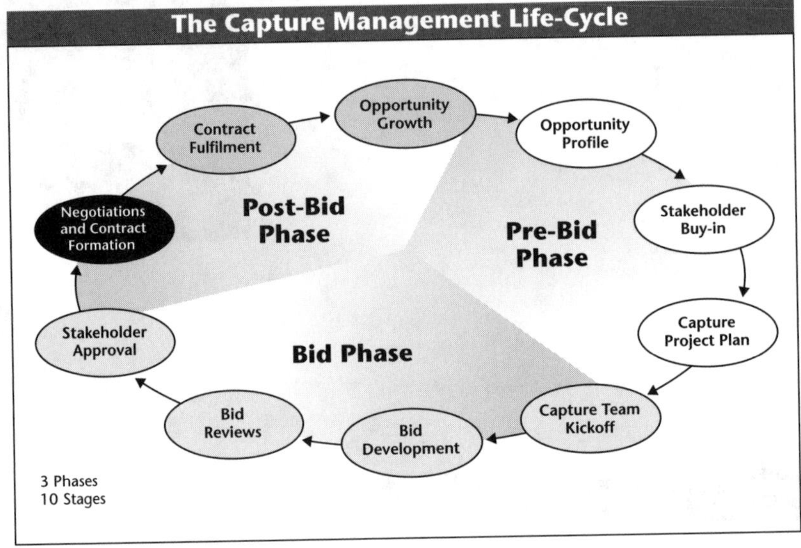

Introduction

The key to successful capture management is contract negotiations, consistently achieving positive results for your organization and having both parties view the deal as a win/win situation. Contract negotiation is a process which must be properly planned and executed, because no one wants to capture a bad deal.

Today, nearly all buyers of products and services talk about the need to build stronger vendor/supplier relationships. Likewise, nearly all sellers of products and services talk about the need to improve customer loyalty via customer relationship management techniques. However, the regrettable reality is that in many organizations it is just talk. In fact, many organizations worldwide maintain very adversarial relations with other parties, and that includes both buyers and sellers.

Chester Karass, author and negotiation consultant has said "You do not get what you deserve, You get what you have the ability to negotiate." Many successful negotiators believe the above statement to be true. According to numerous psychology surveys, two things which many people dislike or fear are public speaking and direct confrontation with another person. Thus, contract negotiation, which may involve some degree of public speaking and may involve some degree of confrontation with other people, is a role which most people would rather someone else perform.

Old school negotiators were often taught to be tough, to use emotional tactics, to wear the other-side down, to view negotiation as a win or lose proposition. During the past 20 years, more research has been conducted into the art and science of negotiations. Simply stated, most of the research has proven that many experienced negotiators are not necessarily good negotiators, because they often fail to effectively plan/prepare their strategy, tactics and countertactics, yielding inconsistent results.

Likewise, some sales people think all they need to do is promise the customer whatever they want, wine and dine them, take them golfing, and they will get a great deal. Unfortunately, too many sales people still have not learned that making promises is easy, but consistently delivering on promises is indeed difficult. Remember, negotiation begins as soon as a seller starts communicating with a potential buyer!

Today, most organizations and companies outsource a great deal of their products and services to other companies. Many of the outsourcing deals are routinely conducted electronically via simple price-based competition for off-the-shelf commercial products and services, typically from pre-qualified suppliers. Often, the biggest and most important deals, which will make or break a company, are still done via face-to-face negotiations forming detailed and complex contracts.

Negotiations & Contract Formation Stage

Negotiation is the process by which two or more competent parties reach an agreement to buy or sell products and/or services. Contract negotiations may be conducted formally or informally and may involve many people or just two - a representative for the buyer and a representative for the seller. Contract negotiation may take a few minutes or may involve many discussions over days, months or years.

The desired result of the negotiation process is a contract. Contract formation is the process of documenting the essential elements of the parties' agreement, including any special items that are unique to the agreement, see Figure 6-1.

Figure 6-1. Negotiations & Contract Formation Stage

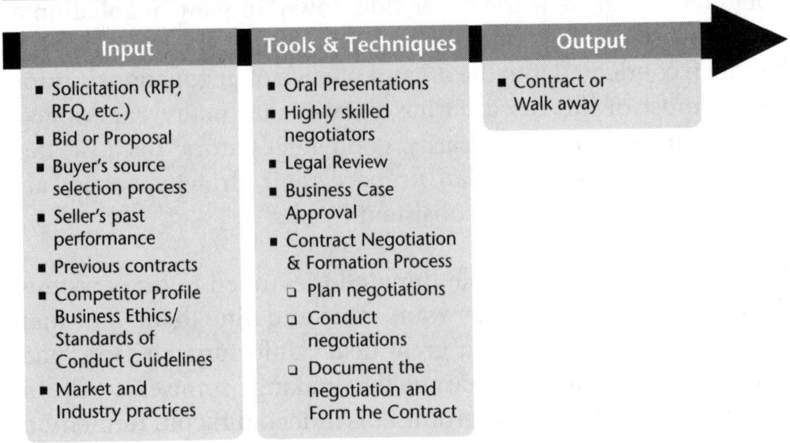

Input	Tools & Techniques	Output
▪ Solicitation (RFP, RFQ, etc.) ▪ Bid or Proposal ▪ Buyer's source selection process ▪ Seller's past performance ▪ Previous contracts ▪ Competitor Profile Business Ethics/ Standards of Conduct Guidelines ▪ Market and Industry practices	▪ Oral Presentations ▪ Highly skilled negotiators ▪ Legal Review ▪ Business Case Approval ▪ Contract Negotiation & Formation Process ❑ Plan negotiations ❑ Conduct negotiations ❑ Document the negotiation and Form the Contract	▪ Contract or Walk away

Input

The input to negotiations and contract formation consists of the following items:

Solicitation

The solicitation is either an oral or written request for an offer (RFP, RFQ, ITB, etc.) prepared by the buyer and provided to one or more potential sellers.

Bid or proposal

The bid or proposal is either an oral or written offer by potential sellers to provide products or services to the buyer, usually in response to a solicitation. It includes all supporting documentation, such as delivery plans, assumptions and cost/price models.

Buyer's source selection process

Source selection is the process by which a buyer selects a seller or source of supply for products or services. Buyers typically apply evaluation criteria to select the best seller to meet their needs.

This source selection process is seldom an uncomplicated one because:

- Price may be the primary determinant for an off-the-shelf item, but the lowest proposed price may not be the lowest cost if the seller proves unable to deliver the product in a timely manner.

- Proposals are often separated into technical/delivery and pricing/contractual sections, with each evaluated separately.

- Multiple sources may be required for critical products.

Bids or proposals may be simple, requiring only one person to evaluate the sources and select the best alternative; they may be complex, requiring a panel of experts. In fact, some proposal evaluations may require a consultant's assistance.

- *Source Selection Evaluation Criteria:* Developing the evaluation criteria for source selection requires three prerequisites. First, the buyer must understand what goods or services it wants to buy. Second, the buyer must understand the industry that will provide the required goods or services. And third, the buyer must understand the market practices of that industry. Market research provides this information.

  During requirements analysis and development of the specification or statement of work, the buyer gains an understanding of the required products or services. Understanding the industry means learning about the attributes of the goods or services in question and the firms that make them: What features do those goods or services have? What processes are used to produce or render them? What kinds and quantities of labor and capital are required? What are the cash requirements? Understanding the market means learning about the behavior of buyers and sellers: What are the pricing practices of the market, and what is the range of prices charged? What are the usual terms and conditions of sale?

  After gaining an understanding of these issues, the buyer is ready to develop the evaluation criteria by selecting attributes for evaluation.

- *Source Selection Attributes:* A consumer shopping for an automobile does not evaluate an automobile, per se, but rather selected attributes of the automobile, such as acceleration, speed, handling, comfort, safety, price, fuel mileage, capacity, appearance and so forth. The evaluation of the automobile is the sum of the evaluations of its attributes.

  An automobile has many attributes, but not all are worthwhile subjects of evaluation. The attributes of interest are those that the consumer thinks are important for satisfaction. The attributes that one consumer thinks are important may be inconsequential to another.

In most procurements, multiple criteria will be required for successful performance, for the following reasons. First, buyers usually have more than one objective; for example, many buyers look for both good quality and low price. Second, attributes essential for one objective may be different from those essential for others; for example, in buying an automobile, the attributes essential for comfort have little to do with those essential for quick acceleration.

To complicate matters further, some criteria will likely be incompatible with others. The attributes essential to high quality may be inconsistent with low price; high performance, may be incompatible with low operating cost. Thus, for any one source to have the maximum desired value of every essential attribute – for example, highest quality combined with lowest price – may be impossible. If so, the buyer must make trade-offs among attributes when deciding which source is best. These are considerations that make source selection a problem in multiple attribute decision making, which requires special decision analysis techniques.*

As a rule, source selection attributes fall into three general categories relating to: the sources, as entities, the products or services they offer and the prices they offer. Thus, the buyer must have criteria for each category that reflect the buyer's ideas about what is valuable. The criteria concerning the sources themselves are the *management criteria*, the criteria concerning the products or services offered are the *technical criteria*, and the criteria concerning the prices of the products or services are the *price criteria*.

Seller's past performance

The past performance of a seller is often a critical aspect of contract negotiation. Has the seller delivered previous products and

---

* For more information about multiple attribute decision-making techniques, consult the following references: Ching-Lai Hwang and Kwangsun Yoon, *Multiple Attribute Decision Making Methods and Applications: A State-of-the-Art Survey* (Berlin: Srpinger-Verlag, 1981); Paul Goodwin and George Wright, *Decision Analysis for Management Judgment* (Chichester, England: John Wiley & Sons LTD., 1991); and Thomas Saaty, *Decision Making for Leaders: The Analytic Hierarchy Process for Decisions in a Complex World* (Pittsburgh, Pa.: RWS Publications, 1995).

services on time? Has the seller provided high-quality products and services?

Past performance can be seen as a separate evaluation factor or as a subfactor under technical excellence or management capability. Using the past performance history also reduces the emphasis on merely being able to write a good proposal.

Previous contracts

Has the seller provided products or services to this buyer in the past? If so, what did the previous contract say? How was it negotiated? Who negotiated it?

Competitor profile

The competitor profile, developed during the Pre-Bid Phase provides a written summary of the seller's competitors and their respective strengths and weaknesses compared to the seller's.

Business ethics/standards of conduct guidelines

Ethics is especially important, in light of numerous recent cases of corporate greed, corruption and violations of state, federal or international laws. Every company should have mandatory business ethics policies, procedures and well-defined standards of conduct. Even the appearance of conflicts of interests should be avoided. All business activities should be conducted in a professional and ethical manner.

Market and industry practices

Knowing what competitors are offering (most-favored pricing, warranties, product discounts, volume discounts, etc.) is essential for a successful outcome to negotiation.

Tools and Techniques

The following tools and techniques are used for negotiations and contract formation.

Oral presentations

It is usually better to orally present your bid/proposal to your customer than to merely submit it electronically (e-mail, FAX, CD-ROM) or in paper/binders. Oral presentations, when preformed by a skilled, knowledgeable and persuasive individual can help sell your products, services and/or solution to the buyer. Oral presentations can be used to address questions and clarify concerns, which the buyer may have regarding your proposal.

Contract negotiation process

The contract negotiation process is discussed in detail in "The Negotiation & Contract Formation Process" later in this chapter.

Highly skilled negotiators

Conducting contract negotiation is a complex activity that requires a broad range of skills. Providing negotiators with the best available training in contract negotiation is vital. Top negotiators help their organizations save money and make higher profits.

Case Study: Northrop/Grumman

For more than 25 years, Northrop/Grumman has enjoyed an excellent reputation for building and developing highly skilled contract negotiators and negotiation teams. Northrop/Grumman traditionally ensure their sales managers, contract managers and contract administrators receive appropriate and timely negotiation training, via in-house professional seminars, university-based courses and attendance at educational conferences and seminars. In addition, Northrop/Grumman has for many years developed and maintained a seasoned and highly-skilled major negotiations team, which is tasked to tackle the largest and most important contract negotiations.

Legal review

A legal review should be conducted, if not as a regular part of the contract negotiation process, then at least for all key contracts.

The Negotiations & Contract Formation Process

The negotiations and contract formation process comprises planning, conducting and documenting the negotiation and forming the contract. Table 6-1 describes an effective, logical approach to plan, conduct and document contract negotiations based on the proven best practices of world-class organizations.

Table 6-1. Key Negotiations & Contract Formation Actions

Plan the Negotiation	Conduct the Negotiation	Document the Negotiation and Form the Contract
1. Prepare yourself and your team 2. Know the other party 3. Know the big picture 4. Identify objectives 5. Prioritize objectives 6. Create options 7. Select fair standards 8. Examine alternatives 9. Select your strat- egy, tactics and countertactics 10. Develop a solid and approved team negotiation plan	11.Determine who has authority 12. Prepare the facility 13. Use an agenda 14. Introduce the team 15. Set the right tone 16. Exchange information 17. Focus on objectives 18. Use strategy, tactics and countertactics 19. Make counteroffers 20. Document the agree- ment or know when to walk away	21. Prepare the negotia- tion memorandum 22. Send the memorandum to the other party 23. Offer to write the contract 24. Prepare the contract 25. Prepare negotiation results summary 26. Obtain required re- views and approvals 27. Send the contracts to the other party for signature 28. Provide copies of the contract to affected organizations 29. Document lessons learned 30. Prepare the contract administration plan

- *Plan the Negotiation:* The following ten actions should be performed to properly plan the negotiation:

    1. *Prepare yourself and your team:* Ensure that the lead negotiator knows both his or her personal and professional strengths, weaknesses and tendencies as well as those of other team members. Many self-assessment tools are available, including the Myers-Briggs Type Indicator® assessment. This tool can provide helpful insight on how an individual may react in a situation based on personal or professional tendencies. Preparing a list of the strengths and weaknesses of team members can be an important first step in negotiation planning (see Form 6-1).

Form 6-1. Team Members Strengths, Weaknesses and Interests

Team Member	**Team Member**
Name	Name
Job Title	Job Title
Phone No.	Phone No.
Fax No.	Fax No.
E-Mail:	E-Mail:
Strengths 1	Strengths 1
2	2
3	3
Weaknesses 1	Weaknesses 1
2	2
3	3
Interests 1	Interests 1
2	2
3	3
Date Prepared:________________	Lead Negotiator:________________

2. *Know the other party:* Intelligence gathering is vital to successful negotiation planning. Create a checklist of things to know about the other party to help the team prepare for negotiation (see Form 6-2.)

Form 6-2. Things to Know About the Other Party

Buyer and Seller

- ❑ What is the organization's overall business strategy?
- ❑ What is its reputation?
- ❑ What is its current company business environment?
- ❑ Who is the lead negotiator?
- ❑ Who are the primary decision makers?
- ❑ What are their key objectives?
- ❑ What are their overall contract objectives?
- ❑ What are their personal objectives?
- ❑ Who or what influences the decision makers?
- ❑ What internal organization barriers do they face?

Seller Only

- ❑ When does the buyer need our products or services?
- ❑ How much money does the buyer have to spend?
- ❑ Where does the buyer want our products and services delivered?
- ❑ What benefits will our products and services provide?
- ❑ What is our company's past experiences with this buyer?

Date Prepared:________________ Lead Negotiator:________________

3. *Know the big picture:* In the words of Stephen R. Covey, author of *The Seven Habits of Highly Effective People,* "begin with the end in mind." Keep focused on the primary objectives. Be aware that the ability of either party to be flexible on some issues may be limited because of internal policies, budgets, or organizational politics. One of the proven best practices to keep the negotiation focused is using interim summaries. The key is not to get caught up in small, unimportant details that take the negotiation off track.

4. *Identify objectives:* Know what both you and the other party want to accomplish (see Form 6-3). Successful negotiators know that nearly everything affects price (see Figure 6-2): changes in schedule, technology, services, terms and conditions, customer obligations, contract type, products and other contracting elements.

Form 6-3. Things to Know About the Other Party

Seller Objectives	Buyer Objectives
Personal 1	Personal 1
2	2
3	3
4	4
5	5
Professional 1	Professional 1
2	2
3	3
4	4
5	5
6	6
7	7
Date Prepared:_______________	Lead Negotiator:_______________

Figure 6-2. Importance of Price

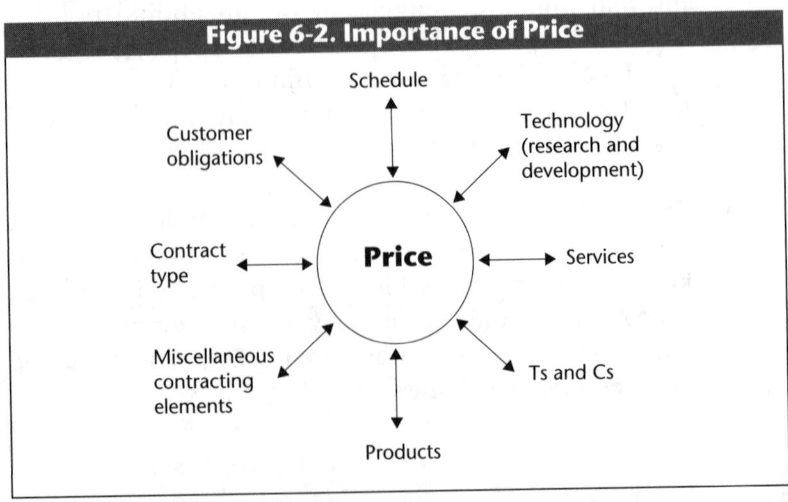

5. *Prioritize objectives:* Although all terms and conditions are important, some are clearly more important than others. Prioritize your objectives to help you remain focused during negotiation (see Form 6-4). Figure 6-3 shows that various terms and conditions affect cost, risk and value.

Form 6-4. Objective Prioritization

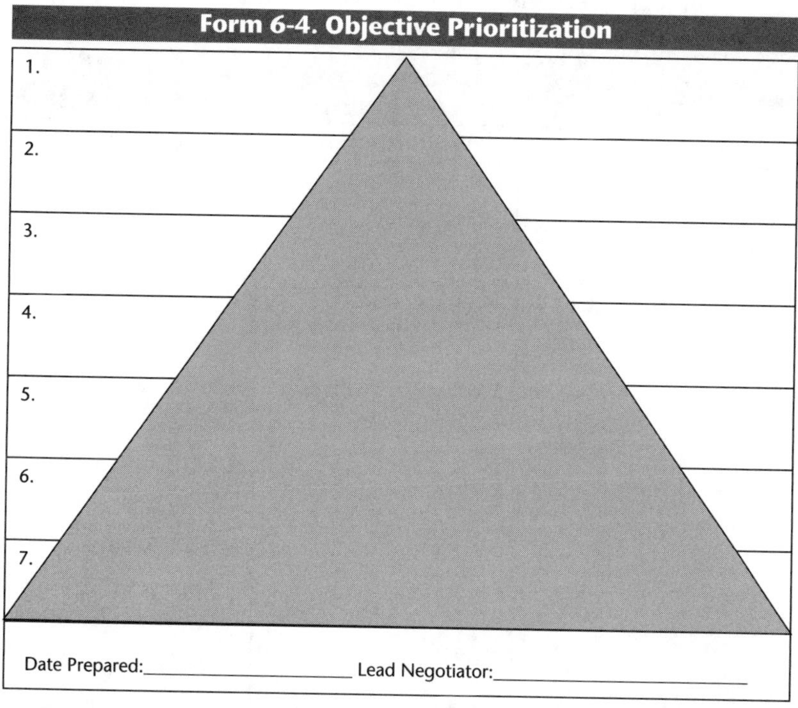

1.
2.
3.
4.
5.
6.
7.

Date Prepared:__________________ Lead Negotiator:__________________

Figure 6-3. Importance of Ts and Cs

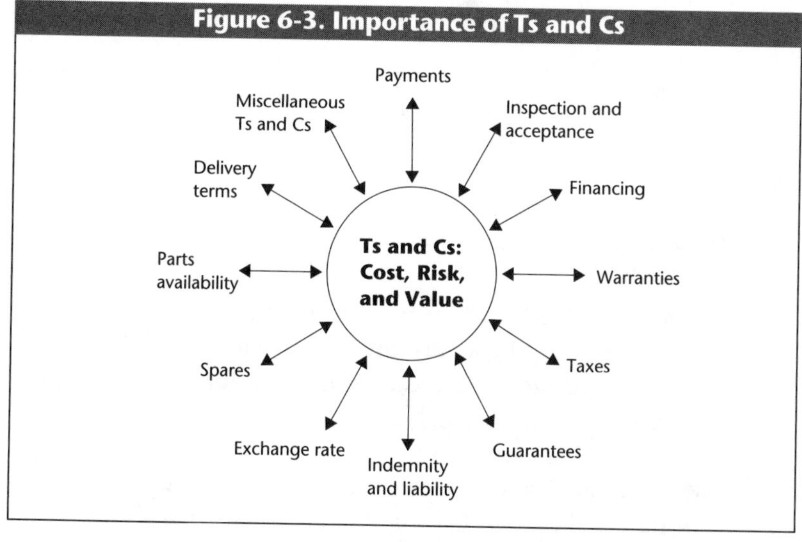

6. *Create options:* Creative problem solving is a critical skill of successful negotiators. Seek to expand options; do not assume that only one solution exists to every problem. Conducting team brainstorming sessions to develop a list of options to achieve negotiation objectives is a proven best practice of many world-class organizations (see Form 6-5).

Form 6-5. Create Options for Achieving Negotiation Objectives

Seller Objectives	Possible Options	Buyer Objectives

Date Prepared:__________________ Lead Negotiator:______________________

7. *Select fair standards:* Successful negotiators avoid a contest of wills by turning an argument into a joint search for a fair solution, using fair standards independent of either side's will. Use standards such as:
   - Uniform Commercial Code
   - United Nations Convention on Contracts for the International Sale of Goods

- American Arbitration Association standards
- ISO 9000 quality standards
- State, local and federal laws
- Market or industry standards

8. *Examine alternatives:* Prepare in advance your alternatives to the important negotiation issues or objectives. Successful negotiators know their best-case, most-likely and worst-case (walk-away) alternatives for all major objectives (see Form 6-6).

Form 6-6. Objectives and Alternatives — Worst Case, Most Likely, and Best Case

Objective:		
Worst Case	Most Likely	Best Case

(Plot your most likely position)

Date Prepared:________________ Lead Negotiator:________________

9. *Select your strategy, tactics, and countertactics:* Negotiation strategies provide the overall framework that will guide how you conduct your negotiation. Negotiation strategies can be divided into two types: win-lose and win-win.

   The win-lose negotiation strategy is about winning today, despite the potential long-term effect tomorrow and beyond. Common characteristics of the win-lose strategy include concealing one's own position and interests, discovering the other party's position and interests, weakening the other party's resolve, and causing the other party to modify its position or accept your position on all key issues. Although the win-lose negotiation strategy is not a politically correct approach, it is a commonly used negotiation strategy worldwide.

The win-win negotiation strategy is about creative joint problem solving, which develops long-term successful business relationships. The win-win negotiation strategy, however, may sometimes be difficult to accomplish. Among the obstacles to developing the win-win business environment are previous adverse buyer-seller relations, lack of training in joint problem solving and conflict resolution, and complex and highly regulated contracting procedures in some organizations, especially large companies and government agencies.

Winning or losing a contract negotiation is, indeed, a matter of perspective, which is based on your knowledge, experience and judgment. The only way to know whether you have won or lost a negotiation is to compare the results to your negotiation plan. Did you get what you wanted? Is what you got closer to your best-case, most-likely or worst-case alternative? Clearly, without a contract negotiation plan, you have no basis against which to evaluate the negotiation outcome.

To achieve your desired contract negotiation results, you need not only a strategy, but also tactics and countertactics, which are a means to a desired end. The key to using tactics successfully is to know what they are, identify the tactic when it is being used, and know how best to counter the tactic.

Table 6-2 presents some common tactics and countertactics used in contract negotiation.

Table 6-2. Negotiation Tactics and Countertactics

Tactics	Countertactics
Attacks (personal insults, emotional reactions, professional insults)	■ Disclose the attack ■ Strike back ■ Give in ■ Break off ■ Explore alternatives
Tricks (false data, no authority to negotiate)	■ Know the truth (have the right data, establish in writing who has authority) ■ Escalate
Arbitrary deadlines	■ Agree with deadline ■ Counter the offer with compromise schedule
Limited availability	■ Refuse to chance schedule ■ Coordinate schedules in advance ■ Counter with your limited availability ■ Be flexible ■ Escalate
Third-party scapegoat (third-party approval required, pretending that such approval is required)	■ Escalate to third party ■ Compromise
Giveaways	■ Disclose them as giveaways ■ Exchange giveaways
Good guy-bad guy	■ Counter with bad guy-good guy ■ Escalate
Prolonging the negotiation	■ Take a break or have a caucus ■ Maintain silence
Delays (submission of data, start of negotiation, return from breaks)	■ Start on time ■ Claim limited availability ■ Leave or create greater delays
Diversions (questions, telephone calls, fax messages, personal breaks)	■ Keep things on track (refocus the team, have no phones in the room, allow no interruptions) ■ Take a break
Stonewall ("take it or leave it," "I shall not move")	■ Give in ■ Say "Yes, and..." ■ Walk away ■ Escalate
End-of-quarter or end-of-year negotiation pressure [management wants to spend money now (buyer) or get the deal now (seller)]	■ Settle next quarter or next year (do not let time pressure you into a bad deal)

Many other negotiation tactics and countertactics are available. Those listed in the table will provide a basis for discussing good and bad tactics and countertactics that may be used by either party while conducting the negotiation.

10. *Develop a solid and approved team negotiation plan:* The conclusion of contract negotiation planning should be the summary and documentation of all planned actions. If necessary, have the negotiation plan reviewed and approved by higher management to ensure that all planned actions are in the best interests of the organization (see Form 6-7.)

Form 6-7. Sample Negotiation Planning Summary

Negotiation Information		
Location	Date	Time
1	1	1
2	2	2
3	3	3

Key Objectives (Plot your most likely position)			
1. Price	Worst Case: $10.5M	$12.0M	Best Case: $12.5M
2. Payments	Worst Case: After Delivery	Progress payments	Best Case: Advance payments
3. Warranty period	Worst Case: 36 months	18 months (Industry average)	Best Case: 12 months
4.	Worst Case		Best Case
5.	Worst Case		Best Case

Form 6-7 Cont'd. Sample Negotiation Planning Summary

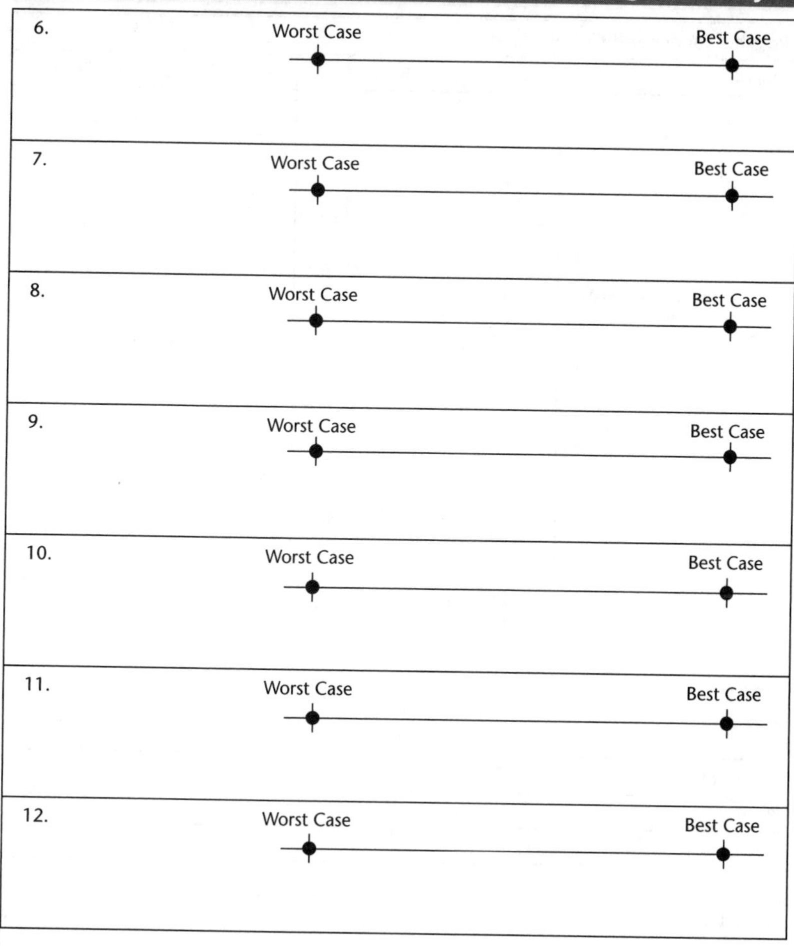

6.	Worst Case	Best Case
7.	Worst Case	Best Case
8.	Worst Case	Best Case
9.	Worst Case	Best Case
10.	Worst Case	Best Case
11.	Worst Case	Best Case
12.	Worst Case	Best Case

Form 6-7 Cont'd. Sample Negotiation Planning Summary

Possible Tactics and Countertactics		
Objective	Planned Tactics - Buyer	Planned Countertactics - Seller

Contract Price
Range
Best Case
Most Likely
Worst Case

Date Prepared:____________________ Lead Negotiator:____________________

Approved by:____________________ Date Approved:____________________

- *Conduct the Negotiation:* The following activities are necessary to conduct the negotiation:

  11. *Determine who has authority:* If possible, before the negotiation, determine who has the authority to negotiate for each party. At the start of the negotiation, ensure that you know who has that authority, who the lead negotiator is for the other party and what limits, if any, are placed on the other party's authority.

  12. *Prepare the facility:* Most buyers want to conduct the negotiation at their offices to provide them with a sense of control. Try to conduct the negotiation at a neutral site, such as a hotel or conference center. Other key facility considerations include the:

      - Size of the room
      - Use of break-out rooms
      - Lighting
      - Tables (size, shape, and arrangement)
      - Seating arrangements
      - Use of audiovisual aids
      - Schedule (day and time)
      - Access to telephone, fax, e-mail/Internet access, restrooms, food and drink

  13. *Use an agenda:* A proven best practice of successful negotiators worldwide is creating and using an agenda for the negotiation. Provide the agenda to the other party before the negotiation begins (see Form 6-8). An effective agenda helps a negotiator to:

      - Set the right tone
      - Control the exchange of information
      - Keep the focus on the objectives
      - Manage time
      - Obtain the desired results

Form 6-8. Negotiation Agenda

Contract	
Title	Date
Location	Time

Topics of Action — Time

- ❑ Introduce team members ____________
- ❑ Provide overview and discuss purpose of negotiation ____________
- ❑ Exchange information on key interests and issues ____________
  - ■ Quantity of products ____________
  - ■ Quality of products and services
  - ■ Past performance
  - ■ Delivery schedule
  - ■ Maintenance
  - ■ Training
- ❑ Have a break ____________
- ❑ Review agreement on all key interests and issues ____________
- ❑ Agree on detailed terms and conditions ____________
- ❑ Agree on price ____________
- ❑ Review and summarize meeting ____________

Date Prepared:____________ Lead Negotiator:____________

14. *Introduce the team:* Introduce your team members, or have team members make brief self-introductions. Try to establish a common bond with the other party as soon as possible.

15. *Set the right tone:* After introductions, make a brief statement to express your team strategy to the other party. Set the desired climate for contract negotiation from the start.

16. *Exchange information:* Conducting contract negotiations is all about communication. Be aware that information is exchanged both orally and through body language, visual aids (pictures, diagrams, photographs, or videotapes) and active listening.

17. *Focus on objectives:* Never lose sight of the big picture.

18. *Use strategy, tactics, and countertactics:* Do what you said you were going to do, but be flexible to achieve your objectives. Anticipate the other party's tactics, and plan your countertactics. Adjust as necessary.

19. *Make counteroffers:* A vital part of conducting the negotiation is providing substitute offers, or counteroffers, when the other party does not accept what you are offering. Document all offers and counteroffers to ensure that both parties understand any changes in the terms and conditions.

When offers and counteroffers are done right, they are part art and part science. A seller should know the approximate range (monetary amount) the buyer intends to spend. Plus, a well prepared seller should know approximately what their competitors are likely to offer and the approximate price. Likewise, well informed and prepared buyer's know what approximate range (monetary amount) sellers are likely to seek. When well prepared Buyers and Sellers enter into the exchange of offers and counteroffers, there should exist a negotiation zone (see Table 6-3).

Table 6-3. Negotiation Zone

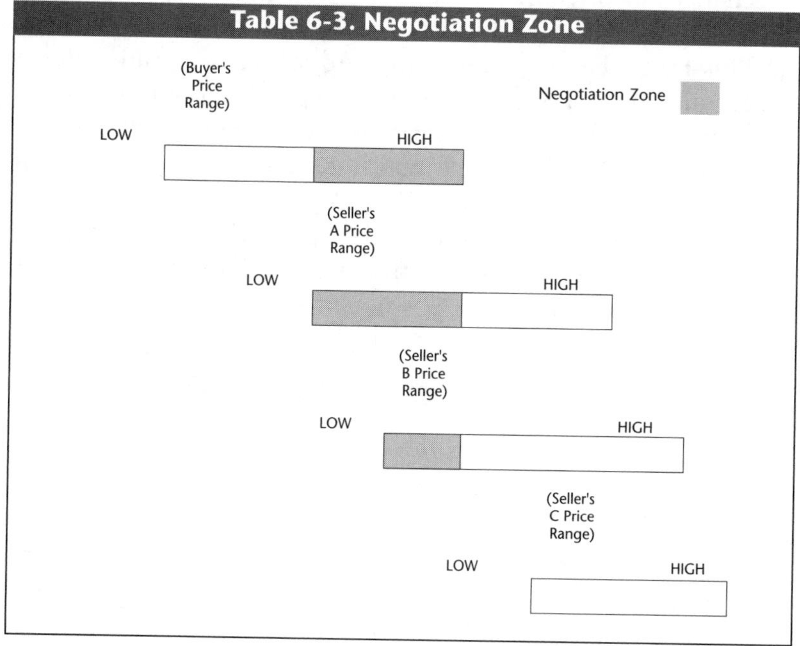

Given a competitive source business environment, sellers must ensure their initial offer is not so high that they will be eliminated from the competition. However, a seller must also ensure they maintain a healthy profit margin and still have room in their offer to give further price reductions if necessary to capture the business. Clearly, every seller must perform a balancing act between their desire to win business and their need to reduce/mitigate risks, while maximizing revenue and profit.

As illustrated in the Negotiation Zone (Table 6-3), every Buyer has a monetary range they expect to spend for their required products and/or services, which vary (low to high) based upon numerous variables typically contained within contract terms and conditions. Further, as depicted in Table 6-3, each Seller (A, B, or C) has a monetary range, typically described in their approved business case, within which they can make offers and counteroffers, based upon their costs, risks, desired profit margin and preferred terms and conditions.

Once both parties have made their initial offer, then the fun really begins. How do you determine how much to move? Do you alter your terms and conditions in conjunction with changes in pricing? Do you offer a different type of pricing arrangement, i.e., Fixed-Price to Time & Materials or Cost-Plus-Fixed Fee (see Table 6-4, Advantages, Disadvantages & Suitability of Various Contract types)? Should you refuse to move to force the other party to counteroffer? The answers to all of the above questions is - it depends! That is why, experienced highly skilled contract negotiators are a valuable asset to every organization involved in detailed, complex and expensive contract negotiations (see Form 6-9).

Table 6-4. Advantages, Disadvantages, and Suitability of Various Contract Types

Fixed Price Contracts (Greatest Risk on Seller)			
Type	Essential Elements and Advantages	Disadvantages	Suitability
FFP	Reasonably definite design or performance specifications available. Fair and reasonable price can be established at outset. Conditions for use include the following: ■ Adequate competition. ■ Prior purchase experience of the same, or similar, supplies or services under competitive conditions. ■ Valid cost or pricing data. ■ Realistic estimates of proposed cost. ■ Possible uncertainties in performance can be identified and priced. ■ Sellers willing to accept contract at a level that causes them to take all financial risks. ■ Any other reasonable basis for pricing can be used to establish fair and reasonable price.	Price not subject to adjustment regardless of seller performance costs. Places 100% of financial risk on seller. Places least amount of administrative burden on contract manager. Preferred over all other contract types. Used with advertised or negotiated procurements.	Commercial products and commercial services for which reasonable prices can be established.
FP/ EPA	Unstable market or labor conditions during performance period and contingencies that would otherwise be included in contract price can be identified and made the subject of a separate price adjustment clause. Contingencies must be specifically defined in contract. Provides for upward adjustment (with ceiling) in contract price. May provide for downward adjustment of price if escalated element has potential of failing below contract limits. Three general types of EPAs, based on established prices, actual costs of labor or material and cost indexes of labor or material.	Price can be adjusted on action of an industry-wide contingency that is beyond seller's control. Reduces seller's fixed-price risk. FP/EPA is preferred over any CR-type contract. If contingency manifests, contract administration burden increases. Used with negotiated procurements and, in limited applications, with formal advertising when determined to be feasible. CM must determine if FP/EPA is necessary either to protect seller and buyer against significant fluctuations in labor or material costs or to provide for contract price adjustment in case of changes in seller's established prices.	Commercial products and services for which reasonable prices can be established at time of award.

Table 6-4. Cont'd

Type	Essential Elements and Advantages	Disadvantages	Suitability
Fixed Price Contracts (Greatest Risk on Seller)			
FPI	Cost uncertainties exist, but there is potential for cost reduction or performance improvement by giving seller a degree of cost responsibility and a positive profit incentive. Profit is earned or lost based on relationship that contract's final negotiated cost bears to total target cost. Contract must contain target cost, target profit, ceiling price and profit-sharing formula. Two forms of FPI: firm target (FPIF) and successive targets (FPIS). FPIF: Firm target cost, target profit and profit-sharing formula negotiated into basic contract; profit adjusted at contract completion. FPIS: Initial cost and profit targets negotiated into contract, but final cost target (firm) cannot be negotiated until performance. Contains production point(s) at which either a firm target and final profit formula, or a FFP contract, can be negotiated. Elements that can be incentives: costs, performance, delivery, quality.	Requires adequate seller accounting system. Buyer must determine that FPI is least costly and award of any other type would be impractical. Buyer and seller administrative effort is more extensive than under other fixed-price contract types. Used only with competitive negotiated contracts. Billing prices must be established for interim payment.	Development and production of high-volume, multiyear contracts.
Cost-Reimbursement Contracts (Greatest Risk on Buyer)			
Cost	Appropriate for research and development work, particularly with nonprofit educational institutions or other nonprofit organizations, and for facilities contracts. Allowable costs of contract performance are reimbursed, but no fee is paid.	Application limited due to no fee and by the fact that the buyer is not willing to reimburse seller fully if there is a commercial benefit for the seller. Only nonprofit institutions and organizations are willing (usually) to perform research for which there is no fee (or other tangible benefits)	Research and development; facilities.
CS	Used when buyer and seller agree to share costs in a research or development project having potential mutual benefits. Because of commercial benefits accruing to the seller, no fee is paid.	Care must be taken in negotiating cost-share rate so that the cost ratio is proportional to the potential benefit (that is, the party receiving the greatest potential benefit bears the greatest share of the costs).	Research and development that has potential benefits to both the buyer and the seller.

Table 6-4. Cont'd

Cost-Reimbursement Contracts (Greatest Risk on Buyer)			
Type	Essential Elements and Advantages	Disadvantages	Suitability
CS	Seller agrees to absorb a portion of the costs of performance in expectation of compensating benefits to seller's firm or organization. Such benefits might include an enhancement of the seller's capability and expertise or an improvement of its competitive position in the commercial market.		
CPIF	Development has a high probability that is feasible and positive profit incentives for seller management can be negotiated. Performance incentives must be clearly spelled out and objectively measurable. Fee range should be negotiated to give the seller an incentive over various ranges of cost performance. Fee is adjusted by a formula negotiated into the contract in accordance with the relationship that total cost bears to target cost. Contract must contain target cost, target fee, minimum and maximum fees, fee adjustment formula. Fee adjustment is made at completion of contract.	Difficult to negotiate range between the maximum and minimum fees so as to provide an incentive over entire range. Performance must be objectively measurable. Costly to administer; seller must have an adequate accounting system. Used only with negotiated contracts. Appropriate buyer surveillance needed during performance to ensure effective methods and efficient cost controls are used.	Major systems development and other development programs in which it is determined that CPIF is desirable and administratively practical.
CPAF	Contract completion is feasible, incentives are desired, but performance is not susceptible to finite measurement. Provides for subjective evaluation of seller performance. Seller is evaluated at stated time(s) during performance period. Contract must contain clear and unambiguous evaluation criteria to determine award fee. Award fee is earned for excellence in performance, quality, timeliness, ingenuity, and cost-effectiveness and can be earned in whole or in part. Two separate fee pools can be established in contract: base fee and award fee. Award fee earned by seller is determined by the buyer and is often based on recommendations of an award fee evaluation board.	Buyer's determination of amount of award fee earned by the seller is not subject to disputes clause. CPAF cannot be used to avoid either CPIF or CPFF if either is feasible. Should not be used if the amount of money, period of performance, or expected benefits are insufficient to warrant additional administrative efforts. Very costly to administer. Seller must have an adequate accounting system. Used only with negotiated contracts.	Level-of-effort services that can only be subjectively measured, and contracts for which work would have been accomplished under another contract type if performance objectives could have been expressed as definite milestones, targets, and goals that could have been measured.

Table 6-4. Cont'd

Cost-Reimbursement Contracts (Greatest Risk on Buyer)			
Type	Essential Elements and Advantages	Disadvantages	Suitability
CPFF	Level of effort is unknown, and seller's performance cannot be subjectively evaluated. Provides for payment of a fixed fee. Seller receives fixed fee regardless of the actual costs incurred during performance. Can be constructed in two ways: *Completion form:* Clearly defined task with a definite goal and specific end product. Buyer can order more work without an increase in fee if the contract estimated costs is increased. *Term form:* Scope of work described in general terms. Seller obligated only for a specific level of effort for stated period of time. Completion form is preferred over term form. Fee is expressed as percentages of estimated cost at time contract is awarded	Seller has minimum incentive to control costs. Costly to administer. Seller must have an adequate accounting system. Seller assumes no financial risk.	*Completion form:* Advanced development or technical services contracts. *Term form:* Research and exploratory development. Used when the level of effort required is known and there is an inability to measure risk.
Time and Materials Contracts			
T&M	Not possible when placing contract to estimate extent or duration of the work, or anticipated cost, with any degree of confidence. Calls for provision of direct labor hours at specified hourly rate and materials at cost (or some other basis specified in contract). The fixed hourly rates include wages, overhead, general and administrative expenses and profit. Material cost can include, if appropriate, material handling costs. Ceiling price established at time of award.	Used only after determination that no other type will serve purpose. Does not encourage effective cost control. Requires almost constant surveillance by buyer to ensure effective seller management. Ceiling price is required in contract.	Engineering and design services in conjunction with the production of suppliers, engineering design and manufacture, repair, maintenance and overhaul work to be performed on an as-needed basis.

Form 6-9. Offers and Counteroffers Summary

Seller	Buyer
Offer	Counteroffer
Offer	Counteroffer
Offer	Counteroffer
Offer	Counteroffer
Date Prepared:________________	Lead Negotiator:________________

20. *Document the agreement or know when to walk away:* Take time throughout the negotiations to take notes on what was agreed to between the parties. If possible, assign one team member to take minutes. To ensure proper documentation, periodically summarize agreements on all major issues throughout the negotiation. At the end of the negotiation, summarize your agreements both orally and in writing (see Form 6-10). If a settlement is not reached, document the areas of agreement and disagreement. If possible, plan a future meeting to resolve differences. Remember: Do not agree to a bad deal – learn to say, "No thank you," and walk away.

Form 6-10. Negotiation Results Summary

Contract Title		Date of Contract
Parties Involved		Date(s) of Negotiation
Brief Product/Service Description		Location
Agreed to Price		
Key changes from Approved Proposal		
Date Prepared:__________________	Lead Negotiator:__________________	

- *Document the Negotiations and Form the Contract:* The following activities are conducted to document the negotiation and form the contract.

21. *Prepare the negotiation memorandum (minutes or notes):* Document what was discussed during the negotiation. After having the memorandum word processed, spell checked and edited, have it reviewed by someone within your organization who attended the negotiation and someone who did not. Then determine whether they have a similar understanding.

22. *Send the memorandum to the other party:* As promptly as possible, provide a copy of your documented understanding of the contract negotiation to the other party. First, e-mail or fax it to the other party. Then send an original copy by either overnight or 2-day mail. Verify that the other party receives your negotiation memorandum by following up with an e-mail or telephone call.

23. *Offer to write the contract:* As the seller, offer to draft the agreement so you can put the issues in your own words. Today, most contracts are developed using electronic databases, which facilitate reviews, changes and new submissions.

24. *Prepare the contract:* Writing a contract should be a team effort with an experienced contract management professional at the lead. Typically, automated standard organizational forms, modified as needed, are used with standard terms and conditions that are tailored during negotiation. At other times, a contract must be written in full. Ensure that no elements of the contract are missing (see Form 6-11). After the initial contract draft, obtain all appropriate reviews and approvals, preferably through electronic data.

Form 6-11. Essential Contract Elements Checklist

Project Name	Prepared by (Print)	Date Prepared
Customer	Telephone/Fax	e-mail

- ❑ Deliverables and prices (provide a listing of deliverables and their prices)
- ❑ Deliverable conformance specifications
- ❑ Requirements in statement of work (determine SOW requirements not listed as deliverables)
- ❑ Delivery requirements (list delivery requirements, deliverable packaging and shipping requirements and service performance instructions)
- ❑ Deliverable inspection and acceptance
- ❑ Invoice and payment schedule and provisions (include in contract tracking summary)
- ❑ Representations and certifications
- ❑ Other terms and conditions

25. *Prepare negotiation results summary:* Prepare an internal-use-only summary of key negotiation items that have changed since originally proposed. Many organizations have found such a summary to be a valuable tool for explaining changes to senior managers.

26. *Obtain required reviews and approvals:* Depending on your organizational procedures, products, services and other variables, one or more people may be required to review and approve the proposed contract before signature. Typically, the following departments or staff review a contract: project management, financial, legal, procurement or contract management and senior management. Increasingly, organizations are using automated systems to draft contracts and transmit them internally for the needed reviews and approvals.

27. *Send the contract to the other party for signature:* Send a copy of the contract to the other party via e-mail or fax, and then follow up with two mailed original copies. With all copies include an appropriate cover letter with a return mail address and time/date suspense for prompt return. Verify receipt of the contract by phone or e-mail. Today, many organizations, as well as the laws of many nations, recognize an electronic signature as valid.

28. *Provide copies of the contract to affected organizations:* The contract is awarded officially after it is executed, signed by both parties and delivered to both parties. Ensure that all other affected organizations or parties receive a copy.

29. *Document lessons learned:* Take the time to document everything that went well during the contract negotiation process. Even more important, document what did not go well and why, and what should be done to avoid those problems in the future.

30. *Prepare the contract administration plan:* At the end of the contract negotiation process, follow a proven best practice by having the team that negotiated the contract help the team that is responsible for administering it develop a contract administration plan.

Table 6-5. Checklist of Tips to Improve Negotiation Results

(Buyer)

- ❑ Know what you want - lowest price or best value
- ❑ State your requirements in performance terms and evaluate accordingly
- ❑ Conduct market research about potential sources before selection
- ❑ Evaluate potential sources promptly and dispassionately
- ❑ Follow the evaluation criteria stated in the solicitation: management, technical and price
- ❑ Use absolute, minimum, or relative evaluation standards to measure performance as stated in your solicitation
- ❑ Develop organizational policies to guide and facilitate the source selection process
- ❑ Use a weighting system to determine which evaluation criteria are most important
- ❑ Use a screening system to prequalify sources
- ❑ Obtain independent estimates from consultants or outside experts to assist in source selection
- ❑ Use past performance as a key aspect of source selection, and verify data accuracy
- ❑ Conduct price realism analysis
- ❑ Create a competitive analysis report
- ❑ Use oral presentations or proposals by sellers to improve and expedite the source selection process

(Buyer and Seller)

- ❑ Understand that contract negotiation is a process, usually involving a team effort
- ❑ Select and train highly skilled negotiators to lead the contract negotiation process
- ❑ Know market and industry practices
- ❑ Prepare yourself and your team
- ❑ Know the other party
- ❑ Know the big picture
- ❑ Identify and prioritize objectives

Table 6-5. Checklist Cont'd

(Buyer and Seller)

- ❑ Create options – be flexible in your planning
- ❑ Examine alternatives
- ❑ Select your negotiation strategy, tactics and countertactics
- ❑ Develop a solid and approved team negotiation plan
- ❑ Determine who has the authority to negotiate
- ❑ Prepare the negotiation facility at your location or at a neutral site
- ❑ Use an agenda during contract negotiation
- ❑ Set the right tone at the start of the negotiation
- ❑ Maintain your focus on objectives
- ❑ Use interim summaries to keep on track
- ❑ Do not be too predictable in your tactics
- ❑ Document your agreement throughout the process
- ❑ Know when to walk away
- ❑ Offer to write the contract
- ❑ Prepare a negotiation results summary
- ❑ Obtain required reviews and approvals
- ❑ Provide copies of the contract to all affected parties
- ❑ Document negotiation lessons learned and best practices
- ❑ Prepare a transition plan for contract administration
- ❑ Understand that everything affects price
- ❑ Understand the Ts and Cs have cost, risk and value
- ❑ Tailor Ts and Cs to the deal, but understand the financial effects on price and profitability
- ❑ Know what is negotiable and what is not

Output

- *Contract:* The output from negotiations and contract formation may be the contract, which is both a document and a relationship between parties.

  Or it may be best to –

- *Walk away:* Do not agree to a bad deal. No business is better than bad business.

Summary

Outsourcing is essential to business in both the public and private sectors. Many simple and smaller value business transactions are routinely done via self-service electronic catalogs or e-shopping carts. However, most large complex business to business transactions still require more formal contract negotiations and formation. Clearly, less face-to-face or in-person interaction is required in today's business environment. This is largely due to advances in communication technologies – video conferences, net meetings, teleconferences, e-mails, e-documents, electronic signatures and electronic funds transfers. However, the need for highly-skilled contract negotiators who understand the process and have mastered all of the inputs, tools and techniques and outputs is more important now than ever before!

Negotiation and contract formation is vital to the success of buyers and sellers worldwide. When skilled contract negotiators follow a proven process approach, successful business agreements are reached. Through effective contract formation practices, win-win contracts are developed and documented, yielding beneficial results for both parties.

Questions to Consider

1. How well does your organization plan your negotiation strategy, tactics and countertactics for your major negotiations?

2. How effectively does your organization negotiate favorable terms and conditions? Do you achieve your negotiation/business plan?

3. Has your organization walked away from any potential bad deals in the past year? If so, how many and why?

4. What actions has your organization taken to help improve/ develop stronger negotiation skills for your sales managers, proposal/bid managers and contract managers?

5. How well does your organization document and share your negotiation lessons learned?

chapter

Post-Bid Phase: Contract Fulfillment

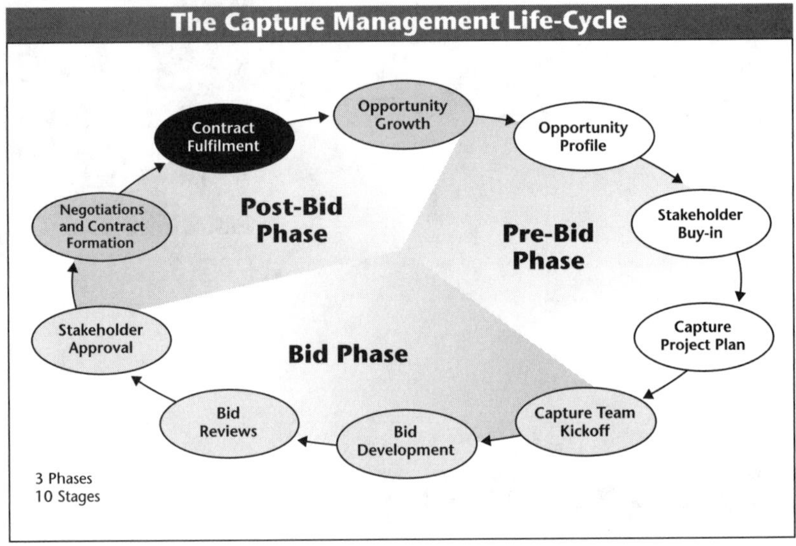

INTRODUCTION

After contract award, during the Post-Bid phase of the capture management life-cycle, there are significant opportunities to win more business with your customers. Many companies, in numerous industries, have fought hard and aggressively priced their bids to win contracts - with the specific intent to closely manage their scope of work through effective project and contract management, to increase revenues and grow profitability. Recognizing the truism that customer/buyer requirements do often change the opportunity to capture more business through contract fulfillment, is both real and significant.

Contract fulfillment is the sum of the joint buyer/seller actions taken to successfully perform and administer a contractual agreement and meet or exceed all contractual obligations, including effective changes management and timely contract closeout.

Contract fulfillment can be straightforward or complex, depending on the nature and size of the project. Administering a contract entails monitoring it throughout the many, varied activities that can occur during project execution. Key contract administration activities are monitoring compliance with contract terms and conditions, practicing effective communication and control, managing contract changes, invoicing and payment and resolving claims and disputes. Getting paid more money for doing more work than was originally agreed to in the contract is both fair and reasonable. Appropriate project management and contract administration procedures are essential to ensure both parties know what is expected of them at all times, to avoid unpleasant surprises and reduce risks regarding requirements, costs, or schedule and to solve problems quickly when they occur.

However, customers do at times consider suppliers who effectively manage their contracts, and actively pursue payment for contract changes to be "nickel and diming" them. Some suppliers/sellers will intentionally "low bid or underprice" the initial bid in order to get the contract, on the bet they can make enough follow-on sales to offset the initial loss and create a profitable long-term business relationship. Often, buyers are so motivated to reduce initial capital expenditures they will essentially entice sellers into an initial low bid/buy-in business model.

Effectively managing the contract scope of work, through proven project and contract management best practices, is wise and financially prudent for both buyers and sellers. Buyers need to ensure they get what they paid for and get it when they need it! Sellers need to ensure they provide the products and/or services as and when they agreed to deliver.

Contract administration is the process of ensuring that each party's performance meets contractual requirements. On larger projects with multiple product and service providers, a key aspect of contract administration is managing the interfaces among the various providers. Because of the legal nature of the contractual relationship, the project team must be acutely aware of the legal implications of actions taken when administering the contract.

Effective contract fulfillment is critical to effective project management because an organization's failure to fulfill its contractual obligations could have legal consequences. Thus, someone must observe performance of contractual obligations. That person is the contract manager, who must always be aware of the legal and financial consequences of an action or a failure to act and who must take steps to ensure required actions are taken and prohibited actions are avoided. In a real sense, a contract manager is a project manager, and the principles of project management apply to his or her work.

Each party to the contract appoints a contract manager, who monitors not only his or her own organization but also the other party to ensure that both parties are keeping their promises. The contract managers must maintain these two perspectives throughout contract performance.

The Contract fulfillment stage, Figure 7-1, includes applying the appropriate contract administration and project management processes to the contractual relationships and integrating the output from these processes into the general management of the project.

Figure 7-1. Contract Fulfillment Stage

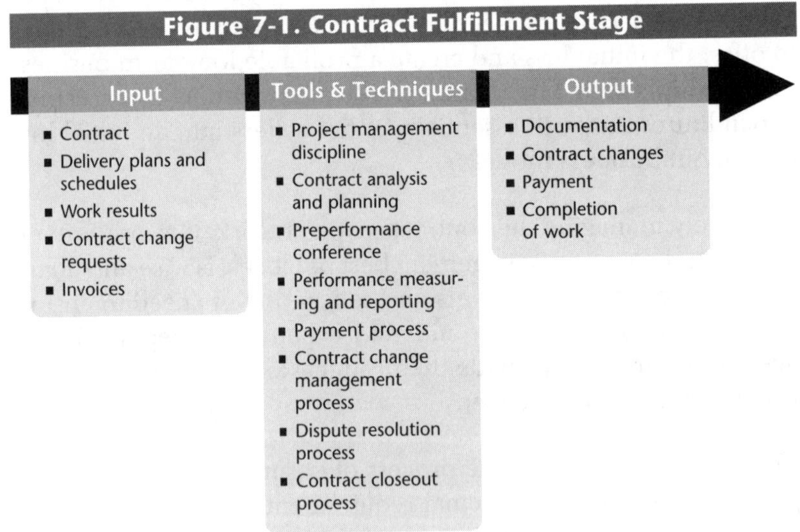

Input

Input to contract fulfillment consists of the following items:

Contract

The contract document is the primary guide for project execution and administering the contract.

Delivery plans and schedules

The project manager shall prepare appropriate plans (i.e., WBS, OBS, RAM) and schedules (i.e., Gantt Chart, Milestone Chart, CPM/PERT Network Schedule, etc.), to ensure the work is properly completed on time, on budget and meets contractual requirements.

Work results

The results of performing the requirement will affect contract administration.

Contract change requests

Contract change requests are a common element of most contracts. An effective process for managing contract changes must be in place to ensure that all requests are handled smoothly. Contract changes may be called amendments, modifications, add-ons, up-scopes or down-scopes. Contract changes are opportunities either to increase or decrease profitability for the seller. Changes are a necessary aspect of business for buyers, because of changes in their needs. Later in this chapter there is a more detailed discussion of Contract Changes Management.

Invoices

An efficient process must be developed for handling invoices throughout contract fulfillment. Few areas cause more concern to sellers than late payment. Buyers can realize savings by developing an efficient and timely payment process, because sellers are often willing to give discounts for early payment.

Tools and Techniques

The following tools and techniques are used for contract fulfillment:

Project management discipline

All work to be performed should be appropriately led, planned, scheduled, coordinated, communicated, tracked, evaluated, reported and corrected as necessary, using the basic guidelines of the Project Management Institute (PMI) Project Management Body of Knowledge (PMBOK).

Contract analysis and planning

Before contract award, each party should develop a contract administration plan and assign the responsibility of administering the contract to a contract manager. To whom should the job be assigned? A project manager could do double duty as contract manager. However in most large companies, contract administration is a specialized function, usually performed by someone in the contracting department, because doing the job requires special knowledge and training. Contract fulfillment is an element of both contract management and project management.

Preperformance conference

Before performance begins, the buyer and the seller should meet to discuss their joint administration of the contract (see Form 7-1, Preperformance Conference Checklist). The meeting should be formal; an agenda should be distributed in advance, and minutes should be taken and distributed. Each party should appoint a person who will be its organization's official voice during contract performance. At the meeting, the parties should review the contract terms and conditions and discuss who will do what. They also should establish protocols for written and oral communication and for progress measurement and reporting and discuss procedures for managing changes and resolving differences. Buyer and seller managers with performance responsibilities should attend the preperformance conference or, at the least, send a representative. Important subcontractors should also be represented. The meeting should be held at the performance site, if possible.

Form 7-1. Preperformance Conference Checklist

Project Name	Prepared by (Print)	Date Prepared
Customer	Contract	Contact Telephone/ e-mail

- ❑ Complete requirements analysis (verify and validate the requirements stated in the contract to ensure that the project, when completed according to the requirements statement, will meet the needs of both parties)
- ❑ Summarize contract requirements (complete the contract requirements matrix Form 7-2)
- ❑ Establish the project baseline (ensure that the baseline and specifications are established)
- ❑ Develop in-scope and out-of-scope listings (develop lists of items that buyer and seller consider within and outside the scope of the contract; these are useful for establishing and managing expectations and for containing contract cost growth)
- ❑ List the seller's assumptions about the buyer's requirements and understanding of the buyer's expectations
- ❑ Establish preliminary schedule of meetings between the parties
- ❑ Inform your team and other affected parties (brief the team members who will attend the meeting, ensuring they understand the basic requirements of the contract and the project)
- ❑ Review meeting findings with all affected people in your organization
- ❑ Document who attended, what was discussed, what was agreed to, and what follow-up actions are required (by whom, where and when)
- ❑ Prepare and send preperformance conference meeting minutes to the other party

Form 7-2. Contract Requrements Matrix

Deliverables				
Description	Contract Reference	Delivery Date or Service Dates	WBS Element	Other Reference

Performance measuring and reporting

During contract fulfillment, the project manager, contract manager and responsible business managers must observe performance, collect information and measure actual contract achievement. These activities are essential to effective control. The resources devoted to these tasks and the techniques used to perform them will depend on the nature of the contract work, the size and complexity of the contract and the resources available.

Payment process

Every contract must establish a clear invoicing and payment process. The buyer and seller must agree to whom invoices should be sent and what information is required. Sellers must submit proper invoices in a timely manner (see Form 7-3). Buyers should pay all invoices promptly (see Form 7-4). Sellers should insist that late payment penalty clauses be included in all contracts, and enforced as appropriate.

Form 7-3. Invoice Request

Accounts receivable: prepare and send an invoice for the following deliverable and send a copy of the invoice to the requestor.

Requestor Information

Name (Print)	Signature	Date
Phone	Fax	e-mail
Project Office	Copies to	

Deliverable Information

Customer	Contract No.	Order No.
Phone	Fax	e-mail
Address		
Deliverable		Invoice Amount

Form 7-4. Invoice and Payment Reconciliation

Project Name	Prepared by (Print)	Date Prepared
Customer	Contact	Contact Telephone/e-mail

Deliverable/ Milestone	Accepted Date	Invoiced Date	Invoice No.	Invoice Amount	Paid Date	Issues/ Comments

Contract Change Management process

As a rule, any party that can make a contract can agree to change it. Changes are usually inevitable in contracts for complex undertakings, such as system design and integration. No one has perfect foresight; requirements and circumstances change in unexpected ways, and contract terms and conditions must often be changed as a result (more information is presented later in this chapter in "Contract Change Management").

Dispute resolution process

No one should be surprised when, from time to time, contracting parties find themselves in disagreement about the correct interpretation of contract terms and conditions. Most such disagreements are minor and are resolved without too much difficulty. Occasionally, however, the parties find themselves entangled in a seemingly intractable controversy. Try as they might, they cannot resolve their differences. If the dispute goes unresolved for too long, one or both the parties may threaten, or even initiate, litigation.

Litigation is time consuming, costly and risky. You can never be entirely sure of its result. Rarely is the outcome a truly satisfactory resolution of a dispute, and it sours commercial relationships. For these reasons, litigation should be avoided. One goal of business managers and contract managers should be to resolve disputes without litigation whenever possible.

The keys to effective dispute resolution are as follows:

- Recognize that contract documents are not perfect
- Keep larger objectives in mind
- Focus on the facts
- Depersonalize the issues
- Be willing to make reasonable compromises

When disputes become intractable, seeking the opinion of an impartial third party can sometimes help. When this approach is formal, and the decision is binding on the parties, it is called arbitration. Many companies include a clause in their contracts that makes arbitration the mandatory means of resolving disputes.

Contract close-out process

Contract closeout refers to verifying that all administrative matters are concluded on a contract that is otherwise physically complete. In other words, the seller has delivered the required supplies or performed the required services, and the buyer has inspected and accepted the supplies or services (see Form 7-5).

Form 7-5. Contract Closeout Checklist

Project Name	Prepared by (Print)	Date Prepared
Customer	Telephone/Fax	e-mail

Activity	Yes	N/A	No		Anticipated Date	Completed Date
1	—	—	—	All products or services required were provided to the buyer.		
2	—	—	—	Documentation adequately shows receipt and formal acceptance of all contract items.		
3	—	—	—	No claims or investigations are pending on this contract.		
4	—	—	—	Any buyer-furnished property or information was returned to the buyer.		
5	—	—	—	All actions related to contract price revisions and changes are concluded.		
6	—	—	—	All outstanding subcontracting issues are settled.		
7	—	—	—	If a partial or complete termination was involved, action is complete.		
8	—	—	—	Any required contract audit is now complete.		
9	—	—	—	The final invoice was submitted and paid.		

Many sellers have a policy that their contract manager sign a contract completion statement confirming that all administrative actions were performed. Standard times for closing out a contract vary depending on many factors.

Contract Change Management Process

With change comes the risk that the parties will disagree on the nature of their obligations to one another. This situation is particularly likely to occur in contracts between organizations in which many people on both sides are in frequent contact with one another. These people may make informal, undocumented arrangements that depart from the contract terms and conditions. Thus, performance may be at variance with expectations, which can lead to misunderstandings and disputes.

Even when the parties formally agree to make contractual changes, they may disagree about who should bear the burden of the effect on cost and schedule. Changes can affect budgets and schedules in unexpected ways, leading to serious disputes. A risk also exists that a proposal for a formal change may provide one party with an opportunity to renegotiate the entire contract based on issues not connected with the change.

Table 7-1. Checklist of Tips to Improve Contract Change Managment

- ❑ Ensure that only authorized people negotiate or agree to contract changes
- ❑ Make an estimate of the effect of a change on cost and schedule, and gain approval for any additional expense and time before proceeding with any change
- ❑ Notify project team members that they must promptly report (to the project manager or contract manager) any action or inaction by the other party to the contract that does not conform to the contract terms and conditions
- ❑ Notify the other party in writing of any action or inaction that is inconsistent with the established contract terms and conditions
- ❑ Instruct team members to document and report in writing all actions taken to comply with authorized changes and the cost and time required to comply
- ❑ Promptly seek compensation for increases in cost or time required to perform, and negotiate claims for such compensation from the other party in good faith
- ❑ Document all changes in writing, and ensure that both parties have signed the contract; such written documentation should be completed before work under the change begins (See Form 7-6)

Form 7-6. Contract Change Request Form

Information

Buyer		Change Request No.	Date Requested
Originator	Department/Company	Phone/Fax	e-mail

Proposed Change

Baseline Description
Change Description
Reason for Change

Affected Documents

WBS No.	SOW Reference	Spec. No.	Drawing No.
WBS No.	SOW Reference	Spec. No.	Drawing No.
WBS No.	SOW Reference	Spec. No.	Drawing No.
Other References			

Seller Authorization

Name (Print)	Signature	Phone/Fax	e-mail

Buyer Disposition

	Approved	Comments (If Appropriate)
	Suspended	
	Disapproved	

Buyer Authorization

Name (Print)	Signature	Phone/Fax	Date

Case Study: Bechtel Corporation

Bechtel, a world-class construction firm, has achieved an outstanding industry reputation for excellent contract fulfillment. Bechtel is well-known for clearly defining roles and responsibilities for their company, their supply chain partners and their customers. Bechtel ensures each contract has a well defined Statement of Work, a project delivery schedule, a contract change management process, clear acceptance criteria and an effective invoice and payment process. Bechtel has demonstrated for many years the importance of tying contract administration and project management together to leverage higher performance and higher profitability.

Managing change means ensuring that changes are authorized, their effect is estimated and provided for, they are promptly identified, the other party is properly notified, compliance and impact are reported, compensation is provided and the entire transaction is properly documented (see Form 7-7).

Form 7-7. Contract Change Log

Project Name	Prepared by (Print)	Date Prepared
Customer	Telephone/Fax	e-mail

Change No.	Description	Date Requested	Date Approved	Effective Date

Contract Change Clauses

Contracts frequently include a clause that authorizes the buyer to order the seller to conform with certain changes made at the buyer's discretion. These are know as Changes clauses. The following clause is an example:

Changes

> ABC Company reserves the right at any time to make changes in the specifications, drawings, samples, or other descriptions to which the products are to conform, in the methods of shipment and packaging, or in the time or place of delivery. In such event, any claim for an adjustment shall be mutually satisfactory to ABC Company and Seller, but any claim by Seller for an adjustment shall be deemed waived unless notice of a claim is made in writing within thirty (30) days following Seller's receipt of such changes. Price increases or extensions of time shall not be binding upon ABC Company unless evidenced by a purchase order change issued by ABC Company. No substitutions of materials or accessories may be made without ABC Company's written consent. No charges for extras will be allowed unless such extras have been ordered in writing by ABC Company and the price agreed upon.

This clause does not expressly tie the amount of the seller's claim to the effect of the change on its cost or time requirements. There is no express mention of reductions in price or time. However, the clause does say that any claim must be "mutually satisfactory" to both parties. It is unclear what, if any, legal significance there is in these subtle differences in language.

The clause also requires that "notice of a claim" by the seller be made in writing within 30 days of the seller's receipt of the change order.

Documentation of Change

Whenever the parties make a change in the contract, it is important that they maintain the integrity of that document as trustworthy evidence of the terms and conditions of their agreement. Logically, a change will add terms and conditions, delete terms and conditions, or replace some terms and conditions with others. Thus, when modifying the contract, the parties should decide what words, numerals, symbols or drawings must be added, deleted or replaced in the contract document.

Parties to a contract will often discuss the change they want to make but fail to describe the change in the context of their contract document. After a few such changes, the document will no longer accurately describe the current status of their agreement, and the parties may dispute what the current terms really are. Such an occurrence should not be a surprise, human communication and memory being what they are.

The best way to avoid this problem is to draft the language of the change carefully in the context of the contract document, ensuring that the new language describes the intent of the parties. This action should be taken before making any attempt to estimate the cost and schedule effect of any change or to perform the work. People sometimes argue that expediency demands that the work proceed before reaching agreement on the precise language of the change. However, this practice is likely to create confusion over just what changed and how. If the parties cannot reach agreement on the language of the change in a reasonable time, they probably are not in agreement about the nature of the change and should not proceed.

Modification of the Contract Document

One party will have the original copy of the contract. The other party will usually have a duplicate original. These originals should remain with the contract manager, or in the contracts department or legal office.

When parties agree to change the contract, they should never alter the original documents. Instead, they should prepare modification documents that describe the contract changes. These changes should follow an agreed to contract change management process, see Figure 7-2. Changes can generally be described in two ways. First, the modification document can include substitute pages in which deleted original language is stricken out and new or replacement language is inserted in italics. Second, minor changes can be described in "pen and ink" instructions that strike out certain words and add others.

Figure 7-2. Sample Contract Change Management Process Flowchart

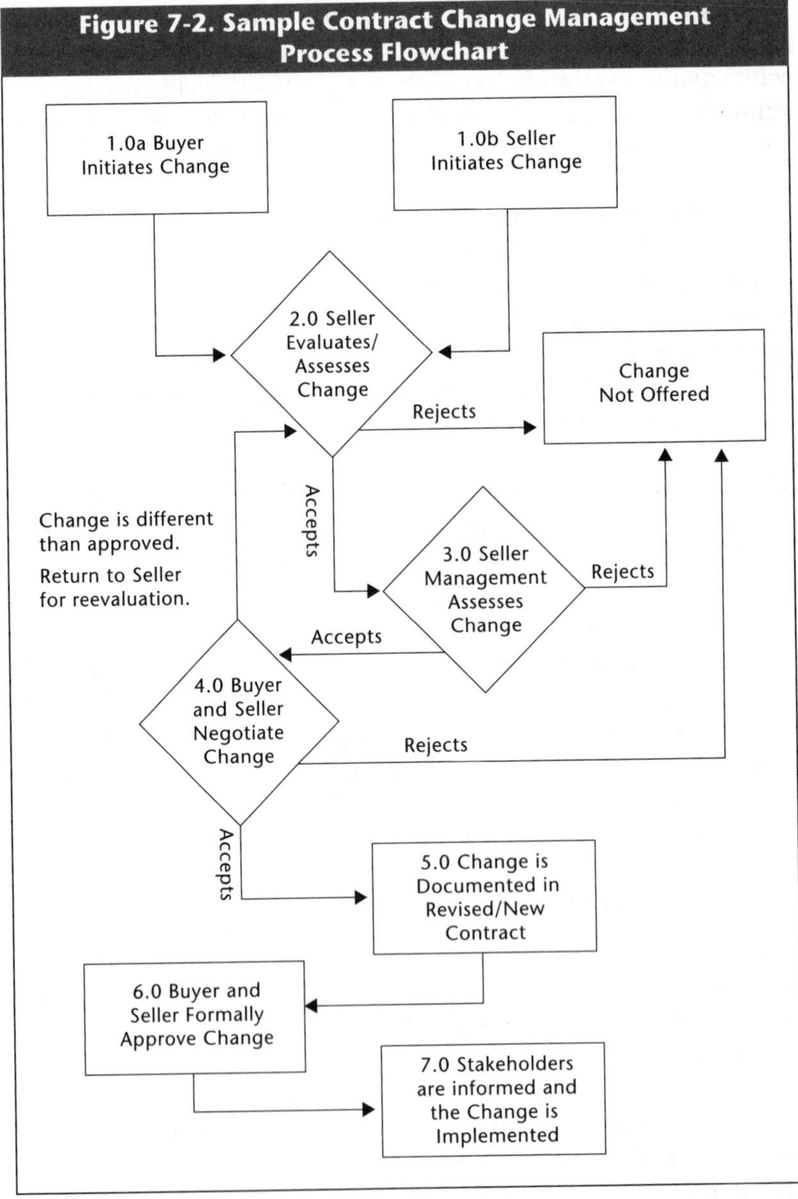

Copies of each modification should be distributed promptly to all project team members who have a copy of the original document. The project manager, contract manager and other key team members should maintain a personal conformed working copy of the contract. This copy should be kept in a loose-leaf binder or electronic database so that pages can be replaced easily. The conformed working copy should be altered as necessary to reflect the current status of the agreement between the parties. Changes should be incorporated promptly. Each team member should always keep the conformed working copy readily available and bring it to meetings. The contract manager should periodically check to ensure that each team member's conformed working copy is up-to-date.

Effect of the Change on Price and Schedule

After the parties are in precise agreement as to how the contract was modified, they should try to estimate the cost and schedule impact of the change. They can do this independently, but the most effective approach is to develop the estimate together, as a team, working out the details and their differences in the process. If the parties are open and honest with one another, this approach can save time and give them greater insight into the real effect of the change on cost and schedule. A well-developed work breakdown structure and project schedule graphic can be of enormous value to this process. Work may proceed based either on an estimate of the cost and schedule impact, with a limit on the parties' obligations, or on a firm-fixed adjustment.

If the parties work out their estimates independently (the traditional approach), an agreement will entail a certain amount of bargaining. This approach can lead to time-consuming haggling and even to deadlock, and such delays can be costly when a change is needed during performance.

Another approach is for the parties to agree that the seller can proceed with the work as changed and submit a claim later. This method can spell trouble for both parties, however, particularly if the adjustments are unexpectedly high. For the buyer, it can mean unpleasant surprises about the effect on prices and schedules for changed work. For the seller, it can mean a dismayed buyer and delays in settling claims. For both, it can mean a damaged relationship. Working out the cost and schedule impact before committing to the change is better for both parties.

If the seller must proceed with the work before the change can be fully negotiated, the parties should agree to limits on their mutual obligations in relation to the change. It is common practice for parties to agree on cost and schedule ceilings when work must begin before agreement is complete. Obviously, such limits should be documented in writing.

Authorization of Performance Under the Change

After the parties have agreed to the change and to either an estimate of the impact on cost and schedule or a final price adjustment, the buyer should provide the seller with written authorization to proceed with the work as changed. The easiest way to accomplish this objective is to prepare, sign and distribute a modification document. If this approach will take too long, a letter or other form of written documentation will suffice. The authorization should include a description of the change, its effective date and a description of any limits on the obligations of the parties.

Submission, Negotiation and Resolution

If price and schedule adjustments are not negotiated before authorizing performance under the change, the parties must negotiate such matters after performance. As a rule, the buyer should try to limit any price adjustments to the cost increases caused by the change, plus reasonable allowances for overhead and profit, and any additional time required to perform the work as changed. However, if the change reduces the cost or time of performance, the buyer should seek a reduction in price or schedule.

The project manager and contract manager should keep detailed records of all costs incurred in complying with changes. They must document the effect of changes on the time required to perform. The party submitting the claim should be able to make a reasonable demonstration of a cause-and-effect relationship between the change and the increased or decreased cost and time requirements. Ideally, the parties will have reached an advance agreement about the nature and extent of claim documentation. The objective of negotiation should be to seek a reasonable settlement that will fairly compensate the seller for performing additional work or fairly reduce the buyer's price when work is deleted.

A word to the wise: if a seller agrees to do work without the buyer's written agreement to pay for said additional products and/or services, then the seller is indeed operating at risk. Further, it is wise to ensure both parties either negotiate a well-defined scope of work and firm pricing arrangement or agree to a not-to-exceed (NTE) amount. Otherwise, one or both parties is likely to be negatively financially impacted and less than satisfied.

Sample Contract Change Management Process

1.0 INITIATOR

1.1a Buyer expresses need for additional service, feature, etc.

1.1b Seller identifies a customer need for additional service(s), feature(s), etc.

2.0 SELLER EVALUATION/ASSESSMENT OF CHANGE

2.1 Change Request Form Completed.

2.2 Seller determines whether change is in scope or out of scope.

2.2.1 Log Request.

2.2.2 Prioritize and Monitor Request.

2.3 Process Request.

2.3.1 Determine Stakeholders and Level of Authority.

2.3.2 Determine if Impact Assessment Required.

2.4 Seller determines the impact of the change from a cost, scope, technical and schedule perspective.

2.4.1 Assess impact on: Mutual Relationship, System Functionality, Operational Functionality, Services/Maintenance; Financials, Implementation Timeline/Schedule impact.

2.5 If the change is not considered to be in seller's interest, the change is not offered.

3.0 APPROVAL

3.1 Analysis of change and required documentation is completed.

3.2 Seller Senior Management, consistent with the Schedule of Authorizations, approves the change.

3.3 After assessing the change proposal, seller may either elect not to pursue the opportunity, or ask members of the program team to revise the change offer before approving it.

3.4 The change offer is communicated to the customer.

4.0 NEGOTIATION

4.1 The Buyer and Seller negotiate the terms and conditions of the change.

4.2 If the terms and conditions differ from what the Seller management originally agreed to, then the revised change opportunity should be reevaluated by the Seller.

4.3 If Buyer and the Seller cannot agree, the change may be withdrawn.

4.4 If Buyer and Seller do agree in principle to the change, appropriate papers are prepared (e.g. Addendum to Contract, Change Request Form).

5.0 DOCUMENTATION

5.1 The negotiated changes are documented formally in a new or revised contract.

6.0 JOINT APPROVAL

6.1 The Buyer and Seller sign the appropriate contract change and tracking forms.

7.0 IMPLEMENTATION

7.1 The change is formally communicated to all stakeholder organizations, such as the program team, supporting functional organizations, subcontractors, customer, etc.

Sample Contract Change Management Process Cont'd

7.2 The baseline commitment for scope, schedule and cost is updated as appropriate.

7.3 Implementation plan developed that includes the following:

- **7.3.1** Change/Commitment Owner.
- 7.3.2 Response Time Commitment.
- **7.3.3** Update/Document of Records to Reflect Approved Changes.
- **7.3.4** Distribute Changes/Feedback to Change Request Originator and Others, as needed.

7.4 The change is implemented.

Output

The following output results from contract fulfillment:

Documentation

Documentation is essential to provide proof of performance, management of changes, justification for claims and evidence in the unlikely event of litigation.

The most important documentation is the official copy of the contract, contract modifications and conformed working copies of the contract. Other important forms of documentation include the following items:

- *External and internal correspondence:* All appropriate contract correspondence should be saved electronically by the contract manager and project managers, with separate files for external and internal correspondence. Each piece of correspondence should be dated and properly stored.

- *Meeting minutes:* Minutes should be electronically recorded for all meetings between the seller and buyer. The minutes should state the date, time and location of the meeting and identify all attendees by name, company or organization and title. They should describe all issues discussed, decisions made, questions unresolved and action items assigned. Copies of the minutes should be provided to each attendee and to others interested in the meeting but unable to attend.

- *Progress reports:* Progress reports should be electronically saved and filed chronologically, by subject.

- *Project diaries:* On large projects, the project manager and contract manager should keep a daily diary either electronically or paper, in which they record significant events of the day. They should update their diaries at the end of each workday. The entries should describe events in terms of who, what, when, where and how. Preferably, the diary should be daily and kept in electronic form or in a perfect-bound book with prenumbered pages.

  A diary supplements memory and aids in recalling events. A diary is also useful as an informal project history when a new project manager or contract manager must take over. It can be of great assistance in preparing, negotiating and settling claims or in the event of litigation. However, a diary may become evidence in court proceedings, so a diarist should be careful to record only facts, leaving out conclusions, speculations about motives and personal opinions about people or organizations.

- *Telephone logs:* Another useful aid to memory is a telephone log, which is a record of all incoming and outgoing calls. It identifies the date and time of each call, whether it was incoming or outgoing, and if outgoing, the number called. It lists all parties to the call and includes a brief notation about the discussion.

- *Photographs and videotapes:* When physical evidence of conditions at the site of performance is important, a photographic or videotape record can be helpful. This record will greatly facilitate communication and will provide an excellent description of the exact nature of the site conditions. Whenever a contract involves physical labor, the project manager, contract manager, or other on-site representative should have a camera and film or digital camera available for use. The purpose of documentation is to record facts and reduce reliance on human memory. Efforts to maintain documentation must be thorough and consistent.

- *Contract changes:* As a result of changes in the buyers' needs, changes in technologies and other changes in the marketplace, buyers need flexibility in their contracts. Thus changes are inevitable. Sellers must realize that changes are not bad, that they are in fact good, because changes are often an opportunity to sell more products or services.

Payment

Cash is important–sellers want their money as quickly as possible. Buyers should seek product or service discounts for early payments. Likewise, sellers should improve their accounts receivable management and enforce late payment penalties.

Completion of work

This last step is the actual accomplishment by the seller of the buyer's requirement for products, services, systems or solutions.

Summary

Ensuring that the parties to the contract communicate with each other is important. A contract is a relationship. Because virtually every contract entails some degree of interaction between the parties, each must keep the other informed of its progress, problems and proposed solutions, so that the other can respond appropriately.

Like all human relationships, contracts are dynamic. As performance proceeds and events unfold, the parties will find that they must modify their original expectations and plans to adjust to real events. As they do so, they must modify the contract terms and conditions to reflect the current status of their agreement. Changes are an inevitable part of contracting, because no one can predict the future with perfect accuracy. However, the parties should make changes consciously and openly, so that they remain in agreement about what they should be doing. Lack of communication can result in dispute over what each party's obligations really are.

An important part of communication and control is the effective management of changes. Effectively managing contract changes includes establishing formal procedures for modifying the contract and limiting the number of people entitled to make changes. It also entails establishing recognition and notification procedures in response to unauthorized changes. Finally, it requires establishing procedures for identifying, estimating, and measuring the potential and actual effect of changes on all aspects of contract performance. Table 7-2 provides a checklist of tips for successful contract fulfillment.

Table 7-2. Checklist of Tips for Successful Contract Fulfillmeent
❑ Develop and implement a project management discipline to ensure on-time delivery and flawless execution
❑ Comply with contract terms and conditions
❑ Maintain effective communications
❑ Manage contract changes with a proactive change management process
❑ Resolve disputes promptly and dispassionately
❑ Use negotiation or arbitration, not litigation, to resolve disputes
❑ Develop a work breakdown structure to assist in planning and assigning work
❑ Conduct preperformance conferences
❑ Measure, monitor and track performance
❑ Manage the invoice and payment process
❑ Report on progress internally and externally
❑ Identify variances between planned versus actual performance
❑ Be sure to follow up on all corrective actions
❑ Appoint authorized people to negotiate contract changes and document the authorized representatives in the contract
❑ Enforce contract terms and conditions
❑ Provide copies of the contract to all affected organizations
❑ Maintain conformed copies of the contract
❑ Understand the effects of change on cost, schedule and quality
❑ Document all communication—use telephone, faxes, correspondence logs, e-mails
❑ Prepare internal and external meeting minutes
❑ Prepare contract closeout checklists
❑ Ensure completion of work
❑ Document lessons learned and share them throughout your organization
❑ Communicate, communicate, communicate!

Conclusion

Contract fulfillment is an important stage of the Post-Bid Phase of the Capture Management Life-Cycle. Simply said, contract fulfillment is the joint buyer-seller actions taken to successfully perform and administer a contractual agreement including effective changes management, and timely contract closeout. The on-going challenge is maintaining open and effective communication, timely delivery of quality products and services, responsive corrective actions to problems, compliance with all agreed-on terms and conditions and effective changes management. After the project is successfully completed, proper procedures are put into place to close out the contract officially. Of course the goal of nearly every seller is to capture the buyer's follow-on business, which is far easier to do if the contract and related project were properly managed by both parties. Remember, achieving a true partnership between a buyer and seller requires dedication and discipline by both parties – not just one!

Remember too, the power of precedent. Your organization is always evaluated based on your past performance and the precedents it sets. Your contract fulfillment, especially change management actions taken years ago affect your organization's reputation today. Likewise, the capture management actions you take today form your organization's reputation for tomorrow. Clearly, the actions taken in the Capture Management Pre-Bid and Bid Phases significantly affect your results in the Post-Bid Phase.

Questions to Consider

1. How well does your organization administer your contracts?

2. How much revenue does your organizaion realize via contract changes management?

3. How much profitability/margin is lost by your organization due to poor contrac administration practices?

4. How effectively does your organization manage the contract payments process?

5. How often and how effectively does your organization conduct customer surveys?

chapter

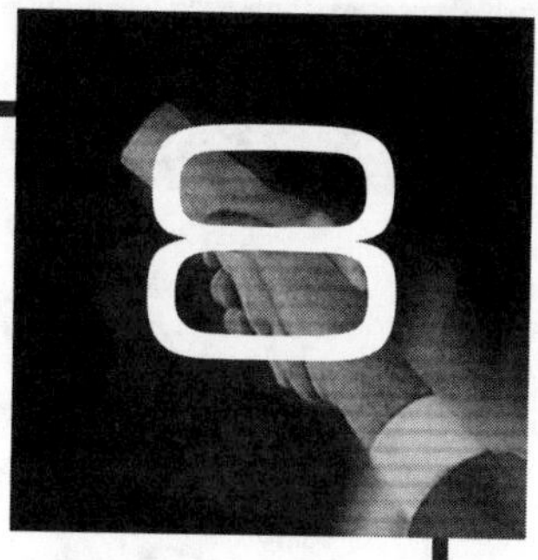

Post-Bid: Opportunity Growth

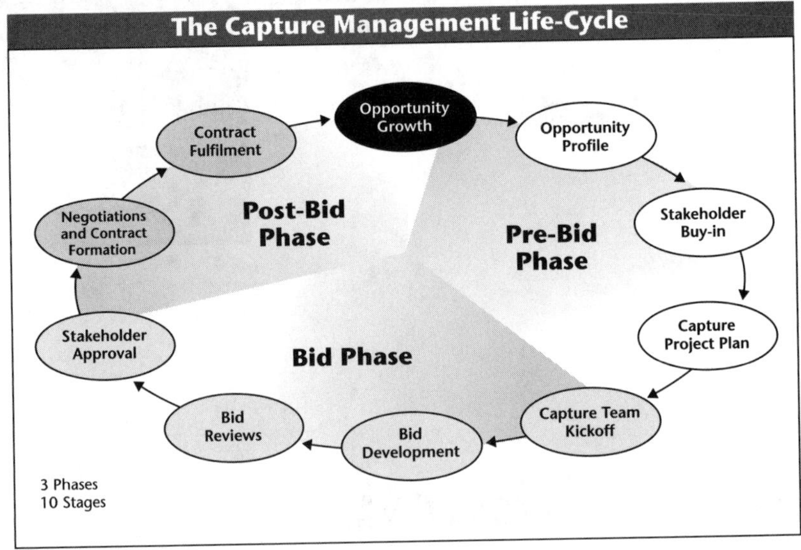

INTRODUCTION

Opportunity Growth is the final stage of the Post-Bid Phase of the Capture Management Life-Cycle. The Opportunity Growth stage is all about leveraging your performance with your existing customer base, to win more business. In order to successfully leverage your past performance you need to ensure your company meets or exceeds your customers' expectations. As stated numerous times throughout this book, talk is cheap, performance is what counts to customers. Customers care about on-time-delivery, reduced cycle-time (from request to delivery), quality products and services, timely customer service, low-to-best value pricing, supplier financing (if available) and breakthrough innovations/technology, not unfulfilled promises.

Opportunity growth is much more than company sales representatives giving gifts to customers or taking them to dinner or golfing. Opportunity growth is all about leveraging your company's knowledge, reputation, past performance and current portfolio of products, services, or solutions to differentiate your company from your competitors in the eyes and mind of your customers. Opportunity growth is about leveraging both facts as well as perceptions, which influence your current customers and potential customers key decision-makers.

In order for a company to successfully grow their business opportunities, they must continually be evaluating their performance from their customers' perspective. You should be looking to obtain feedback throughout the entire Capture Management Life-Cycle, not just at the end of delivery of a contract. Obtaining customer feedback is vital to the success of every supplier and needs to be an ongoing proactive part of your business. Learning how to improve performance, based upon customer feedback, is essential to customer retention. Sellers sharing both lessons learned and best practices within their company and supply chain is critical to sustaining supplier high performance, building trust and achieving lasting customer loyalty.

The following diagram, Figure 8-1, illustrates the inputs, tools and techniques and outputs of the Opportunity Growth Stage of the Capture Management Life-Cycle.

Figure 8-1. Opportunity Growth Stage

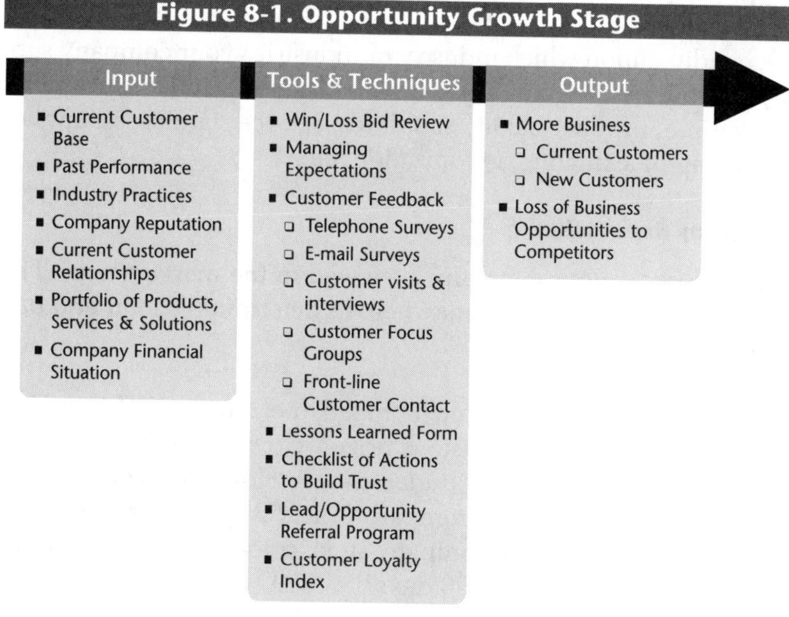

Inputs

The following items are all essentials inputs to the Opportunity Growth stage of the Capture Management Life-Cycle.

Current Customer Base

This is the sum of all of your company's current clients, people and organizations who have purchased products, services and solutions from your firm in the past year, and your firm has a reasonable expectation for continued future business.

Past Performance

This is the summary of all of your company's demonstrated actions over some period of time, usually determined by the customer. Key aspects of past performance typically include the following items, which are of great interest to most customers:

- On-time-delivery to Customer Request Date (track record)
- Cycle-time (from request to delivery)
- Quality of products and services
- Timely customer service/support
- Ease of doing business with
- Number of complaints filed against your company

Industry Practices

Depending upon which industry or industries your company supports, what are the generally accepted business practices, including: cycle-time, product quality standards, service standards, supplier financing (if available), unionization, etc.

Company Reputation

Refers to how your company is viewed in the marketplace. The following list of questions may help in determining a fair and balanced perspective:

- If your company is publicly traded, (i.e., on the NYSE or Nasdaq) – What is current stock price? How many shares of your company are typically traded daily? How does your current company stock price compare to its 52 week high and low? Generally, has your company stock price been moving up or down during the past 90 days?
- Do your top company officers (CEO, CFO, COO, CIO, etc.) have well-known and industry respected reputations (e.g., Andy Grove (Intel), Kent Kresa (Northrup-Grumman), etc.)?
- How do your current customers view your company in comparison to competitors?
- Is your company listed or viewed as one of the top companies in its industry (based upon revenues, quality of products and/or services, etc.)?
- Has your company received recent (last 6 months) positive press, via feature article in major business magazine or industry/professional publications?

Current Customer Relationships

Who you know and how well you know them are extremely important aspects of retaining customers and winning more business. Of course, every company should seek to establish professional business relationships with their customers' senior officers. Plus, smart suppliers proactively seek out the other important customer decision-makers, including: key personnel in purchasing/supply-chain management, engineering, operations, customer service, etc.

Portfolio of Products, Services and Solutions

The sum of what your company offers in terms of goods, services and customized business solutions.

Company Financial Situation

Customers have become increasingly concerned about the financial stability of any party/supplier they choose to do business with. Customers do not want to become involved with a company which may not be able to deliver on their promises/commitments due to their poor financial management.

Tools and Techniques

The following items are all proven effective tools and techniques, which may be used and appropriately tailored for your company's actions, during the Opportunity Growth stage of the Capture Management Life-Cycle.

Win/Loss Bid Reviews

There are two perspectives from which an organization can conduct a Win/Loss Bid review: (1) Customers perspective – obtain customer feedback on why your company won or lost the opportunity and (2) the Company/Supplier's internal perspective of what did we do well or where can we improve?

Although there are valuable insights to be gained from an internally focused Win/Loss Review, the customer's perspective will produce learnings with the most value, so first priority should always be given to a customer focused Win/Loss Review. If you opt to conduct an internally focused Win/Loss Review of a lost bid, you should carefully manage the situation to ensure it does not turn into a "witch-hunt" to identify "who lost the bid."

Typically, customer evaluation factors include the items contained in the Win/Loss Review Outline (Form 8-1).

Form 8-1. Win/Loss Review Outline

Key Customer Evaluation Factors	A Reason For	
	Win (Strength)	Loss (Weakness)
■ Lowest Price	❑	❑
■ Best-Value Deal	❑	❑
■ Innovative/Break-Through Technologies	❑	❑
■ Current Customer Relationship	❑	❑
■ Highest Perceived Quality	❑	❑
■ Speed of Delivery	❑	❑
■ Past Performance Record	❑	❑
■ Company Reputation	❑	❑
■ Supplier Financing	❑	❑
■ Extended Warranties	❑	❑
■ Ease of Doing Business With	❑	❑
■ Best Technical Solution	❑	❑
■ Quality of Talent/Personnel	❑	❑
■ Unique Products/Services	❑	❑
■ Feedback from Other Customers	❑	❑
■ Company Financial Situation	❑	❑
■ Portfolio of Products, Services & Solutions	❑	❑

When conducting Win/Loss Bid Reviews with customers it is important to focus on facts vs. interesting trivia. Some customers have a difficult time in providing hard or disappointing information to suppliers, while other customers give bad news to their suppliers with great ease. The key for suppliers is to focus on what actions the customer considers your company has done well and on what actions the customer feels your company needs to improve. Remember – it is the customer's perspective that counts! It is important to conduct Win/Loss Bid Reviews with your customers both when you win, as well as when you lose! The essential elements are what real actions you take with the information you obtain, to help your company win more business in the future.

Managing Expectations

In our current dynamic high-speed world of e-business, expectations are incredibly high. Too often, people expect the impossible to be achieved without knowing all the facts or details. Of course, sometimes companies can create virtual miracles, but in many cases, they fall well short of their customers' unrealistic expectations.

No one in business can avoid setting expectations. Everything companies say or do – or don't say or do – sets some form of expectation in the minds of others. Most companies try to set expectations through their advertising and marketing. However, companies' real market expectations are typically set by their actual performance in comparison to their promises, commonly referred to by result-oriented business leaders as the Hype-to-Results index. The real key to successfully managing expectations and honoring commitments is understanding the process (see Figure 8-2).

The process of managing expectations is primarily a communications process. Figure 8-2 depicts a variety of simple ways to describe the essential elements. Understanding process is good; applying it is even better. Unfortunately, because of the speed of business today, companies frequently react to partial information based upon inaccurate assumptions, rather than truly listening and understanding their customers' needs and desires. Often, sellers do not properly distinguish the real difference between a buyer's needs vs. desires.

Figure 8-2. The Managing Expections Process

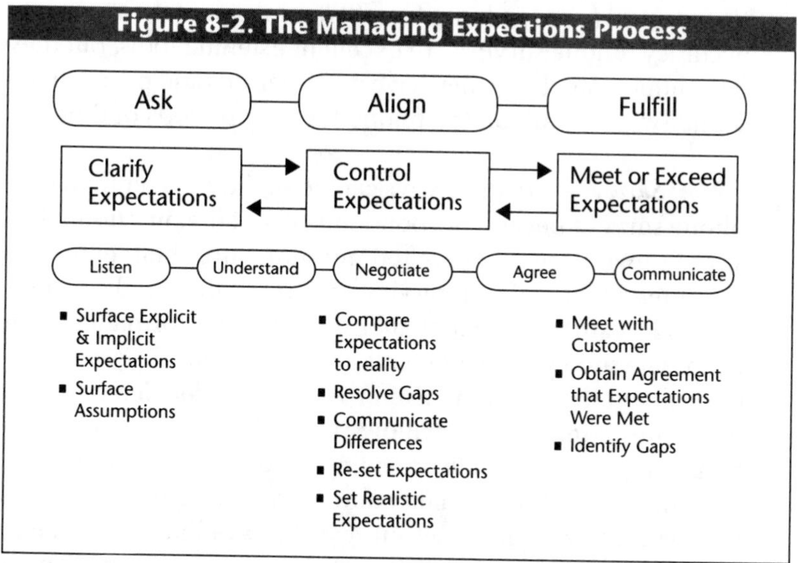

Adapted from: "Managing Expectations" by Dorothy Kirk, PM Network, August 2000

Aligning expectations to reality is a critical step in the managing expectations process. Aligning expectations does not mean reducing objectives or requirements to the lowest level. Aligning expectations is about negotiating a challenging but achievable set of objectives for all parties, based upon the realities of the situation (i.e., technology maturity, schedule, budget, scope of work, mutual priorities and resource availability).

In order to meet or exceed customer expectations, a company must first agree upon, preferably in writing, what is required. These requirements, often referred to as acceptance criteria, include price, schedule, quality, quantity, etc. It is clearly in the best interest of both parties to ensure the agreed-to products, services or solutions will meet or exceed the documented acceptance criteria.

Customer Feedback

There are many proven effective techniques available that will allow your company to obtain valuable customer information, including the following:

- *Telephone Surveys* – Phone surveys are excellent methods to use if time is of the essence, the questions are not intrusive and the survey is not too long. Great care must be taken to verify accuracy. Phone surveys are excellent listening tools, but they have limitations, since they have no visual aids and people often do not want to talk on the phone for long periods of time.

- *e-Mail Surveys* – e-mail surveys can be slightly longer than telephone surveys because respondents fill out the questionnaires at their own pace. Well crafted questionnaires help eliminate the potential bias of an interviewer. E-mail surveys allow companies to gather a much greater quantity of information than telephone surveys. Respondents also have more opportunity to think about their answers and provide more detailed information. Plus, e-mail surveys allow respondents to answer questions anonymously, while providing the business opportunity to present itself in a high-quality and more standardized manner to its customers. But e-mail surveys do have limitations. First, the response rate on e-mail surveys is generally lower than on other survey tools. Second, the survey may get lost or discarded with other e-mails. Third, respondents may not complete the entire survey.

- *Customer Visits & Interviews* – One of the best ways to gather customer information and assess customer satisfaction is by going to the customer's location and conducting an interview. This allows you to ask customers directly what they like and do not like about your company, products or services and what they perceive to be your company's strengths and weaknesses. A major advantage of customer visits and personal interviews is that the interviewer(s) can gather information via verbal and non-verbal responses to questions. But customer visits are very expensive, especially if your customers are spread over a wide geographic area. Form 8-2 provides a Checklist of Tips for Suppliers Conducting Customer Interviews.

Form 8-2. Checklist of Tips for Suppliers Conducting Customer Interviews

- ❑ The interviewer must have a professional appearance
- ❑ The interviewer must have a thorough knowledge of the specific characteristics and requirements of the customer's projects
- ❑ The interviewer should clarify the roles and responsibilities of the suppliers key personnel who interface with the customer
- ❑ The interviewer should seek to understand what the customer perceives as both your companies strengths and areas for improvement
- ❑ The interviewer should understand what are the customers key performance areas and metrics

- *Customer Focus Groups* – These consist of individuals who represent a number of your customers, brought together to participate in discussions concerning a series of topics, questions, products or services. Customer focus groups are sometimes referred to as user-groups and can prove to be very effective when dealing with improvements to existing products, product features and customer support services. Limitation to customer focus-groups include:
  - ❑ A dominant individual can overly influence discussions
  - ❑ An ineffective moderator may allow discussions to go off-topic
  - ❑ Time constraints

- *Front-line Customer Contact* – Perhaps the most valuable of customer feedback is the daily personal discussions, e-mails, telephone calls, conference calls and actual work your company employees engage in with your customers and the communication they share with each other.

- *Lesson Learned Form* – Documenting lessons learned based upon the collective knowledge your company gains from participating in the entire Capture Management Life-Cycle is critical to continuous improvement and winning more business. In fact, you may opt to represent an internal Win/Loss Review more as a "Lessons Learned Review" to keep the team focused on providing constructive feedback. Lessons Learned, Form 8-3 provides a simple but effective means to document company lessons learned to identify what went well and what must be improved. At the completion of every customer project, the key team members should take the time to clearly and concisely document their individual and collective lessons learned.

Suppliers should develop a Customer Lessons Learned database to ensure appropriate best practices and suggestions for improvement are being shared, followed-up and properly implemented throughout their organization and supply-chain. Customers really dislike it when suppliers do not learn from their mistakes. Conversely, customers often appreciate a supplier who does learn from their mistakes based upon constructive feedback.

Form 8-3. Lesson Learned

PROGRAM NAME	PREPARED BY	DATE PREPARED

What did we do well? Why?

How do we perpetuate the good things?

What did we do poorly? Why?

How do we avoid repeating the bad things?

Are we doing activities that don't add value?

Building Trust Checklist

One of the biggest challenges in creating and maintaining a successful long-term business partnership is building trust. Trust is like quality; it is difficult to accurately describe, but you know it when it's there.

Trust is typically earned by doing what you say you are going to do on a repeated basis; in other words, by honoring commitments. A company can also instill trust when it comes to the rescue of another company in a time of urgent business need.

Building trust in business partnerships can take years to accomplish, but sometimes can be lost very quickly.

It is important to keep your customers well informed of the facts, by providing them program status reports, whether on a contract or program basis, business professionals must learn to deliver the truth, both good and bad. No business partnership goes perfectly, but communicating the good, the bad, and at times the ugly, goes a long way to building trust. What a company does to overcome business obstacles and successfully communicate those actions with customers can be vital to building trust, even when the final results are not the best.

Form 8-4 provides a checklist of actions for building trust between customers and suppliers.

Form 8-4. Checklist of Actions for Building Trust

- ❑ Listen to the customer
- ❑ Under stand the customer's needs vs. desires
- ❑ State the obvious
- ❑ Be accessible
- ❑ Return phone calls, voice-mails and e-mails in a timely manner
- ❑ Provide regular communication on contract, program and partnership status
- ❑ Develop a project plan for every deal (scope of work, integrated schedule, work breakdown structure, responsibility assignment matrix and acceptance criteria)
- ❑ Develop a risk management plan
- ❑ Disclose problems early and mitigate negative impacts
- ❑ Back up all verbal agreements and conversations with written documentation
- ❑ Develop a changes management process
- ❑ Provide frequent communication via multiple media
- ❑ Be prepared to deliver both good and bad news at multiple levels, both internally and with customers
- ❑ Be flexible; develop alternatives
- ❑ Set challenging but achievable objectives
- ❑ Demonstrate passion in honoring commitments
- ❑ Recognize that trust is the most important thing in a successful business relationship
- ❑ Learn from mistakes and openly communicate lessons learned
- ❑ Celebrate joint success
- ❑ Document and share best practices

Lead/Opportunity Referral Program

Another key technique for growing business opportunities is to develop a Lead/Opportunity Referral program within your company. A Lead/Opportunity Referral program will help your organization identify new potential clients, track your progress in developing future sales opportunities, and often provide a recognition and reward program for the individuals who help identify the lead/opportunity and those who help make the potential opportunity become a sales reality.

To be effective, a Lead/Opportunity Referral program needs to create a simple means for all individuals in your company who have customer contact (e.g., service, installation, program management, etc.) to forward potential sales leads to the sales representative. This can be done as simply as establishing a single number to call with sales leads (e.g., the Lead/Opportunity Referral Hotline), or an e-mail mailbox, or a form which can be faxed. Basic information to be collected includes the name of the individual making the referral, their contact information, the customer to be contacted, and what the potential opportunity is. Collecting this centrally allows you to route it quickly to the right sales representative, and more importantly, to track the lead to see how many and which ones result in a sales.

Most Lead/Opportunity Referral programs offer some kind of nominal recognition or reward (e.g., a gift certificate) to the individual who referred the lead if it results in a sale. This provides motivation for individuals to forward quality leads, since only leads which result in sales qualify for a reward. It also helps create a sense that everyone is part of the team that helps generate new business.

Customer Loyalty Index

In addition to all of the tools and techniques previously mentioned, more and more suppliers are combining their collective customer knowledge and customer feedback to develop an overall Customer Loyalty Index rating to help them measure their performance (monthly, quarterly, annually, etc.) using the "Voice of the Customer."

Outputs

Simply said, the outputs for the Opportunity Growth stage are either more business, with your current customers and new customers, or a loss of business opportunities to your competitors.

Case Study — Microsoft

Few companies have been as successful as Microsoft in retaining customers and capturing new customers, especially so in the highly competitive world of computer software and operating systems. Microsoft's dominance is more than mere legend, it is an undisputed reality. Microsoft's co-founder and former CEO Bill Gates has created his best practices or 12 new rules of how companies should function in the digital business infrastructure (see Table 8-1).

Table 8-1. Bill Gate's New Rules
1. Insist that communications flow through e-mail
2. Study sales data online to share insights easily
3. Shift knowledge workers into high-level thinking
4. Use digital tools to create virtual teams
5. Convert every paper process to a digital process
6. Use digital tools to eliminate single-task jobs
7. Create a digital feedback loop
8. Use digital systems to route customer complaints immediately
9. Use digital communication to redefine boundaries
10. Transform every business process into just-in-time delivery
11. Use digital delivery to eliminate middlemen
12. Use digital tools to help customers solve problems for themselves

Case Study — Cisco Systems

By employing its own Internet strategy and solutions, Cisco Systems has successfully maintained its agility, culture of empowerment and competitive advantage. All of Cisco's business operations, including finance, supply-chain management and employee communications are Internet-based. Today, Cisco transacts nearly 90 percent of orders and 82 percent of customer support inquiries over the Web.

Using outsourcing and the Internet has allowed Cisco to create a virtual manufacturing system that seamlessly manages 37 global plants as one.

Cisco's Internet technology and global real-time project level accounting allow the company to conduct a virtual close on their financial books each fiscal quarter within 24 hours.

To help Cisco stay in close touch with its customers, Cisco conducts regular customer surveys via the internet, customer focus groups and frequent customer visits and interviews with key customer decision-makers worldwide. Cisco is well respected for how they have successfully leveraged their supply-chain and knowledge of their customers to grow profitable business opportunities in both good and challenging times.

SUMMARY

In retrospect, the Opportunity Growth Stage consists of many actions, some of which occur at the completion of bids, contracts and projects (i.e. conducting Win/Loss Bid Reviews, collecting customer feedback and documenting Lessons Learned), and some actions which are on-going and lead to new or follow-on business opportunities (i.e. managing customer expectations, taking actions to build trust, implementing a Lead/Opportunity Referral Program and Measuring Customer Loyalty). The Opportunity Growth stage is clearly at the core of the Capture Management Life-Cycle, a company must continually take positive actions to: (1) manage customer expectations, (2) build customer trust, (3) learn from mistakes and (4) seek customer feedback to improve performance. The discipline required to deliver on commitments combined with the actions taken to build a strong customer relationship, based on mutual respect and trust, is what allows companies to professionally and ethically win more business.

QUESTIONS TO CONSIDER

1. Does your organization routinely conduct or participate in Win/Loss Bid Reviews with its customers?

2. How well does your organization manage customer expectations?

3. How effectively does your organization obtain customer feedback? What methods does your organization use to gather customer feedback?

4. Does your organization document and share lessons learned, in order to improve performance?

5. Does your organization have an effective Lead/Opportunity Referral Program?

chapter

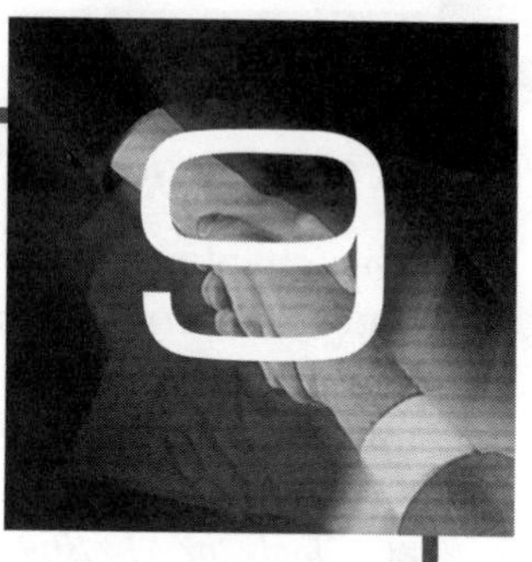

Capture Management: Information Technology Tools

Introduction

This chapter is intended to provide a survey view of the various types of information technology tools available to support the Capture Management Life-Cycle model. The chapter is divided into the following sections for ease of use and reference:

- *Tools for Meetings*
- *Tools for Sharing Documents*
- *Tools for Proposal Development and Production*
- *Integrated Tools to Manage the Capture Management Life-Cycle*
- *Information Security*

Increasingly, people are separated by geography, time and, as your company goes global, language and culture. Information technology tools will help you address these separations and allow you to create a seamless virtual corporate environment which supports the pursuit of new business. Companies which can create this seamless virtual corporate environment are the ones who will succeed because they know how to leverage their resources on a global basis providing them a tremendous advantage over competitors. The key to creating this environment is understanding the depth and breadth of information technology tools available, and picking the right ones for your company.

Vendors and applications are constantly changing and evolving to bring more capabilities to the desktop. The intent of this chapter is to focus on the types of tools available, with illustrative examples of each. While numerous specific vendors and applications are cited throughout this chapter, no endorsement or recommendation is being made of any particular vendor or application.

Tools for Meetings

Technology has made it possible to conduct meetings in a wide variety of mediums which are constantly evolving. While not an exhaustive list, the following are the fundamental types of tools available for meetings, along with the advantages, disadvantages and best applications for each. For many meetings, it is likely you will have a mix of mediums allowing for maximum engagement of all participants. All of the tools mentioned can be used by companies of all sizes; however, there are security considerations to keep in-mind if you use them over the Internet or public phone network.

When considering tools for meetings, one also needs to consider the communication needs in-terms of the communication flow. Communication flows fall into three basic types: Broadcast (i.e., one-way send), Exchange (i.e., send and receive) and Collection (i.e., one-way receive). Figure 9-1 shows the communication flow for each of the key meetings during the Pre-Bid and Bid Phase.

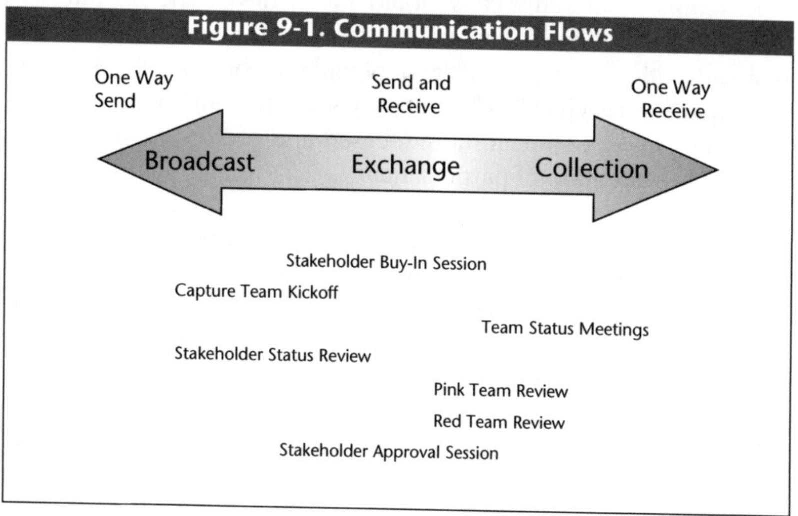

Face-To-Face Meetings – With advances in technology and a continued competitive focus on reducing expenses, face-to-face meetings are often overlooked as a critical tool in winning new business. As you invest in information technology tools, don't naively believe you will (or more importantly should) eliminate face-to-face meetings. Face-to-face meetings are essential to building relationships and developing trust and are an irreplaceable tool for customer meetings, contract negotiations and discussions with suppliers or partners. Don't be "penny wise" and "pound foolish" by investing entirely in technology tools at the exclusion of all face-to-face meetings.

Conference Bridges – Voice conference bridges have become the primary alternative to face-to-face meetings. Voice conference calls have the advantage of being easy to use and allow participation from remote locations, thus saving travel expenses and time. Conference bridges are very effective for dissemination of information to a large audience, the exchange of information between a small number of speakers or short meetings. They do have the disadvantage of only providing voice interaction. However, with a little prior planning, presentation materials can be distributed in advance to participants which significantly increases their effectiveness.

Due to their ease of use and relative affordability, conference bridges are also frequently misused to the detriment of many companies wasting countless hours of potentially productive time on the part of participants. Conference calls should always have a specific purpose, agenda and time limit. Avoid endless "marathon" or "open ended" type calls with a large group in favor of multiple shorter calls with fewer participants on each call. This not only saves the time of participants, it will also make each call more focused and productive as you will not lose the attention of participants.

Conference bridges have become so common-place in their use, that many fail to take appropriate precautions to ensure against eavesdropping by unwelcome participants. Always use a conference bridge which provides audible tones when someone joins or leaves the call, or one that screens participants by name or with an access code, and always take roll. Many conference bridges now offer two access codes, one for participants and one for the host. This not only provides additional security, it also protects against unwanted use of the bridge by someone other than the host. Finally, be sure to change bridge numbers and access codes regularly and only publish them to the participants needed for the call.

Collaboration Software – Recent developments have created a number of software collaboration tools, such as Microsoft NetMeeting, Intel ProShare and Sun Systems ShowMe. These tools allow for the real-time exchange of visual information using personal computers. Not only can all users see the information being shown (e.g., a presentation, spreadsheet or document) on their PC screen, if permitted by the host, they can be given control to make changes to the information. These tools are ideal for meetings where you want to exchange and edit information, such as strategy sessions, solution development session or possibly even during a Pink Team Review session. They can also be used effectively for strategy sessions and Stakeholder Review sessions, if all stakeholders have PC access and the collaboration software.

Most collaboration software tools also permit simultaneous voice on the same data connection, although the voice quality can be very poor. If you find this to be the case, you can use a collaboration software tool in conjunction with a voice conference bridge. While this does require a separate voice and data connection, it provides the best of both worlds, high quality voice along with interactive sharing of visual information using PCs.

If you have a private data network protected by a firewall, you have some built-in security against eavesdropping by unwelcome participants. Most collaboration software tools either provide or can be used in conjunction with other software applications to provide as much as 128-bit security encryption. While this does make it more difficult for others to eavesdrop, no method is failsafe, so do not share highly proprietary or sensitive information using such tools over public networks or the Internet.

Video Web Conference – Until recently, video conferences required expensive equipment and network infrastructure thus limiting widespread use. With the introduction of inexpensive PC web cameras, it is now possible to have a video conference as easy as making a telephone call. Video web conferencing can be done using many of the collaboration software tools mentioned previously, or stand-alone packages. Although the quality of such video conferences often leaves something to be desired, they can be useful for one-on-one meetings and especially in a broadcast mode to give remote participants a greater sense of connection for something like a kickoff meeting. Video conferencing raises the same security considerations as software collaboration tools.

Interactive Chat – The last tool which can be used for meetings is interactive chat software, such Microsoft Windows Messenger, Netscape AOL Instant Messenger and Yahoo!Messenger. Interactive chat allows you to establish a connection between one or more parties and exchange text or graphics via a virtual bulletin board. While this tool is very useful for short, frequent communication between a small number of parties, it can also be used quite effectively as a coaching tool by managers with employees who are not co-located. On conference calls, you can establish an Instant Messenger connection with a new employee on the same call and use this connection to provide tips or even answer questions with the individual. This real-time feedback is invaluable in helping the new employee learn faster, handle problems better and establish credibility quicker with others.

Tools to Share Documents

Traditionally, distributing or mailing documents was the only means to share them with others. Thanks to advent of modern communications technology, there are a variety of mediums available that permit the near instantaneous sharing of documents with large numbers of individuals. Consequently, there are frequently so many documents being shared from so many sources that team members are overwhelmed by the volume and find it incomprehensible. One of the biggest challenges in pursuit of new business will be to ensure the right people on your team have access to and use the most current information. In order to overcome this challenge, you are likely to use a mix of tools, such as those described in this section.

e-mail – e-mail has become the most common tool to exchange documents and collect inputs to develop proposals. If possible with your e-mail service, establish a team e-mail or broadcast list which can be used by the team to easily share information with everyone. If your e-mail is traveling over a public network or the internet, be aware that it's not as secure as you may think. Be wise about what to send via e-mail and caution all team members of the same.

Extremely easy to use and nearly universally accessible, it is also one of the most frequently abused tools for sharing documents. Don't constantly broadcast e-mail messages to your team – take the time to write concise, clear and articulate e-mails. If you are using e-mail to exchange documents, be aware of the size of the files and how long this may take team members to download your e-mail. Compress large files using applications such as WinZip, PKZIP, Stuffit or Tar, and try to limit the number of times documents are sent and re-sent by the team. Table 9-1 provides some of the most important e-mail tips to share with the team.

Table 9-1. E-Mail Etiquette Tips

1. Be concise and to the point
2. Answer all questions, and pre-empt further questions
3. Use proper spelling, grammar & punctuation
4. Make it personal
5. Use templates for frequently used responses
6. Answer swiftly
7. Do not attach unnecessary files
8. Use proper structure & layout
9. Do not overuse the high priority option
10. Do not write in CAPITALS
11. Don't leave out the message thread
12. Add disclaimers to your e-mails
13. Read the e-mail before you send it
14. Do not overuse Reply to All
15. Mailings > use the bcc: field or do a mail merge
16. Take care with abbreviations and emoticons
17. Be careful with formatting
18. Take care with rich text and HTML messages
19. Do not forward chain letters
20. Do not request delivery and read receipts
21. Do not ask to recall a message.
22. Do not copy a message or attachment without permission
23. Do not use e-mail to discuss confidential information
24. Use a meaningful subject
25. Use active instead of passive
26. Avoid using URGENT and IMPORTANT
27. Avoid long sentences
28. Don't send or forward e-mails containing libelous, defamatory, offensive, racist or obscene remarks
29. Don't forward virus hoaxes and chain letters
30. Keep your language gender neutral
31. Don't reply to spam
32. Use cc: field sparingly

Source: www.emailreplies.com

War Room – A project workroom, traditionally referred to as a "war room" has tremendous value for companies with a geographical concentration of employees. The term "war room" is a reference to a command center in the military where information on the battle is collected and displayed to support decisions by the battle commander and staff. A war room provides the team a secure (i.e., lockable) dedicated work space where information can be collected and posted for use by the team, promoting team building and creating continuity on large projects or those which may span long periods of time. The use of war rooms to support the capture of large bids continues to be the norm with successful government contractors such as *Lockheed-Martin, General Dynamics, Boeing, Raytheon, SAIC,* and others.

Share Point – With new technology, war rooms are being replaced with "virtual war rooms." One common way to do this is by using a server on your company network to establish a file sharing point accessible to the team. There is a wide range of file sharing point applications from the simple to the sophisticated including such applications as Microsoft Share Point, Open Text Live Link and IBM Lotus QuickPlace.

One of the major considerations in the type of share point you create is who has access to view documents and who has access to edit and add documents. You should make documents readily available to the team; however, you generally do not want them to be changed or over-written. Most applications allow you to set some users as "read-only" to prevent them from over-writing documents.

There are also considerations of access to information within the team and between teams, so you need to consider how information can be partitioned. For example, not everyone on the team needs access to pricing information, and even fewer should have access to the internal business case information. Most applications allow access permissions to be established for each "folder" of files and many permit limiting access on a file-by-file basis. Be sure to wisely balance the need for security with the costs, if you establish file-level permissions, someone will have to establish and monitor them as files are created and new team members join the project.

Intranet Website – You can also establish a share point by creating an intranet website to post documents for the team, using applications such as Microsoft FrontPage or HTML. One of the inherent benefits of an intranet website is that only the web administrator can add or edit documents. There are a variety of ways to limit access. The simplest is to create User IDs and passwords for each project.

Tools for Proposal Development and Production

With the proliferation of PCs, printers and desktop publishing software, many companies naively assume that proposal development and production requires no special equipment or advance planning. While technology is certainly more affordable and available, there are some key considerations in terms of tools needed to establish and maintain a highly effective and efficient proposal development and production capability.

A state-of-the art proposal development and production team needs at minimum personal computers, word processing and graphics software, high quality color and black and white printers, CD-ROM burners, scanners and one or more servers. The quantity and quality of each required will be determined by the number, type and size of proposals to be produced. In order to maximize productivity, you should consider centralizing proposal development and production in your company.

The following are considerations which were excerpted from "Proposal Production – A Primer on Quality Drivers, Lead Times and Production Task Scope" by Suzanne Kelman , APMP Proposal Management Journal, Spring/Summer 2002. These paraphrased excerpts are summarized in Table 9-2, Tips on Proposal Development & Production.

Table 9-2. Tips on Proposal Development & Production

	Tool	Consideration
Equipment	Memory	Memory, server and local hard disk space
	Software	Full-scale word processing and graphic editing software tools
		Software compability between applications
	Backup	Internal and external backup capability
	Security	Establish reliable communication practices and security standards
Training	File Management	Centralized network drive and consistent file naming structure
	Applications	Customers may require specific software versions or electronic deliverables
	Writer Style	Writing style, allocated page limits
		Regional grammar and dialect (e.g., U.S. to U.K. English)
Graphics	Font Selection	Use standard widely accepted fonts or ones specified by your customer
	Logos	Ensure quality of customer logo is print-ready and color matches
	Templates	Develop template with color palette, line weights, fonts, styles and sizes
	Photographs	Be aware of copyright laws, or use royalty-free artwork
	Scanners	High quality scanner, especially for photographs and artwork
	Production	Ensure you have properly estimated time to develop graphics
	Covers	Be aware of customer response intructions and rules on covers
	CD-ROM Labels	Be aware of customer response intructions and rules on labels
Physical Media	Paper	Be aware of customer requirements on type and size (e.g., metric), single sided or duplex, color restrictions, foldout-page restrictions
	Dummy Book	Set-up to estimate size of total proposal and binding requirements
	Tabs	Consider volume required and various methods to produce tabs
	Binding	Ensure have wide variety of shapes, colors, ring designs and sizes
		For metric paper proposals usually 4-ring binders are common
Navigation	Cross Reference	Hyperlinked electronic proposals require time to cross-reference and review
	Acronyms	Need to be reviewed for accuracy in list and throughout proposal
	Table of Contents	Extremely valuable if available as automated software feature
	List of Figures	Extremely valuable if available as automated software feature
Printing	Outsource	If security and time permits, consider as cost savings
	In-House	Be wary of mixing in-house and outsourced items - they may not match
	Printer Quality	Have multiple printers as well as a backup printer capability
	Consumables	Have plenty of print cartridges, toner, developer, etc. on-hand
	Server Space	Ensure print server has plenty of disk space and buffer for optimal output
	Collation	Consider RIP Time and use of automatic collation on large proposals
	Book Check	Leave time to review each printed copy of proposal page-by-page
Electronic Media	CD-ROMs	Invest in a reliable read/write CD-ROM
	Labels	Check each CD-ROM for readibility before affixing labels
	Hyperlinks	Make sure hyperlinks actually work on finished CD-ROMs
	Front End Design	Ensure CD-ROMs are "read only" and CD-ROMs are readable
	Burning	Be sure to estimate time required to duplicate all CD-ROMS required
Shipping	Packaging	Ensure you comply with any customer packaging/labeling requirements
	Shipping	Always use reliable shippers and understand their limitations
	Contingency	Consider contingency plans for mulitiple shipments on critical proposals
		Consider the most unusual delivery requirement you have come across

Equipment – Use the best equipment and production technology available including PC, high quality printers, and scanners; with plenty of hard disk space and memory. Have full-scale word processing and graphic editing software tools and make sure they are all compatible with each other. Provide a means to backup files using either internal or external devices such as a CD-ROM writer or Iomega® Zip®-disk drive. Establish reliable communication practices and security standards.

Training – Use a centralized network drive to store files and ensure everyone knows how to use it. Ensure the team is trained on specific software versions or electronic deliverables required by your customer. Train the writers on the style for the proposal, any page limits, and consider editors to address regional dialect and grammar (e.g., U.S. to U.K. English).

Graphics – Stick to widely accepted fonts and develop templates for use by with color palette, line weights, fonts, styles and sizes. Be sure customer logos are print-ready and adhere to copyright laws or use royalty-free artwork. Use only high quality scanners, especially with photographs. Be sure to allow adequate time to develop graphics, and follow any customer instructions on covers and labels.

Physical Media – Be aware of customer requirements on physical media such as paper type, size, single-side or duplex printing, color restrictions or foldout-page restrictions. Set-up a dummy proposal to estimate size, production time and tabs. Ensure you have ample variety of binder shapes, colors, sizes and ring designs (e.g., metric paper requires 4-ring binders).

Navigation – Hyperlinked electronic proposals are in increasing demand by customers, especially those with embedded graphics, sound files and compressed video files (e.g., *.mpg) and require training and time to cross-reference.

Printing – One major consideration is whether to print in-house or consider outsourcing. While outsourcing may appear cheaper on the surface, keep in mind factors such as security, turnaround time and quality of output. If printing in-house, you should have multiple printers, as well as, a backup printer capability (e.g., access to another printer for emergencies), and plenty of print cartridges, toner, etc. Be sure the print server is adequately sized with disk space and memory for optimal output and raster image processor or RIP time.

Electronic Media – Invest in reliable quality read/write CD-ROM media. Make sure hyperlinks work, files are readable, and disks are "read only" before affixing labels.

Shipping – Be sure to package and label in accordance with customer requirements. Have a reliable shipper and understand their pick-up and delivery times. Have a contingency plan for late shipments which miss the standard pick-up (e.g., night drop-off, FedEx Same Day Air). Consider multiple shipments or delivery methods on extremely large and critical responses.

Integrated Tools to Manage the Capture Management Life-Cycle

If your company has the resources and volume, you should consider either purchasing or developing your own system with integrated tools to manage the Capture Management Life-Cycle. An integrated system which provides the ability to track opportunities and retain key documentation throughout the Capture Management Life-Cycle can save your company considerable time and money, both in-terms of manpower savings and ensuring key information is retained and available. The breadth of the system, in terms of size and scope, will of course depend upon the type and size of your business.

Commercially Available Packages – Appendix B (pages 263–281) is adapted from "Proposal Automation Tools," by Greg Wilson (APMP Proposal Management Journal, Spring/Summer 2001), and provides a survey of commercially available packages. All the information from the original 2001 article was updated in January-February 2003 to include current products, capabilities and pricing. This will provide the reader with a perspective on the types of systems available, the major vendors, and rough pricing. This can serve as a starting point for a formal investigation of packages for use by your company.

In-House Tools – If commercially available packages do not suit the needs of your business, you should consider developing an in-house tool. When considering your needs, you may find commercial tools have too many features you will not use or alternatively too few of the features you need. You may also find your existing information technology infrastructure lends itself to creating an in-house tool with minimal investment and training. Table 9-3 shows the trade-offs considerations between Commercial Products and In-House Tools.

Table 9-3. Commercial Products vs. In-House Tools

	Commercial Products	In-House Tools
Strengths	Robust tools with impressive number of features. Extensive documentation, impressive front-ends, and maintenance support. Can truly automate the proposal process.	Usually do not involve a significant investment. Develop by and for users. Are flexible, customized, and address the specific needs of the proposal organization. Employ the "common sense" approach, and do not contain unnecessary options. Can often be developed using previously purchased software.
Weaknesses	Require significant investment of company resources, including a financial investment and time investment for employee training. Are sometimes very compicated and overwhelming to the new user. Often suffer from a lack of flexibility.	Do not carry the large number of options and features, support documentation, and maintenance servcies that are present in most commercial products. Harder to "upgrade", and frequently use older software because they have been slowly developed over time.

CACI Case Study – CACI International, Inc. is a large information technology company with approximately 5,700 employees and approximately $650 million in revenues for fiscal year 2002. The vast majority of their revenues come from contracts with the federal government, including the Department of Defense. Most of this business is acquired by responding to Requests for Proposals (RFPs). Because CACI already had an existing Lotus Notes environment company-wide, they found it would be cheaper to develop an in-house tool.

The CACI system is based on four fundamental toolsets. The first is the "Proposal Manager's Toolkit," which includes all the capabilities needed to manage a proposal. The second is the "Best of Class Proposal Knowledgebase," which is a repository populated with the company's very best proposals. The third is the "Proposal Repository," which contains all information related to a particular proposal. The fourth is the "Proposal Database," which serves both as a section management and review tool on large and complex proposal efforts. Since creating their tool, CACI subsequently researched numerous commercially available products, but found none can adequately or cost-effectively replace the in-house developed tool.

Information Security

One would be remise in a discussion of Information Technology Tools not to discuss the subject of information security. Information security starts with recognizing that nearly all the information related to the pursuit of new business is competitively sensitive and is generally considered "proprietary" as it is valuable to your competitors.

Managing Sensitive Information – Before discussing information technology security, one also needs to first address the basics of identifying and managing disclosure of sensitive information. Denise Rhea-McKenzie (2002) of Titan Systems, a major defense contractor, cited several steps to take to protect sensitive data. These are:

- Ensure all teammates, subcontractors and contractors have signed a Non-Disclosure Agreement (NDA) before they obtain access to information
- Ensure all proposal documentation is labeled with a restrictive legend
- Use a sign-in sheet that attendees must sign for every meeting with a clearly visible statement that all information discussed is proprietary

Titan Systems Case Study – Titan Systems uses the following disclaimer on the cover page of all proposals and material sent outside the company:

> *"This document includes data that shall not be disclosed other than to employees of* **<Company Name>**, *on a need to know basis, and shall not be duplicated, used or disclosed in whole or in part, for any purpose other than to support* **<Proposal or Business Development Effort Name>**. *This restriction does not limit* **<Company Name>***'s right to use information contained in this data if it is obtained from another source without restriction. The data subject to this restriction are contained on all sheets."*

Titan uses the following statement on all sign-in sheets for every meeting:

> *We, the undersigned, hereby acknowledge that the presentation by and/or discussions with Titan Systems ("Titan") regarding the XXXXXXXXX Proposal (XXXXX), on this date* **<date>**, *contain information of a proprietary, confidential and/or competition-sensitive nature. By signing below and attending this meeting, we hereby agree to not disclose to any*

> *third party any information presented by Titan on this date, and acknowledge that any such disclosure would result in substantial and irreparable harm to Titan.*

Although these measures identify sensitive information, marking it for distribution, and place all individuals on notice that such information is sensitive and must not be shared, additional precautions must be taken to address how this same information is stored and shared in an information system.

Information Security Threats – Tom Cavanaugh, computer consultant and former defense contractor analyst, stated threats to proposal (i.e., information) security fall into three main categories: Benevolent Threats, Indifferent Threats and Malevolent Threats. Benevolent threats are actions by well-intentioned people in your own company that result in the loss of information. Indifferent Threats are related to physical events which can damage or impair hardware or software resulting in the loss of information. Malevolent Threats are engineered by outside organizations to compromise your system to extract and/or change information.

Benevolent threats are the most common, and are also the easiest to protect against. The first step is to ensure all project files are kept on a central server. The next step is to make frequent back-ups of the server files on another server, CD-ROM or other off-line storage media (e.g., Iomega® Zip® Disk Drive).

Indifferent threats are the next most common, and are also easy to protect against. Make sure computer equipment and the server is in a safe protected environment where it isn't likely to be knocked around, have things dropped on it, have water or other liquids (like coffee) spilled on it, or otherwise be damaged. Protect against power failures with an Uninterruptible Power Source (UPS) with enough power to provide time to save all open files and safely power-down the system.

For your server, you may want to consider a Redundant Array of Independent Drives (RAID) which was developed by the University of California, Berkeley, in an effort to improve the performance and reliability of hard disk drives. A RAID 0 configuration provides two drives each of which stores half the information. A RAID 1 configuration, often referred to as mirroring, also uses two drives, but both store all your data. A RAID 5 configuration uses multiple drives to store some of the information, and an extra drive to store redundant information. For a more thorough explanation of RAID, visit the Web sites of either Advanced Computer Network Corporation at *http://www.acnc.com/04_01_000.html* or Finite Systems Ltd. at *http://www.finitesystems.com/PRODUCT/raid/raid.html.*

Other protections against indifferent threats are to eliminate the use of screen savers, as they use PC resources and are no longer needed to protect monitors from "burning-in." Systems should always be loaded with virus software that is current and scans files looking for viruses, and be sure firewalls are used for all internet connections.

Malevolent threats are the least common, yet can be the most damaging when they do occur. Protect against these by controlling who has access to information. Use passwords and require users to change them routinely. Wireless networks are becoming increasingly popular; however, be aware of the security weaknesses even when proper encryption methods are used. Finally, keep files on your server and ensure users are aware of the risks and their responsibilities to protect files which are copied onto PDAs, laptops, CD-ROM or other portable devices or media.

Summary

There are countless information technology tools available to support the Capture Management Life-Cycle. The intent of this chapter has been to provide a survey view of the types of tools available and not an exhaustive inventory, which is neither possible nor practical given the constant evolution and introduction of new and better applications. The material in this chapter should be considered a starting point or reference point in your journey to finding the right information technology tools for your company.

The key to effectively using information technology tools is the same as what you will do with your customer's to win new business. First, understand the problem or objective. Second, consider the potential solutions available. Third, select the solution which best solves the problem and meets your financial constraints.

Questions to Consider

1. How well does your organization use information technology tools in support of the Capture Management Life-Cycle?

2. How effectively does your organization identify, assess and adopt the use of new information technology tools? Is the introduction of new information technology tools driven through a top-down (i.e., formal pro-active) or bottom-up (e.g., informal re-active) process? How savvy are the employees in your organization on the use of new information technology tools?

3. Does your organization have documented processes or offer training on the use of information technology tools?

4. What actions has your organization taken to improve/develop the skills of your Sales managers, capture/proposal managers and contract managers on the use of information technology tools?

5. How well does your organization document and share your lessons learned on the use of information technology tools?

chapter

Going Global—Opportunities & Challenges

Introduction

Capturing business opportunities on a multi-national basis requires an organization to go through the Capture Management Life-Cycle, discussed in Chapter 2 and thoroughly reviewed by each phase and stage in Chapters 3 – 8 of this book. Of course, the nature of the products, services, and/or solution, the complexity, volume, dollar magnitude, risk and criticality are all important factors which will determine the extent to which each of the capture management stages are vital to success and which tools and techniques need to be employed. With the above stated understanding of the Capture Management Life-Cycle in mind, there are additional opportunities and challenges an organization or company faces when going global. The focus of this chapter is to highlight the additional opportunities and challenges an organization may encounter when doing business on a multi-national basis.

Key points of discussion in the chapter include the following:

- *Globalization – What is It?*
- *Global Thinking*
- *Globalization is a Paradigm Shift*
- *Multi-national Trade Organizations and Agreements*
- *Global Marketing and Sales*
- *What it Takes to Win Business Globally*

Globalization—What is it?

Globalization can be defined in several ways depending on the level you choose to focus on. You can speak of globalization of the entire world, a single country, a specific industry, a specific company or even a particular line of business or function within a company. At the worldwide level, globalization refers to the growing economic interdependence among countries as reflected in increasing cross-border flows of goods, services, capital and know-how. At the level of a specific country, globalization refers to the extent of the interlinkages between a country's economy and the rest of the world. At the level of a specific industry, globalization refers to the degree to which a company's competitive position within that industry in one country is interdependent to that in another country (Financial Times, London, 1998).

Clearly, since the terrible terrorist attacks of September 11, 2001, the entire world has been forced to reevaluate how the complex process of globalization will continue to evolve. In fact, most organizations and companies are continually evaluating the changing characteristics that shape the global business environment, see Table 10-1, which lists these key characteristics.

Table 10-1. Key Characteristics Shaping the Global Business Environment

1980s and Before	1990s and After
■ Continuity	■ Change
■ Planning	■ Coping with the unexpected
■ Adjustment	■ Transformation
■ Diversification	■ Focus and segmentation
■ Management	■ Leadership
■ Instruction	■ Facilitation & learning
■ Individuals	■ Project teams
■ Knowledge	■ Competence
■ Scale	■ Flexibility & speed
■ Uninformed customers	■ Knowledgeable & demanding customers
■ National boundaries	■ Freedom of movement

* Adapted from: Colin Coulson-Thomas, Creating the Global Company, New York, McGraw-Hill, 1992.

Global Thinking

In order to make globalization work, you must practice global thinking. There are three critical dimensions to global thinking:

- Understand Global Sources of Demand!
- Understand Global Sources of Supply!
- Understand Global Marketing, Sales and Execution!

Or said differently, know the following better than your competitors:

- How to market to worldwide buyers
- How to source more efficiently
- How to sell, manufacture, and distribute more effectively

Global Sources of Demand – *IBM*, *Toys R Us* and *NCR* are three very different companies with very different products and services, yet all three have successfully mastered global thinking and the art of globalization. All three understand the multinational demands for their respective products and services, especially in developed countries with higher per capita income.

Toys R Us for example has learned the opportunities and challenges one must face in the $6 Billion Japanese toy market. Likewise, *NCR* has worked hard and made considerable international investments in Europe, Japan and South America to penetrate the multi-billion dollar Automated Teller Machines (ATMs), optical scanners and computer cash registers markets. *IBM* likewise realizes the tremendous global demand of businesses both large and small to outsource computer support services.

Global Sources of Supply – *The Limited* is regarded as one of the world's most successful retailers of apparel. While all of *The Limited's* retail outlets are located inside the United States, it has successfully established global sourcing practices. The process of product design to shipment of garments to the individual stores takes less than 60 days, which is a dramatically reduced cycle-time compared to its competitors. In addition, superior global supply-chain management allows *The Limited* to have their garments designed by numerous companies throughout Europe, produced in Asian and other countries by local manufacturers and shipped via global logistics networks to Columbus, Ohio, where they are distributed to thousands of retail outlets including *The Limited Express, Victoria's Secret, Abercrombie and Fitch, Lerner* and *Henri Bendel.*

Global Sales, Manufacturing and Execution – *ABB* has successfully learned that as companies become global in scope, managers face increased responsibility for marketing and sales to foreign countries and managing adaptation to significant cultural differences. *ABB* helps key managers develop their cultural awareness skills, foreign language skills, and provides them the opportunity to manage multi-national programs while fully utilizing the support of local subcontractors and local country hires for much of the execution of the actual work.

Global thinking is critical to the success of many companies. Globalization is not limited to just large corporations like *General Mo-*

tors (GM), IBM, Sony, Phillips, Ikea, Honda, McDonalds, etc. Because of size, small firms tend to be more flexible, which allows them to quickly and effectively adapt to local markets often far better than large firms. In fact, over 80 percent of the more than 100,000 companies in the U.S. that export are small businesses.

Both large and small business throughout the United States and worldwide are forming partnerships or alliances to leverage strengths, in order to help each of the partners sell more products and services. In November 2002, *Sun Microsystems* and *Lucent Technologies* announced their global partnership to target sales of their products and related services for wireline, wireless and enterprise customers worldwide.

Globalization is a Paradigm Shift

Figure 10-1 illustrates the paradigm shift which must take place to allow globalization to be successful.

Figure 10-1. The Paradigm Shift

Old paradigm	New paradigm
1. Firms were primarily domestic-oriented	1. Firms are evolving to a global orientation for survival and growth
2. Demand exceeded supply in many industries	2. Greater emphasis on quality, custom design, speed, & small-lot size
3. Single large national concern dominated the market	3. Multiple, smaller businesses are created within a global umbrella
4. Companies competed through increasing the size and number of employees	4. Complexities of global commerce are forcing companies to form partnerships/alliances and reduce permanent staffing
5. Focus was on strategic planning and continuous improvement	5. Focus is on strategic thinking, vision, planning and execution
6. Strategy was product driven	6. Strategy is market driven and often lead by services

Adapted from "The Global Challenge", by Moran and Riesenberger, McGraw-Hill, 1994.

Multi-national Trade Organizations and Agreements

The first real attempt to form a world trade organization, after World War II, failed because the U.S. Congress refused to ratify the proposed agreement. Later in 1947, 23 nations signed a document called, "General Agreement on Tariffs and Trade" (GATT). Almost 40 years later, the Secretariat of the GATT effectively evolved into the World Trade Organization (WTO).

GATT

GATT essentially served as an international forum focused on increasing international trade. GATT accomplished its mission by bringing member nations together in meetings called rounds to negotiate reductions in their respective import duties. GATT also served as an important forum for discussion and settlement of trade disputes. The coverage of GATT expanded to more than 100 nations.

The Uruguay Round

The Uruguay Round of GATT lasted for several years and resulted in numerous agreements, which were signed by 113 countries on May 3, 1994, in Morocco. The governments signed GATT 1994, plus agreements in the following areas of international trade.

- Agriculture
- Preshipment Inspection
- Import Licensing Procedures
- Rules of Origin
- Trade in Services
- Trade-Related Aspects of Intellectual Property Rights
- Rules and Procedures Governing Settlement of Disputes
- Trade in Civil Aircraft
- Government Procurement
- Dairy Products
- Others

The WTO

The World Trade Organization (WTO) was established April 15, 1995, in Morocco. The mission of the WTO is to provide a common framework for the conduct of international trade among member nations. The WTO holds a meeting of its trade ministers every two years. WTO meetings were held in 1996, 1998, 2000 and 2002, at various cities worldwide including Singapore (1996) and Seattle (2000). Despite some protests at each of the meetings, the WTO has grown in both members and influence since its inception. Today 141 nations are members of the WTO, including China, which joined in January 1, 2002.

The WTO has numerous councils that meet more often than the general meeting. The WTO Councils include the General Council, that acts as a forum to settle trade disputes, a Council for Trade in Goods, a Council for Trade-Related Aspects of Intellectual Property Rights, and others. In addition, the WTO has established numerous committees including: Trade and Development Committee, Budget Committee, Finance and Administration Committee and others. The former Secretariat of the GATT became the Secretariat of the WTO. Simply said, the WTO is a legal entity which serves as the champion of fair trade worldwide.

NAFTA

The North American Free Trade Agreement (NAFTA) was signed in December 1992, and was ratified by the United States, Canada and Mexico on January 1, 1994. NAFTA to a large extent was an expansion of the U.S. - Canada Free Trade Agreement, which was ratified fives years earlier. The mission of NAFTA is to increase trilateral trade and investment, through the elimination of both tariff and non-tariff barriers over time.

NAFTA requires a special Certificate of Origin form which must be used for all shipments for which NAFTA duty rates are requested. NAFTA also covers trade in services, investment, protection of intellectual property rights and settlement of disputes. NAFTA has been successful in increasing both trade and investments between all three countries. For more information, see the official NAFTA web site *www.nafta-sec-alen.org*.

EU and EFTA

The European Union (EU) has grown to 15 nations and may continue to grow. The EU cooperates closely with the European Free Trade Association (EFTA), which consists of seven additional countries, not currently in the EU. Clearly, the EU and EFTA have placed the U.S. and Canadian exports to Europe at a disadvantage, because they face entry barriers that are not faced by any of the member nations of the EU and EFTA. Mexico faces far fewer barriers when exporting to Europe, because it receives special consideration under the EU's Generalized System of Preferences. For more information about the EU, see the web site, *www.s700.uminho.pt/ec.html.*

Global Marketing and Sales

In the late 1990's the international business theme of *ABB* and other successful multinational enterprises was to "Think Globally, but Act Locally." Today, the new global business theme is to "Think Globally and Locally, but Act Appropriately." It is far harder to sell many products and services worldwide than just in a single country. Globalization presents both great sales opportunities and significant business challenges/expenses.

Figure 10-2 illustrates the key determinants of market competitiveness in the globalizing industries and the external forces which act upon each of the key determinants.

Figure 10-2.

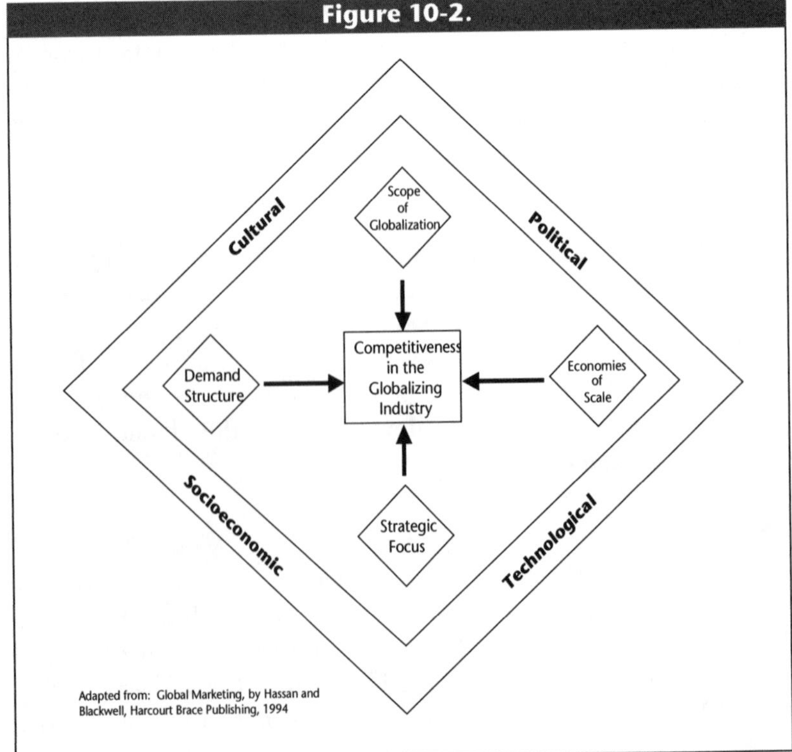

Adapted from: Global Marketing, by Hassan and Blackwell, Harcourt Brace Publishing, 1994

Scope of Globalization – A company's decision as to how much or how far they want to expand their marketing and potential for sale of their respective products and/or services in a particular industry dictates the degree of standardization of the marketing program and process. The greater the multi-national presence the more customized marketing and increased local investment is required.

Economies of Scale – A company's decision to go global can expand the sourcing opportunities for labor and subcontracting, it can also provide for increased economies of scale in research and development, product design, manufacturing, assembly, testing and packaging procedures, thus reducing unit costs. However, some savings associated with economies of scale will be offset by increased costs associated with investments in localizing the product or services to a specific market.

Strategic Focus – When going global, a company must decide which countries to target, which market segments to focus on within the selected countries and how much are they willing to spend to penetrate said markets to win more business.

Demand Structure – Real competitiveness in the globalizing industries can only be achieved by understanding the needs of the customer, adapting to local requirements and establishing close partnerships with customers and suppliers. Local investments for manufacturing, subcontracting, local offices, local country hires, etc. are becoming more critical to global success.

External Forces – There are numerous factors which potentially impact a company's ability to successfully market and sell more products and services on a multinational scale, including:

Socioeconomic Forces

- Inflation rate
- Unemployment rate
- New and evolving markets
- Labor rates
- Tariffs/taxes
- Standard of living
- Customs process
- Exchange rate
- Stock market stability

- Currency stability
- Degree of competition in the market

Technological Forces

- Technology adaptation rate
- Telecommunications infrastructure
- Internet availability & usage
- Rate of technological change
- Degree of technical standards
- Technology transfer requirements

Political Forces

- Protectionism laws and regulations
- Support of multinational enterprises
- Political stability
  - Legislative changes
  - Judicial changes
  - Executive changes
- Local hiring regulations
- Commercial sales code
- Counter trade requirements
- Offset rules
- Co-production requirements
- Licensing/taxes

Cultural Forces

- Local customs
- Language
- Need for local presence (office/facilities)
- Local country hires
- Currency

If a company is serious about going global, the aforementioned key determinants of market competitiveness and the related external forces must all be appropriately factored into the opportunity and risk assessment.

What it Takes to Win Business Globally

Some people believe that globalization is an attitude, not knowledge or information. Stephen Rhinesmith has stated that a global mindset is a requirement of a global business manager who will guide institutions and organizations into the future. He defines a mindset as:

> A predisposition to see the world in a particular way that sets boundaries and provides explanations for why things are the way they are, while at the same time establishing guidance for ways in which we should behave. In other words, a mindset is a filter through which we look at the world.

Rhinesmith explains that people with global mindsets approach the world in a number of specific ways, including:

1. Look for the big picture, they look for multiple possibilities.
2. Understand the world is very complex and business is interdependent.
3. Are process-oriented, understanding that all business follows a process of inputs, tools & techniques and outputs.
4. Consider diversity in people as a real asset and valued resource, know how to work effectively in multicultural teams.
5. Are comfortable with change and ambiguity.
6. Are open to new experiences, and enjoy a challenge.

While a global mindset or attitude is vital to winning business worldwide, there are several additional factors or competencies which are essential for success. The following diagram, Figure 10-3, illustrates the globalization essentials and individual key competencies of a successful global business manager/executive.

Figure 10-3. Individual Globalization Compentencies

Vision	Strategy		Structure	Implementation
Global Attitude	Leadership	Competencies Required to make it Work!	Discipline	Execution
■ Possess a global mindset	■ Motivates employees to excellence	Demonstrated abilities/actions	■ Focused on process improvement	■ Leverages supply-chain partners
■ Ability to work with a highly diverse team	■ Facilitates organiza-tional change		■ Serves as a team or force multiplier	■ Skillfully executes the deployment cycle
■ Possess a long-term orientation	■ Sets high expectations		■ Holds employees accountable	■ Plans and tracks performance with appropriate metrics
	■ Leads by example			

*Adapted from The Global Challenge, by Moran & Riesenberger, New York, McGraw-Hill, 1994

In addition to the individual competencies required for successful global business managers/executives, there are numerous core organizational competencies required for a company to win more business worldwide. Table 10-2 lists the core organizational competencies necessary for global business success.

Table 10-2. Organizational Globalization Competencies

Core Competencies	Worldwide Organizational Solution
1. **Global Vision** - Where the corporation intends to go, emphasis is on acceptance	Unified, understood and accepted by all employees
2. **Strategic Focus** - Competitive advantages of the organization	Growth through coordinated centralization and local adaptability
3. **Control** - Flow of strategic direction from headquarters	High
4. **Local Autonomy** - Degree of freedom allocated to the subsidiary to change/modify products or services	High
5. **Coordination** - Degree of Teamwork between subsidiary, headquarters and 3rd parties	High
6. **Domestic** - Subsidiary Relationship - Flow of information - sharing	High, shared and interdependent
7. **Corporate Culture** - Characteristics that unite people in an organization	Central and unified
8. **Management Selection** - Strong Leadership trait, team-builder and results-oriented	Flexibility, best candidate available from any country
9. **Employee Selection** - Combine country of origin and corporate management staff	Best available candidate
10. **Decision Processes** - Control and flow of decision-making	Shared and complex emphasis on the customer and empowering employees
11. **Information Processes** - Control and flow of information and knowledge	Shared and complex, real-time data, accurate information
12. **Performance-Oriented** - Results focused management and employees	Shared and understood performance goals and metrics, with pay tied to performance

*Adapted from The Global Challenge, by Moran and Riesenberger, New York, McGraw-Hill, 1994

SUMMARY

In retrospect, this chapter has reinforced the need for companies to understand the holistic nature of capturing business via the Capture Management Life-Cycle, while providing valuable insights into the opportunities and challenges companies face when going global.

Clearly, globalization requires global thinking from both individuals and whole organizations working in harmony. Globalization for many organizations is a paradigm shift in both thinking and doing. Understanding key global trade agreements and how they impact your business is critical to success. Finally, understanding how to translate the knowledge of doing business internationally into a practical list of actions for both individuals and organizations is what will ultimately determine your success or failure in capturing business on a multi-national scale. As in all business, talk, while important, is cheap, it is your execution – demonstrated performance, which will help your company build trust and maintain customer loyalty both domestically and globally.

Appendix 

Capture Management Organizational Assessment Tool (CMOAT)

Overview

The Capture Management Organizational Assessment Tool (CMOAT) is designed to support a multi-functional assessment of an organization's ability to win business. It should be completed by representatives from sales, marketing, proposal management, contract management, project management and organization executives.

The Capture Management Organizational Assessment Tool (CMOAT) is designed to help sellers/suppliers of products, services or solutions improve their current capture management win rate. CMOAT contains three critical elements: (1) a ten question organizational capture management capability assessment, (2) a ten question organizational capture management performance assessment and (3) a model/matrix to illustrate the organization's assessed capture management capability and performance. Completing CMOAT helps an organization to focus their critical resources on the key aspects which will enable them to win more business.

The CMOAT

The process for performing the capture capability and performance assessment using the Capture Management Organizational Assessment Tool involves three basic steps:

- *Evaluating capture capability.* A series of ten questions on Capture Capability Analysis are answered with a score calculated for each. The questions are weighted on a scale of 1 (low weight) to 5 (high weight) in terms of their relative importance to each other. This score is calculated by multiplying the raw score (Capability Factor (C)) by a pre-established weight value (W). After each question is scored, a total capability score is calculated by determining the sum of the individual question scores. The Capability Factor (C) and total capability score for each question should then be recorded and totaled on the scoring summary.

- *Evaluating capture performance.* A series of ten questions on Capture Performance are to be answered, with a score calculated for each. The score is calculated by multiplying the raw score (Performance Factor (P)) by the pre-established weight value (W). The Performance Factor (P) and total performance score for each question should then be recorded and totaled on the scoring summary.

- *Mapping the capability and performance scores to the model.* The total scores for capture capability and performance as reflected on the scoring summary are then be plotted on the matrix provided within the model. The location of this score on the matrix helps determine the level of capture capability and relative capture performance and serves as an indicator of the level of risk that needs to be managed or actions taken in order to win more business.

- *Answering the questions.* Answer the questions in the context of key projects or the majority of projects pursued or delivered by your organization.

Timing

The questions provided in this tool can be applied to an organization at any time during the sales cycle. The tool is designed so that it should be completed by a Core Team in a hour or less.

Interpreting the Results

Once the scores have been mapped on the model's matrix, the organization's leadership, Sales Team and others can determine the next appropriate step. Normally, a meeting with management is held to review the assessment results. This meeting should include management representation from each of the organizations responsible for performing the assessment. These same organizations will ultimately be responsible for execution of any needed changes to ensure business success.

Capture CAPABILITY Analysis
The Seller's Perspective

Weight Factor (W)	x	Capability Factor (C)	=	Total Score (W x C)

1. **Seller's Demonstrated Leadership Commitment to Winning More Business**

Seller's leadership commitment is a vital factor in the success of winning more business. Committed leadership will place a high degree of importance on capture management and will make it part of its business plan. Committed leadership will apply resources, such as dedicated capture management teams to win more business, as well as a budget and appropriate staffing to successfully implement the project.

Capability Factor (C)

Has the seller's Leadership demonstrated their commitment to win more business?

Weight Factor (W)	x	Capability Factor (C) 1 2 3 4	=	Total Score (W x C)
5	x	☐☐☐☐	=	______

1. The Seller has not assigned personnel or a budget.
2. The Seller has assigned personnel, but no budget.
3. The Seller has assigned a budget, but little personnel.
4. The Seller has assigned appropriate personnel and sufficient budget to win more business.

Notes

Capture CAPABILITY Analysis
The Seller's Perspective

Weight Factor (W)	x	Capability Factor (C)	=	Total Score (W x C)

2. Seller's Resource Utilization

A sales opportunity may be highly desirable if it makes good use of the Seller's resources and assets that are either currently or projected to be underutilized. Even a deal that might otherwise be declined may be desirable for its positive impact on the Seller's resource and asset utilization. The impact on sales, project management, and support personnel and the use of Technical facilities and equipment should be considered. What is the organization's current resource utilization and the number and type of projects currently underway. Consider how senior management would react to requests for additional resources?

Capability Factor (C)

What is the Seller's organization's current resource utilization and how would potential deals impact staffing in key roles?

__3__ x [1] [2] [3] [4] = ______

1. The organization is currently understaffed and future business will negatively impact current projects.
2. The organization has limited resources for growth, but can handle all current business.
3. The organization is flexible and able to adapt to reasonable peaks and valleys regarding business opportunities.
4. The organization is currently overstaffed/ underutilizing resources and has the ability to do significant more work with current resources.

Capture CAPABILITY Analysis
The Seller's Perspective

Weight Factor (W)	x	Capability Factor (C)	=	Total Score (W x C)

3. Seller's Availability of Leading-edge Technology and Products

Consider the maturity of the technologies and products which are sold. Many products available today are so widely used that they have been accepted as industry standards. Products that have a substantial field population and have been in use for a year or more are considered mature. These types of products are typically very reliable and pose little risk, but often have reduced sales potential. However, newly released products, or products using leading-edge technology, pose greater risks, but often have very significant potentials sales.

Capability Factor (C)

What percentage of the products needed to achieve customer requirements on future business dealsare leading-edge vs. mature?

3 x [1 | 2 | 3 | 4] = ______

1. All requirements can be satisfied with mature released products, with limited sales potential.
2. Less than 10% of the products will be prereleased or new products, or products using leading-edge technology, with high sales potential.
3. Between 10% to 30% of the products will be prereleased or new products, or products using leading-edge technology, with high sales potential.
4. 30% or more of the products will be prereleased or new products, or products using leading-edge technology, with high sales potential.

Capture CAPABILITY Analysis
The Seller's Perspective

Weight Factor (W)	x	Capability Factor (C)	=	Total Score (W x C)

4. Seller's Ability to Leverage their Supply Chain

Most sales opportunities will require some products and/or services by other suppliers as subcontractors to the Seller. How effective is the organization in managing their supply chain to obtain the highest quality products, to accelerate delivery, and reduce costs of products and services offered to customers?

Capability Factor (C)

Which of the following describes the organization's supply change management capabilities?

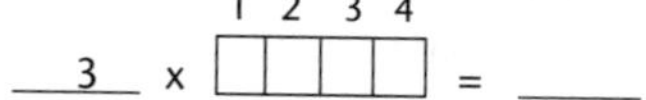

3 x 1 2 3 4 = ____

1. The organization has little to no ability to leverage their suppliers to reduce costs or accelerate delivery.
2. The organization has marginal ability to leverage suppliers to reduce costs and/or accelerate delivery.
3. The organization has demonstrated the capability of leveraging a few suppliers to reduce costs and/or accelerate delivery.
4. The organization has a robust supply chain management capability which consistently demonstrates the ability to leverage suppliers to achieve significant cost reductions and dramatic acceleration in product and services deliveries.

Notes

Capture CAPABILITY Analysis
The Seller's Perspective

	Weight Factor (W)	x	Capability Factor (C)	=	Total Score (W x C)

5. **Buyer Favors the Seller**
   Potential sales opportunities involving Buyer(s), key decision makers, who favors the Seller before the project has been proposed (for reasons other than price) is highly desirable. Buyer's may prefer the Seller for any number of reasons, including technology, reputation, past experience, industry commitment, and so on. Of course, they may favor the competition for the same reasons. Consider the number of competitors vying for the deal, as well as the Buyer's past experience with the Seller and/or the competition.

Capability Factor (C)

How does the Buyer view the Sellers organization in comparison to the competition for future deals?

3 x [1 | 2 | 3 | 4] = ______

1. Buyers favor the competition and is negative towards the Seller for future business.
2. Buyers favor the competition and is neutral towards the Seller for future business.
3. Buyers are neutral towards all potential suppliers for future business.
4. Buyers prefer the Seller for future business.

Notes

Capture CAPABILITY Analysis
The Seller's Perspective

	Weight Factor (W)	x	Capability Factor (C)	=	Total Score (W x C)

6. **Seller's Past Experience and Performance**
Experience with previous projects that are similar to expected future business can reduce risk. Determine how many of the potential sales opportunity requirements can be met using products, technologies, and/or skills that have been previously provided by the Seller on past projects.
Consider:
- The skills available at the local level to manage and carry out expected future business.
- How much of the system solution needs to be developed as opposed to having been done before somewhere within the Seller's organization or supply chain.
- The Seller's experience with the non-seller's products needed for possible future business.
- The Seller's track-record of successful performance, including on-time-delivery.

Capability Factor (C)
What is the Seller's organizational experience with projected future customer needs? 4 x [1 2 3 4] = ____

1. None of the Seller's past experience will be useful in obtaining future business.
2. A small amount of the Seller's past experience will be useful in obtaining future business.
3. A majority (50% or more) of the Seller's past experience will be useful in obtaining future business.
4. The Seller's past experience and performance will be critical factors in the determination of future business opportunities.

Capture CAPABILITY Analysis
The Seller's Perspective

Weight Factor (W)	x	Capability Factor (C)	=	Total Score (W x C)

7. **The Seller's Participation in Proposal & Project Requirements**
   Many Buyers develop proposal requirements without the participation of those who will bid on the projects. In this type of situation, those who bid will have little or no input regarding schedules, technology, product selection, and so on. The less the Seller is involved in the development of the requirements, the higher the risk of winning the business.

   Capability Factor (C)
   Does the Seller have any involvement in the development of the proposal and project requirements for future business?

Weight Factor (W)	x	Capability Factor (C) 1 2 3 4	=	Total Score (W x C)
2	x	☐☐☐☐	=	______

   1. The Seller had no involvement in developing the requirements.
   2. The Seller was asked for comments after requirements were developed.
   3. The Seller guided the Buyer in developing requirements.
   4. The Seller developed many of the proposal and project requirements for the Buyer.

   Notes

Capture CAPABILITY Analysis
The Seller's Perspective

	Weight Factor (W)	x	Capability Factor (C)	=	Total Score (W x C)

8. Seller's Future Business Potential

Successful projects often result in better opportunity for future business. Successful past performance often provides the means to enter a new account, or may be required to protect an existing account. Participation in the project (either in whole or in part) may be required for the Seller to be considered for future business.

Capability Factor (C)

What impact has successful past performance had on future Seller opportunities with their current customers or new customers? __1__ x [1 2 3 4] = ____

1. Positive Past Performance has little or no bearing on future business.
2. Future business is possible as a result of positive past performance.
3. Future business is likely as a result of positive past performance.
4. Future business is assured as a result of positive past performance.

Notes

Capture CAPABILITY Analysis
The Seller's Perspective

Weight Factor (W)	x	Capability Factor (C)	=	Total Score (W x C)

9. Executive for Bid/Proposal/Contract Management Assessment of Organization's Capture Capability

The Executive responsible for Bids & Proposals or Contract Management, should provide an overall assessment of the capabilities of the organization as a whole to win future business.

Capability Factor (C)

On a scale of 1 (low) to 10 (high), which is the Executive's overall assessment of the organization's capability to win this future business?

2 x [1 | 2 | 3 | 4] = ______

1. 5 or less
2. 6 or 7
3. 8 or 9
4. 10

Reasons for overall assessment:

____

____

____

____

____

____

____

____

____

____

____

____

____

____

____

Capture CAPABILITY Analysis
The Seller's Perspective

Weight Factor (W)	x	Capability Factor (C)	=	Total Score (W x C)

10. Sales Executive Assessment of Organization'sCapture Capability

The Sales executive should provide an overall assessment of the capabilities of the organization as a whole to win future business.

Capability Factor (C)

On a scale of 1 (low) to 10 (high), which is the Sales Executive's overall assessment of the organization's capability to win future business?

3 x [1 2 3 4] = ____

1. 5 or less
2. 6 or 7
3. 8 or 9
4. 10

Reasons for overall assessment:

Capture PERFORMANCE Analysis
The Seller's Perspective

	Weight Factor (W)	x	Capability Factor (C)	=	Total Score (W x C)

1. **Seller's Actual Revenue Recognized vs. Sales Plan**
   How well has the organization been able to meet or exceed their quarterly and annual revenue targets/plan?

   Performance Factor (P)
   What was the actual revenue recognized by the organization during the past quarter or year in comparison to their respective targets/plan?

   4 x [1 2 3 4] = ______

   1. The organization missed by more than 25% their revenue targets/plan for the past quarter and/or past year.
   2. The organization missed by less than 25% their revenue targets/plan for the past quarter and/or past year.
   3. The organization met their respective revenue targets/plan for the past quarter and/or past year.
   4. The organization exceeded their respective revenue targets/plan for the past quarter and/or past year.

   Notes

Capture PERFORMANCE Analysis
The Seller's Perspective

Weight Factor (W)	x	Capability Factor (C)	=	Total Score (W x C)

2. **Seller's Actual Margin Achieved vs. Margin Plan**

How well has the organization been able to meet or exceed their quarterly and annual margin targets/plan?

Performance Factor (P)

How does the actual gross margin achieved by the organization compare to the percentage margin goals stated in the quarterly and annual plan?

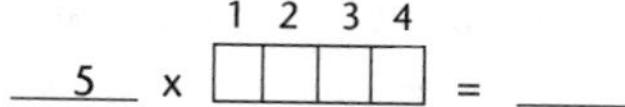

1. Negative margins, or break-even.
2. Margins up to 50% of annual plan.
3. Margins greater than 50%, but less than 100% of annual plan.
4. Margins equal to or in excess of annual plan.

Example: An organization's annual plan states a 32% GM goal for a given year. For a project that is projected to generate up to 16% margin, you should select the second answer.

Capture PERFORMANCE Analysis
The Seller's Perspective

	Weight Factor (W)	x	Capability Factor (C)	=	Total Score (W x C)

3. **Seller's Alignment of Deals to Organization's Strategic Direction**

   Does the organization properly focus on winning business which is vital to the seller's core business and strategic direction?

   Does the seller's organization focus on winning business which:

   - ❑ Supports your strategic market direction.
   - ❑ Supports your focus on key accounts.
   - ❑ Utilizes your knowledge of specific industries.
   - ❑ Represents an excellent example of the type of business Seller seeks and will serve as a reference for future sales efforts with other accounts.

   The more of these attributes your sales opportunities have, the higher the potential to win profitable business. If properly executed, deals with all of the above attributes promote the Seller as an industry leader.

   Performance Factor (P)

   How many of the Seller's major strategies as Outlined above are matched by the key deals (or majority of deals) they pursue.   5 x [1 2 3 4] = ____

   1. One
   2. Two
   3. Three
   4. Four

Capture PERFORMANCE Analysis
The Seller's Perspective

	Weight Factor (W)	x	Capability Factor (C)	=	Total Score (W x C)
4. Seller's Project Management Executive Assessment of Recent Projects					

The Project Management Executive or equivalent team should provide an overall assessment of how well the organization was able to satisfy the customers requirements, ensure on-time-delivery, mitigate potential problems, manage the scope of work, and control cost.

Performance Factor (P)

On a scale of 1 (low) to 10 (high), what is the Project Management Executive's overall assessment of the Seller's ability to successfully manage past projects? 4 x [1 | 2 | 3 | 4] = ____

1. 5 or less – Poor Overall Performance
2. 6 or 7 – Satisfactory Overall Performance
3. 8 or 9 – Good Overall Performance
4. 10 – Excellent Overall Performance

Reasons for overall assessment:

____
____
____
____
____
____
____
____
____
____
____
____
____
____

Capture PERFORMANCE Analysis
The Seller's Perspective

Weight Factor (W)	x	Capability Factor (C)	=	Total Score (W x C)

5. **Seller's Recent New Business has Added Important Experience and/or Skills**
   As a result of winning new business, the organization has truly gained valuable experience and/or skills, which will help the organization to grow and succeed.

   Performance Factor (P)
   What is the value of the experience and skills gained from key recent business or the majority of recent Business?

   3 x [1 2 3 4] = ____

   1. Little improvement in existing skills has resulted from recent projects.
   2. Significant improvement in existing skills has resulted from recent projects.
   3. Little improvement in existing skills has occurred, but some new skills and expertise have developed.
   4. Significant improvement in existing skills, new skills, and expertise has resulted from recent projects.

   Notes

Capture PERFORMANCE Analysis
The Seller's Perspective

Weight Factor (W)	x	Capability Factor (C)	=	Total Score (W x C)

6. **Seller's Presale Expense**

Every project has presale expense associated with it. The amount of presale expense varies greatly from bid to bid. Some projects are largely a replication of an existing project with the same account or another account. In other projects, a significant amount of planning and even a demonstration of the system (including a benchmark, trial or live test demonstration) is required before the bid is considered by the account. Projects with little presale expense are more desirable. Examples of items that increase the level of presale expense include:

- ❑ Additional local resources beyond those normally assigned to the account.
- ❑ A benchmark system to be constructed.
- ❑ Non-seller's product(s) to be acquired for evaluation before the proposal is generated.
- ❑ Resources from other organizations, such as country or group home office.
- ❑ Professional services from outside the seller's sources.

Performance Factor (P)

What is the estimated level of presale expense for the key projects or the majority of projects? (Use the items listed above as a guide).

3 x [1 | 2 | 3 | 4] = ______

1. High (all of the above apply).
2. Moderate (three or four of the above apply).
3. Low (one or two of the above apply).
4. Minimal presale expense is expected (none of the above).

Capture PERFORMANCE Analysis
The Seller's Perspective

	Weight Factor (W)	x	Capability Factor (C)	=	Total Score (W x C)
7. Seller's Actual Bid/Proposal Win Rate How many bids/proposals did the organization win in comparison to how many bids they submitted? Also, how many opportunities did theorganization choose not to bid?					
Performance Factor (P) What was the Seller's organizational bid/ proposal win rate during the past year?	3	x	1 2 3 4	=	______

1. The Seller won less than 20% of the bids/ proposals they submitted.
2. The Seller won between 21% to 50% of the bids/ proposals they submitted.
3. The Seller won between 51% to 80% of the bids/proposals they submitted.
4. The Seller won more than 80% of the bids/proposals they submitted.

Notes

Capture PERFORMANCE Analysis
The Seller's Perspective

	Weight Factor (W)	x	Capability Factor (C)	=	Total Score (W x C)

8. Seller's - Customer Loyalty Index Rating

Does the organization survey their respective customers and assess a Customer Loyalty Index Rating? If so, how does their Customer Loyalty Index Rating compare to other organizations in the same industry?

Performance Factor (P)

What is the Seller's - Customer Loyalty Index Rating for the past quarter or year? 3 x [1 | 2 | 3 | 4] = ____

1. The Seller does not survey their customers for a Customer Loyalty Index rating.
2. The Seller's Customer Loyalty Index rating is below the ratings of their competitors.
3. The Seller's Customer Loyalty Index rating is comparable to the ratings of their competitors.
4. The Seller's Customer Loyalty Index rating exceeds the ratings of their competitors.

Notes

Capture PERFORMANCE Analysis
The Seller's Perspective

	Weight Factor (W)	x	Capability Factor (C)	=	Total Score (W x C)

9. Seller's - Actual Number of Days of Sales Outstanding vs. Plan

How well has the organization been able to meet or exceed their quarterly and annual number of Days of Sales Outstanding vs. plan?

Performance Factor (P)

What was the actual number of Days of Sales Outstanding during the past quarter or year in comparison to the plan?

2 x [1 | 2 | 3 | 4] = ____

1. The organization missed, by more than 25%, their number of Days of Sales Outstanding target for the past quarter or year.
2. The organization missed, by less than 25%, their number of Days of Sales Outstanding target for the past quarter or year.
3. The organization met their respective number of Days of Sales Outstanding target for the past quarter or year.
4. The organization exceeded their DSO target (lower number of days) for the past quarter or year.

Notes

Capture PERFORMANCE Analysis
The Seller's Perspective

Weight Factor (W)	x	Capability Factor (C)	=	Total Score (W x C)

10. Revenue Generated via Changes Management vs. Plan

How successful was the organization in capturing more revenue via the contract changes management process in comparison to their plan?

Performance Factor (P)

What was the actual revenue recognized by the organization, via the changes management process, during the past quarter or year in comparison to their targets/plan?

Weight Factor (W)	x	Capability Factor (C) 1 2 3 4	=	Total Score (W x C)
2	x	☐☐☐☐	=	____

1. The organization missed, by more than 25%, their changes management revenue targets/ plan for the past quarter and/or past year.
2. The organization missed, by less than 25%, their changes management revenue targets/ plan for the past quarter and/or past year.
3. The organization met their changes management revenue targets/plan for the past quarter and/or past year.
4. The organization exceeded their changes management revenue targets/plan for the past quarter and/or past year.

Notes

Capture Management Organizational Assessment Tool (CMOAT)

Scoring Summary

Capture Capability Analysis (*W x C = Score)				
1.	5	x	____	= ____
2.	3	x	____	= ____
3.	3	x	____	= ____
4.	3	x	____	= ____
5.	3	x	____	= ____
6.	4	x	____	= ____
7.	2	x	____	= ____
8.	1	x	____	= ____
9.	2	x	____	= ____
10.	3	x	____	= ____

Total Capability Score = ____

Capture Performance Analysis (*W x C = Score)				
1.	4	x	____	= ____
2.	5	x	____	= ____
3.	5	x	____	= ____
4.	4	x	____	= ____
5.	3	x	____	= ____
6.	3	x	____	= ____
7.	3	x	____	= ____
8.	3	x	____	= ____
9.	2	x	____	= ____
10.	2	x	____	= ____

Total Performance Score = ____

*Weights pre-assigned based upon cross-industry surveys

Capture Management OrganizationalAssessment Tool (CMOAT)

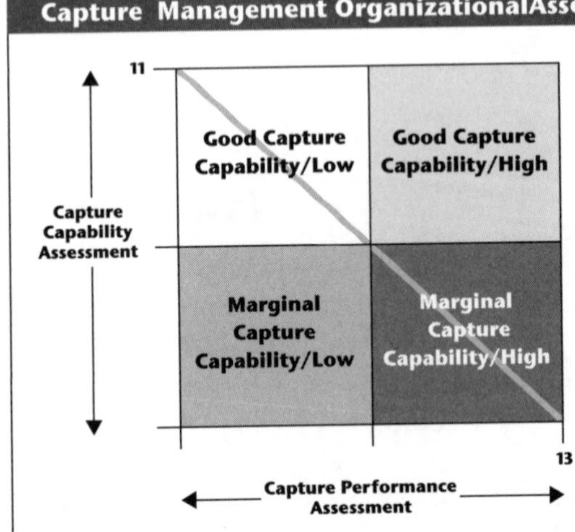

Total scores for capture capability and performance that fall on or below the diagonal line require the greatest need for management support,improvement actions, contingency planning, and so on.

Appendix 

Proposal Automation Products Matrix

Adapted from "Proposal Automation Products" by Greg Wilson from Journal of the Association of Proposal Management Professionals, Spring 2001 edition (*www.apmp.org*)

Note: All information updated by vendors January/February 2003

Product Name	Vendor [Listed alphabetically]	Platform / Configura-tion	Description—General	Features / Capabilities *	
				Capture Phase	Proposal Development
RESTRIEVE	Applied Solutions, Inc. 3959 Pender Drive, Suite 306 Fairfax, VA 22030 Voice: 703-691-3004 Fax: 703-691-3006 Email: *asi@appliedsolutions.com* Web: *www.appliedsolutions.com* Primary Application: Government and Commercial procurement	Windows 95, 98, NT, ME, 2000, XP Single and multi-user Stand-alone and network Compatible w/ MS Word, Word Perfect, Excel	RESTRIEVE is an advanced applicant and skills tracking system combined with résumé generation and management capabilities. RESTRIEVE includes a comprehensive data entry system and extensive queries and reports to assist in identifying the most qualified and cost effective team of professionals to submit with your proposal. RESTRIEVE can generate standard résumés and project abstracts/history formatted to meet any custom set of specifications.		■ Capture/ maintain proposal text ■ Allow export to other applications packages
As-One	AS-ONE, Inc. Sterling, VA Marketed by: Advantage Consulting, Inc. 7611 Little River Turnpike, 204W Annandale, VA 22003 Voice: 703-642-5153 Fax: 703-658-0159 Email: *jbender@acibiz.com* *Web: www.acibiz.com* Primary Application: Government and commercial procurements and projects	Intranet/ extranet Windows NT, 2000, XP, Sun Solaris, HP-UX, IBM AIX, and Linux operating systems. Requires MS SQL Server, Oracle, or Sybase DBMS	Web-based collaboration and project management solution, designed to support Knowledge Management, Project Management, Team Collaboration, and Process Improvement. Communicates business development, proposal, and project delivery information Allows customer and partner limited access to the same system company manages with	■ Opportunity management ■ Capture collaboration ■ Win strategy development ■ Activity history ■ Contact management ■ Discussion groups	■ Capture/ maintain proposal text ■ Capture/ maintain proposal graphics ■ Configuration/ version control of proposal sections ■ Proposal distribution to key players ■ History of document changes ■ Action item assignment ■ Discussion groups ■ Proposal calendar (Events)

Features / Capabilities *			Introduction / Maturity	Training & Support *	Pricing *
Proposal Database Components	**Pricing Activity**	**Other**			
■ Resume library ■ Project abstracts and history	■ Materials/ hardware estimate capability		Product introduced 1994 Current Version 6.1 released 11/00 Current customers: 4 New Web-based version available 4th quarter of 2003	Training and 90 days of support included in purchase price	$2,500 for single user standard addition $14,000 for multi-user site license for standard addition. Add-on component providing full Project capability starts at $1,600
■ Shared reference document library ■ Resume library ■ Previous proposal library ■ Past performance library ■ Integration with other corporate data bases	■ Work breakdown structure ■ Earned value calculations ■ Links with timesheet systems	■ Customizable workspace for each user ■ Customer portal ■ Search/query ■ Access control (security for employees, customers and partners) ■ Export to other applications ■ Synchronization with MS Outlook ■ Bi-directional interface with MS Project	Introduced 2000 Current version = 6.0 SEI CMM Level 3 process	Included in initial packages Annual, support, maintenance & updates: Small business - $2,116.50 Enterprise – $11,900.00 Additional training available: $3,500 per course (12 students max).	Packages include license, installation, customization and training: Small business - $12,450 Enterprise – $70,000 ASP/Rental, multi-server pricing available

Product Name	Vendor [Listed alphabetically]	Platform / Configuration	Description—General	Features / Capabilities *	
				Capture Phase	Proposal Development
WinAward	Bayesian Systems, Inc. Gaithersburg, MD Marketed by: Advantage Consulting, Inc. 7611 Little River Turnpike, 204W Annandale, VA 22003 Voice: 703-642-5153 Fax: 703-658-0159 Email: *jbender@acibiz.com* Web: *www.acibiz.com* Primary Application: Government and Commercial procurements	Windows 98,Me,2000, NT,XP Single and Multi-user Standalone or Network Web-enabled MS Access or SQL Server versions available	Track business opportunities through entire life cycle with continual assessment of business case and win probability. Communicates business development and capture Interfaces with Microsoft's Outlook contact management	■ Pipeline building ■ Opportunity tracking ■ Win strategy assessment ■ Competitive assessments ■ Capture planning ■ Bid/no bid analysis ■ Activity tickler ■ Historical data base for win probability calc	■ Bid/Win Strategies
Deltek CRM & Proposals	Deltek Systems, Inc. 13880 Dulles Corner Lane. Herndon, VA 20171 Voice: 703-734-8606, 800-456-2009 Fax: 703-734-1146 Web: *www.deltek.com* Primary Application: Government and Commercial procurement	Windows 95, 98, NT and 2000 Compatible w/ MSWord, Adobe Pagemaker, WordPerfect, Quark Scalable client/server architecture, WAN, Winframe/ Metaframe, WTS	Deltek CRM & Proposals is a fully integrated, Web-based suite of client focused proposal generation and information tracking applications aimed at increasing the productivity of Professional Services Organizations (PSOs) by automating key business processes. Custom Proposals component provides search and retrieval capabilities, customized formats, creation an unlimited catalog of custom templates, proposal status tracking, data sharing tools, and proposal review tools. The Government Proposals component includes SF255/ SF254 generators allowing users to retrieve stored information into government forms.	■ Opportunity tracking ■ Prompt response tactics ■ Prompt, capture & track competition/ risk assessment ■ Security/ controlled access	■ Import an electronic RFP ■ Allocate and link RFP requirements ■ Allocate "win factors" to sections ■ Capture/ maintain proposal text ■ Capture/ maintain proposal graphics ■ Allow export to other applications packages ■ Security/ controlled access

Features / Capabilities *			Introduction/ Maturity	Training & Support *	Pricing *
Proposal Database Components	Pricing Activity	Other			
		■ Search/query ■ Access control (security) ■ Export to other applications ■ Links to email ■ Imports from: ePipeline, Govcon, Fed Sources, Input, and Eagle Eye services	Introduced 1996 Current version = 5.0 Current users: over 1,000.	Training- Admin (1 day) User (1/2 day) Warranty: 6 mos support & upgrades Annual support avail at 15% of current price; includes phone support, upgrades, user group & news	Concurrent user pricing on 1 server: 1– $2,900 5– $9,000 10– $16,000 15– $22,000 25– $30,000 Multi-server and enterprise pricing available
■ Resume library ■ Previous proposal library ■ Past performance library ■ Integration w/ other corporate data bases	■ Work break-down structure (WBS) correlation	Core features include: ■ Custom proposal style sheets ■ Web-based ■ Full integration between CRM and Proposals components ■ Dynamic section builder ■ Graphical relational report writer ■ Build resume by query ■ Proposal tracking	Originally introduced in 1986 – Proposal Component introduced in 2000 Over 675 customers	Training courses able and listed at *www.deltek.com.* Training CD, on-site training, portable wireless classroom, training space available at Deltek locations 60 day money back guarantee	There are several pricing options for Deltek CRM & Proposals. If buy-ing the solution stand-alone, the CRM module can be purchased for $90/employee for companies with up to 100 employees, and $55/employee for up to 1000 employees. For the Proposals module (with Govt. Forms 254/255) the cost is $93/employee for companies with up to 100 employees, and $68/employee for up to 1000 employees. Deltek CRM and Proposals can also be purchased as part of the Deltek Vision PSA suite, ranging in price from $1800 for a 10 person firm to $114000 for a 1000 person firm.

Product Name	Vendor [Listed alphabetically]	Platform / Configuration	Description— General	Features / Capabilities *	
				Capture Phase	Proposal Development
SLATE **V6.5**	EDS PLM Solutions (formerly TD Technologies) 5400 Legacy Dr. M/S C3-2C-13 Plano, TX 75024 Parent Company: EDS Voice: 972-604-3423 Fax: 972-604-2333 Email: *info@slate.sdrc.com* Web: *www.eds.com/products/plm/teamcenter/slate* Primary Application: Government Procurement	Unix and PC platforms. HPUX, Solaris, Win 2000, NT, XP Compatible with office suites such as MS Office 2000, XP, Visio, Project, and Framemaker Multi-User groupware accessible via standard clients, "live" desktop integrations (such as Excel-live), and Web Stand-alone or network	SLATE provides a set of Object Oriented building blocks for capturing proposed systems and relating those systems back to RFP/RFI document elements (providing complete traceability and realtime decision support to entire development/ proposal teams. SLATE captures documents, identifies customer requirements, captures approaches, organizations, processes, etc. and associates quantifiable information (such as cost/time to various approaches) and exports to standard word processors finished proposals with complete traceability.	■ Opportunity tracking ■ Prompt, capture, & track win strategy ■ Prompt response tactics ■ Capture & track response strategy ■ Prompt, capture, & track competition/ risk assessment ■ Prompt, capture, & track capture plan ■ Bid/no bid analysis ■ Security/ controlled access	■ Import an electronic RFP ■ Import RFP data through manual means only ■ Capture/build proposal outline ■ Parse RFP ■ Allocate and link RFP requirements to/by author or to/by capture requirements ■ Allocate "win factors" to sections ■ Allocate "evaluation criteria" to sections ■ Produce/maintain completed storyboards ■ Capture/maintain proposal text ■ Capture/maintain proposal graphics ■ Allow export to other applications packages ■ Facilitate amendment/ rqmts. changes ■ Configuration/ version control ■ History of document changes ■ Security/controlled access
Virtual Proposal Center **Version 5.1.4**	Intravation, Inc 1113 Hewitt Drive Des Plaines, IL 60016 Voice: 847-299-6423 Fax: 847-299-6428 Email: *info@intravation.com* Web: *www.intravation.com* Primary Application(s): Government and Commercial procurement	Windows 95/98/NT/ 2000/XP Unix Compatible w/ all desktop applications software including graphic packages Multi-user through browser across an intranet/ Internet network. Can set up multiple instances on same server.	Collaborative, workflow-enabled intranet/Internet application that helps manage, support, and simplify the proposal development process. Allows user to plan, assemble, review, store, and disseminate proposal information.	■ Opportunity tracking ■ Capture & track win strategy ■ Capture & track response strategy ■ Capture & track competition/ risk assessment ■ Capture & track capture plan ■ Security/ controlled access	■ Import an electronic RFP ■ Capture/build proposal outline ■ Allocate "win factors" to sections ■ Produce/maintain completed storyboards ■ Capture/maintain proposal text ■ Capture/maintain proposal graphics ■ Allow export to other applications packages ■ Configuration/ version control (of proposal sections and volumes) ■ History of document changes ■ Security/controlled access

Features / Capabilities *			Introduction / Maturity	Training & Support *	Pricing *
Proposal Database Components	Pricing Activity	Other			
■ Previous proposal library ■ Integration with other corporate data bases	■ Materials/ hardware estimate capability ■ Work breakdown structure correlation ■ Correlation/link to standard application packages (Word, Excel, Lotus, Visio, Project)	■ All documents, decisions, and rationale captured ■ Automatic generation/ maintenance of traceability matrices	Introduced July 1994 V6.5 released January 2003 In use at over 700 organizations ~10,000 licenses in use	Customer service included in maintenance cost 90-day warranty	Based on enabled features (i.e. req. mgmt list price is $3995) Price for features enabled - $9,495 Add-ons are typically $2,000 Web client access - $2000 Prices are for simultaneous access, floating licenses
■ Shared reference document library ■ Resume library ■ Previous proposal library ■ Past performance library ■ Integration w/ other corporate data bases		■ Search ■ Version control with check-in/ check-out ■ Work Plan (status view) w/ automatic updating & Import/Export to MS Project ■ Notification ("due" alerts) ■ User to user e-mail with threads. ■ Document viewing in any file format ■ Proposal metrics	Introduced in January 1998 V5.1.4 released January 2003 Current number of customers or installations: 15	Training – 1-3 days on customer site included with software license purchase, tailored to customer Annual technical support (normal business hours) at 17% of license fee. Includes all upgrades. Additional support available on request.	Server license: $8,000 "Active" user license: $1,500 Users with "read only" access do not count towards license total

<table>
<tr><th rowspan="2">Product Name</th><th rowspan="2">Vendor [Listed alphabetically]</th><th rowspan="2">Platform / Configuration</th><th rowspan="2">Description—General</th><th colspan="2">Features / Capabilities *</th></tr>
<tr><th>Capture Phase</th><th>Proposal Development</th></tr>
<tr><td>The Proposal Assembler v5

Proposal Express v5</td><td>Pragmatech Software, Inc.
4 Limbo Lane
Amherst, NH 03031

Voice:
603-672-8941
800-401-9580
Fax:
603-672-7132

Web:
www.pragmatech.com
Email:
info@pragmatech.com

Primary Application(s):
Government and Commercial Procurement</td><td>■ Windows 98, Windows NT 4.0 SP6 or later, Windows 2000, or Windows XP
■ Single and Multi-user
■ Stand alone or network
■ Compatible w/ MS Office</td><td>■ Automates the production of RFP responses, proposals, and other sales documents
■ Offers simplified database creation
■ Ensures consistency of message across the sales force, sales support, marketing channels, and others</td><td></td><td>■ Allocate "win factors" to sections
■ Allocate "evaluation criteria" to sections
■ Capture/maintain proposal text & graphics in one, central knowledge base
■ Configuration/ version control (of proposal sections and volumes)
■ History of document changes</td></tr>
<tr><td>e-Proposals v5</td><td>Pragmatech Software, Inc.

[Same as above.]</td><td>■ Windows 98, Windows NT 4.0 SP6 or later, Windows 2000, or Windows XP
■ Single and Multi-user
■ Stand alone or network
■ Compatible w/ MS Office</td><td>■ Combines the proven benefits of traditional sales proposals with the power, flexibility, and ubiquity of the Web
■ Guides buyers through content selection using intuitive web-based Forms
■ Delivers proposal document to recipient electronically
■ Provides a wireless handheld proposal generation option</td><td></td><td>■ Match prospects' requirements through delivery of targeted, customized selling documents
■ Ensure delivery of consistent, accurate, and professional messaging to prospects and clients immediately upon demand
■ Accommodate the diverse document generation needs of global and mobile enterprises</td></tr>
</table>

Features / Capabilities *			Introduction / Maturity	Training & Support *	Pricing *
Proposal Database Components	**Pricing Activity**	**Other**			
■ Shared reference document library ■ Previous proposal library ■ Integration with other corporate databases		■ Template- and Forms-based proposals	■ Introduced in 1995 ■ Current customers: over 1,800 ■ Over 35,000 installations	Training: ■ The Proposal Assembler: 4-day course ■ Basic Blueprints and Forms: 1-day course ■ Intermediate Blueprints and Forms: 2-day course ■ Advanced Blueprints and Forms: 2-day course Support: Annual Support and Maintenance (18%) includes: ■ Unlimited access to Technical Support Center on the Web ■ Telephone support ■ Email support ■ All upgrades and enhancements for a 1-year period	Per named user: ■ The Proposal Assembler: $5,000 ■ Proposal Express: $1,000
		■ Allows for high-volume proposal generation and rapid response to demands for content	■ Introduced in 2001 ■ Current customers: over 1,800	Support: Annual Support and Maintenance (18%) includes: ■ Unlimited access to Technical Support Center on the Web ■ Telephone support ■ Email support ■ All upgrades and enhancements for a 1-year period	Server License: ■ e-Proposals: call for pricing

Product Name	Vendor [Listed alphabetically]	Platform / Configuration	Description—General	Features / Capabilities *	
				Capture Phase	Proposal Development
The RFP Machine v5 **RFP Express v5** **RFP Express Server v5**	Pragmatech Software, Inc. [Same as above.]	■ Windows 98, Windows NT 4.0 SPG or later, Windows 2000, or Windows XP ■ Single and Multi-user ■ Stand alone or network ■ Compatible w/ MS Office	■ Automates the production of RFP responses, proposals, and other sales documents ■ Offers simplified database creation ■ Ensures consistency of message across the sales force, sales support, marketing channels, and others		■ Import an electronic RFP ■ Capture/build proposal outline ■ Parse RFP ■ Allocate and link RFP requirements to/by author and to/by capture requirements ■ Facilitate amendment/ requirements changes ■ Allow export to other applications
The RFP Tracking System v5	Pragmatech Software, Inc. [Same as above.]	■ Windows 98, Windows NT 4.0 SPG or later, Windows 2000, or Windows XP ■ Single and Multi-user ■ Stand alone or network ■ Compatible w/ MS Office	■ Tracks proposal activity, including issuer of RFP/RFI, person responsible for the response, win/loss status, and other important information	■ Opportunity tracking ■ Capture & track response strategy ■ Capture & track competition/ risk assessment ■ Capture & track capture plan	

Features / Capabilities *			Introduction / Maturity	Training & Support *	Pricing *
Proposal Database Components	Pricing Activity	Other			
		■ Automatically reads RFP questions, presents possible answers from DB, & inserts answer (under user control) into document	■ Introduced in 1995 ■ Current customers: over 1,800 ■ Over 50,000 installations	Training: ■ The RFP Machine: 3-day course Training: ■ Regional RFP Machine: 3-day course ■ Online RFP Machine: 4 segments of 5 hours each ■ Intro to Document Preparation: 2-hour online course ■ Authoring Foundations: 1-day course ■ RFP Express: 1-day course ■ Online RFP Express: 4-hour online course Training: ■ RFP Express Train-the-Trainer: 1-day course ■ Online RFP Express Train-the-Trainer: 1-day course Support: Annual Support and Maintenance (18%) includes: ■ Unlimited access to Technical Support Center on the Web ■ Telephone support ■ Email support ■ All upgrades and enhancements for a 1-year period	
■ Past performance library			■ Introduced in 1995 ■ Current customers: over 1,800 ■ Over 35,000 installations	Training: ■ The RFP Tracking System: 1-day course ■ Online RFP Tracking System: 4-hour course Support: Annual Support and Maintenance (18%) includes: ■ Unlimited access to Technical Support Center on the Web ■ Telephone support ■ Email support ■ All upgrades and enhancements for a 1-year period	Per named user: ■ The RFP Tracking System: $495

Product Name	Vendor [Listed alphabetically]	Platform / Configura-tion	Description—General	Features / Capabilities *	
				Capture Phase	Proposal Development
PropLibrary.com	PropLibrary.com. Annandale, VA Marketed by: Advantage Consulting, Inc. 7611 Little River Turnpike, 204W Annandale, VA 22003 Voice: 703-642-5153 Fax: 703-658-0159 Email: *jbender@acibiz.com* Web: *www.acibiz.com* *www.proplibrary.com* Primary Application: Government and Commercial procurements	Web-hosted ASP Use with any browser Fixed price per-proposal with unlimited users	Provides a document creation and proposal management system for immediate use via the Internet. Use Proplibrary.com for coordinating dispersed writers or reviewers and version control of proposal documents and files	■ Win strategy development ■ Discussion groups	■ Capture/build proposal outline ■ Link Win Factors, RFP requirements and personnel to sections ■ Produce/maintain storyboards ■ Capture/maintain proposal text ■ Capture/maintain proposal graphics ■ Produce compliance matrices ■ Configuration/ version control of proposal sections ■ Discussion groups

Features / Capabilities *			Introduction / Maturity	Training & Support *	Pricing *
Proposal Database Components	**Pricing Activity**	**Other**			
■ Shared reference document library ■ Resume library ■ Previous proposal library ■ Past performance library		■ Access control (security) maintained by Proposal Manager	Introduced 2002.	On-line help Wash DC local on-site training & support	$1,000/proposal or $5,000/month subscription Discounts for multi-proposal packages or extended subscription periods.

Product Name	Vendor [Listed alphabetically]	Platform / Configuration	Description—General	Features / Capabilities *	
				Capture Phase	Proposal Development
Proposals Organized to Win—POW2000™ version 1.0	Ransone Associates, Inc. 5320 Jessie Dupont Memorial Highway Wicomico Church, VA 22579 Voice: 804-580-5929 Fax: 804-580-4028 Email: *Ransone@aol.com* Web: *www.ransone.com* Primary Application: Government, Commercial, and International procurement	Windows 95/98, ME, 2000, NT, XP POW2000 compatible w/ MS Office 2000 Professional and MS Project 98/2000 Multi-user Network or Stand-alone	Win Strategy development, proposal scheduling, RFP shredout to proposal, CDRL tracking to proposal, text and illustrations tracking, Integrated Program Management, CWBS, CSOW, IMP/IMS, Cost/Pricing tracking, risk assessment and management planning, Storyboards, Red Team Review, CR/DR response, Oral Presentations. Also includes a unique "Proposal RunningStart™" function that provides an online, MS Word-based continuum from RFP requirements to Storyboards/ Instructions to Authors/Proposal Drafting.	■ Opportunity tracking ■ Prompt, capture & track win strategy ■ Prompt, capture & track response strategy ■ Prompt, capture & track competition/ risk assessment ■ Prompt, capture & track capture plan ■ Bid/no bid analysis	■ Import an electronic RFP ■ Capture/build proposal online ■ Parse RFP ■ Allocate and link RFP requirements to/by author or capture rqmts. ■ Allocate "win factors" to sections ■ Allocate "evaluation criteria" to sections ■ Produce online storyboard forms ■ Produce/maintain completed storyboards ■ Track proposal text and illustrations ■ Allow export to other applications packages ■ Facilitate amendment/ requirements changes ■ Configuration/ version control (of proposal sections and volumes) ■ History of document changes
RFPMaster 5.0	The Sant Corporation 10260 Alliance Road, Suite 210 Cincinnati, OH 45242 Voice: 888-448-7268 Fax: 513-791-4580 Email: *info@santcorp.com* Web: *www.santcorp.com* Primary Application(s): Commercial and government	Windows 95 and above Compatible w/ MS Word 97 and above Single or multi-user; stand-alone or network.	Manages the process of responding to RFPs. Questions/ requirements can be assigned to team members with due dates. Users can search a comprehensive library of answers automatically. Shows answers that match criteria and lets user choose best one, or combine several. Compiles the final proposal in Word and includes an optional compliance matrix.	■ Prompt response tactics, messaging	■ Import electronic RFP, or import manually ■ Capture, build & maintain proposal outline ■ Parse RFP ■ Capture/maintain proposal text & graphics ■ Data base library for: - ref. documents, - resumes, - previous proposals - past performance

Features / Capabilities *			Introduction / Maturity	Training & Support *	Pricing *
Proposal Database Components	Pricing Activity	Other			
	■ WBS correlation ■ Correlation/link to standard application packages (MS Excel, ProCyon) ■ POW can export the ILS detailed tasks to Excel for cost/pricing ■ Export IMS tasks to MS Word for BOE ■ Address IMS detail tasks for Risk assessment and mitigation plans	■ Oral Presentation and Proposal support ■ Online self training ■ Online help ■ Pop-up help topics ■ User-friendly user interface ■ All functions, interface screens, and output easily customizable to user's needs	■ Introduced in 1988 (DOS) ■ POW95 v1.0 for Office 95 released 1997 ■ POW95 v1.1 released 1999 ■ POW2000 v1.0 released 2002 ■ Current customers: 15	■ One-Day or two day Training and OJT ■ 6 months free telephone support ■ 30-day money back guarantee, 6 month warranty program ■ One free upgrade	Price: $9,500 Corporate discounts Site licensee may load software on all computers at one proposal organization Licensee may load software on teammate computers temporarily for duration of a proposal. CD includes self-training program and user's Tour Guide
		■ Access control (security) ■ Automatically creates a compliance matrix ■ Integrates with other corporate data bases ■ Creates an MS Word document.	RFP Master 4.0 released January 1998 First introduced in 1994 Currently over 20,000 RFPMaster users.	Training & workshops available 30 days free technical support	$595 per user

Product Name	Vendor [Listed alphabetically]	Platform / Configuration	Description—General	Features / Capabilities *	
				Capture Phase	Proposal Development
eRFP Master 5.0	The Sant Corporation [Same as above.]	Server OS: Windows NT 4.0 or Windows 2000 Client OS: Windows 98 or above Compatible w/ MS Word 97 or above	Web-based version of RFPMaster. [Not just "web enabled."] eRFPMaster runs completely through the browser, requiring no special software on the user's computer.	[Same as above.]	[Same as above.] Also: ■ Broadcast email to team members
Proposal-Master 5.0	The Sant Corporation [Same as above.]	Windows 95 or above Single or multi-user; stand-alone or network. Compatible w/ MS Word 97 and above & PowerPoint 97 and above	Allows user to create formal proposals, letter proposals, or sales letters quickly. Asks questions about the opportunity/ prospect, then creates a professional proposal (in Microsoft Word) that user can modify. Users can customize the structure of their documents and create new documents.	■ Connects with any Customer Relationship Management (CRM) system	■ Capture/build proposal outline ■ Capture/maintain proposal text ■ Data base library for: - ref. documents, - resumes, - previous proposals ■ Integrates with other corporate data bases ■ Allows export to MS Word ■ Powerful reporting
eProposal-Master 5.0	The Sant Corporation [Same as above.]	Server OS: Windows NT 4.0 or Windows 2000 Client OS: Windows 98 and above Compatible w/ MS Word 97 & above and MS PowerPoint 97 and above	Web-based version of ProposalMaster. eProposalMaster runs completely through the browser, requiring no special software on user's computer. [Functions same as above.]	[Same as above.]	[Same as above.]

Features / Capabilities *			Introduction / Maturity	Training & Support *	Pricing *
Proposal Database Components	Pricing Activity	Other			
		■ SQL Server ■ Automatic compliance matrix ■ Integrates with other corporate DBs ■ Creates an MS Word document.	eRFPMaster released July 2000	[Same as above.]	$795 per user $2,995 server
	■ Correlates / links to standard application packages including MS Excel, Calico, Trilogy, Exactuim	■ Architecture includes standard proposal elements: - Cover letter - Executive summary - Needs analysis - Benefits - ROI graphs - Solution statement ■ Architecture can also be changed to match client's needs ■ Generates mngt reports ■ Configuration control ■ Presentation Builder module creates PowerPoint presentation.	Introduced in 1993. Current users: over 70,000	Training & workshops available 30 days free technical support	Standard: $395 per user Enterprise: $695 per user Presentation-Builder: $95 per user
	[Same as above.]	[Same as above.]	First version introduced in November 2000	[Same as above.]	Standard: $595 per user Enterprise: $895 per user Server license: $3,995 Presentation-Builder included

Product Name	Vendor [Listed alphabetically]	Platform / Configuration	Description—General	Features / Capabilities *	
				Capture Phase	Proposal Development
Thinkwire Version 2.0	Thinksmith Corporation 20 Camden St., Suite 200, Toronto, Ontario Canada, M5V 1V1 Parent Company: Impact Mobile Voice: 416-516-1600 Fax: 416-925-5903 Email: *info@thinksmith.com* Web: *www.thinksmith.com* Primary Application: Government, Commercial, and International procurement	OS; Windows, Unix and Linux; requires Internet Explorer or Netscape Navigator browser with Java VM enabled. Multi-user, Network configuration Compatible w/ Internet Explorer or Netscape Navigator browser with Java VM enabled	Web-native and client-free document creation tool that enables users to work on-line — at any time — to discuss, research and build RFPs, RFQs, RFIs, plans, budgets, proposals, etc. Includes: graphical organization and navigation of elements/ideas; document assembly; instant updating; fast and easy team evaluations and decision-making; in-line editing of team decisions and responses; HTML output of complete document; automatic storage and archiving of all team comments/ decisions/responses; web-native encrypted access from browsers.	■ Opportunity tracking ■ Prompt, capture, and track win strategies ■ Prompt response tactics ■ Capture and track response strategy ■ Prompt, capture and track capture plan ■ Bid/no-bid analysis ■ Security/ controlled access	■ Import an electronic RFP ■ Capture/build proposal outline ■ Parse RFP ■ ments to/by author and capture requirements ■ Allocate "win factors" to sections ■ Allocate "evaluation criteria" to sections ■ Capture/maintain proposal text ■ Capture/maintain proposal graphics ■ Allow export to other applications packages ■ Facilitate amendment/ requirements changes ■ Configuration/ version control (of proposal sections and volumes) ■ History of document changes ■ Security/controlled access

* **Note:** Information listed is considered reliable but not guaranteed. Pricing current as of January/February 2003. In most cases, prices subject to change without notice. Other discounts, features, and/or options may be available or apply. Please contact vendor for additional information, pricing, and features specific to your needs.

Features / Capabilities *			Introduction / Maturity	Training & Support *	Pricing *
Proposal Database Components	Pricing Activity	Other			
■ Shared reference document library ■ Resume library ■ Previous proposal library ■ Past performance library ■ Integration with other corporate data bases	■ Work breakdown structure correlation	■ Archives information/ process ■ web-based researching & filesharing	First released October, 1999 V2.0 released 2001 Current customers: 10 Note: This product is only available on a limited basis to new customers. Please contact the vendor for details.	Customer service available 24x7 via toll free number and e-mail Product and service 100& guaranteed Training features "Quickstart Workshop," a three day introductory course	The vendor does not have an established price list for this product. Pricing is avilable from the vendor as a custom quote.

Glossary of Key Terms

absolute standards

A type of standard used in competitive negotiations to evaluate a proposal. Includes both the maximum acceptable value and the minimum acceptable value for all selected evaluation criteria.

acceptance

(1) Taking and receiving of anything in good part, and as if it were a tacit agreement to a preceding act, which might have been defeated or avoided if such acceptance had not been made. (2) Agreement to the terms offered in a contract. An acceptance must be communicated, and (in common law) it must be the mirror image of the offer.

acquisition cost

Money invested up front to bring in new customers.

acquisition plan

A plan for an acquisition that serves as the basis for initiating the individual contracting actions necessary to acquire a system or support a program.

acquisition strategy

The conceptual framework for conducting systems acquisition. It encompasses the broad concepts and objectives that direct and control the overall development, production and deployment of a system.

act of God

An inevitable, accidental or extraordinary event that cannot be foreseen and guarded against, such as lightning, tornadoes or earthquakes.

actual authority

The power that the principal intentionally confers on an agent or allows the agent to believe he or she possesses.

actual damages

See *compensatory damages.*

affidavit

A written and signed statement sworn to under oath.

agency

A relationship that exists when there is a delegation of authority to perform all acts connected within a particular trade, business or company. It gives authority to the agent to act in all matters relating to the business of the principal.

agent

An employee (usually a contract manager) or other person empowered to bind his or her organization legally in contract negotiations.

allowable cost

A cost that is reasonable, allocable and within accepted standards, or otherwise conforms to generally accepted accounting principles, specific limitations or exclusions or agreed-on terms between contractual parties.

alternative dispute resolution

Any procedure that is used, in lieu of litigation, to resolve issues in controversy, including settlement negotiations, conciliation, facilitation, mediation, fact finding, mini-trials and arbitration.

amortization

The process of spreading the cost of an intangible asset over the expected useful life of the asset.

apparent authority

The power the principal permits a perceived agent to exercise, although not actually granted.

as is

A contract phrase referring to the condition of property sold or leased; generally pertains to a disclaimer of liability. Property sold in as-is condition is generally not guaranteed.

assign

To convey or transfer to another, as to assign property, rights or interests to another.

assignment

The transfer of property by an assignor to an assignee.

audits

The systematic examination of records and documents and/or the securing of other evidence by confirmation, physical inspection, or otherwise, for one or more of the following purposes: determining the propriety or legality of proposed or completed transactions, ascertaining whether all transactions have been recorded and are reflected accurately in accounts, determining the existence of recorded assets and inclusiveness of recorded liabilities, determining the accuracy of financial or statistical statements or reports and the fairness of the facts they represent, determining the degree of compliance with established policies and procedures in terms of financial transactions and business management and appraising an account system and making recommendations concerning it.

base profit

The money a company is paid by a customer, which exceeds the company's cost.

best value

The most favorable combination of competing factors for a particular purchase requirement. The key to successful best-value contracting is consideration of life-cycle costs, including the use of quantitative as well as qualitative techniques to measure price and technical performance trade-offs between various proposals. The best-value concept applies to acquisitions in which price or price-related factors are not the primary determinant of who receives the contract award.

bid

An offer in response to an invitation for bids (IFB).

bid development

All of the work activities required to design and price the product and service solution and accurately articulate this in a proposal for a customer.

bid phase

The period of time a seller of goods and/or services uses to develop a bid/proposal, conduct internal bid reviews and obtain stakeholder approval to submit a bid/proposal.

bilateral contract

A contract formed if an offer states that acceptance requires only for the accepting party to promise to perform. In contrast, a unilateral contract is formed if an offer requires actual performance for acceptance.

bond

A written instrument executed by a seller and a second party (the surety or sureties) to ensure fulfillment of the principal's obligations to a third party (the obligee or buyer), identified in the bond. If the principal's obligations are not met, the bond ensures payment, to the extent stipulated, of any loss sustained by the obligee.

breach of contract

(1) The failure, without legal excuse, to perform any promise that forms the whole or part of a contract. (2) The ending of a contract that occurs when one or both of the parties fail to keep their promises; this could lead to arbitration or litigation.

buyer

A party contracting for goods and/or services with one or more sellers.

cancellation

The buyer's withdrawal of the requirement to purchase goods and/or services from the seller.

capture management

The art and science of winning more business.

capture management life cycle

The art and science of winning more business throughout the entire business cycle.

capture project plan

A document or game plan of who needs to do what, when, where, how often and how much to win business.

change in scope

An amendment to approved program requirements or specifications after negotiation of a basic contract. It may result in an increase or decrease.

change order/purchase order amendment
A written order directing the seller to make changes according to the provisions of the contract documents.

claim
A demand by one party to a contract for something from another party, usually for more money or more time. Claims are usually based on an argument that the party making the demand is entitled to an adjustment by virtue of the contract terms or some violation of those terms by the other party. The word does not imply any disagreement between the parties, although claims often lead to disagreements. This book uses the term dispute to refer to disagreements that have become intractable.

clause
A statement of one of the rights and/or obligations of the parties to a contract. A contract consists of a series of clauses.

collaboration software
Automated tools that allow for the real-time exchange of visual information using personal computers.

collateral benefit
The degree to which pursuit of an opportunity will improve the existing skill level or develop new skills which will positively affect other or future business opportunities.

compensable delay
A delay for which the buyer is contractually responsible that excuses the seller's failure to perform and is compensable.

compensatory damages
Damages that will compensate the injured party for the loss sustained and nothing more. They are awarded by the court as the measure of actual loss, and not as punishment for outrageous conduct or to deter future transgressions. Compensatory damages are often referred to as "actual damages." See also incidental and punitive damages.

competitive intelligence
Information on competitors or competitive teams which is specific to an opportunity.

competitive negotiation

A method of contracting involving a request for proposals that states the buyer's requirements and criteria for evaluation; submission of timely proposals by a maximum number of offerors; discussions with those offerors found to be within the competitive range; and award of a contract to the one offeror whose offer, price and other consideration factors are most advantageous to the buyer.

condition precedent

A condition that activates a term in a contract.

condition subsequent

A condition that suspends a term in a contract.

conflict of interest

Term used in connection with public officials and fiduciaries and their relationships to matters of private interest or gain. Ethical problems connected therewith are covered by statutes in most jurisdictions and at the federal level. A conflict of interest arises when an employee's personal or financial interest conflicts or appears to conflict with his or her official responsibility.

consideration

(1) The thing of value (amount of money or acts to be done or not done) that must change hands between the parties to a contract. (2) The inducement to a contract – the cause, motive, price or impelling influence that induces a contracting party to enter into a contract.

constructive change

An oral or written act or omission by an authorized or unauthorized agent that is of such a nature that it is construed to have the same effect as a written change order.

contingency

The quality of being contingent or casual; an event that may but does not have to occur; a possibility.

contingent contract

A contract that provides for the possibility of its termination when a specified occurrence takes place or does not take place.

contra proferentem

A legal phrase used in connection with the construction of written documents to the effect that an ambiguous provision is construed most strongly against the person who selected the language.

contract

(1) A relationship between two parties, such as a buyer and seller, that is defined by an agreement about their respective rights and responsibilities. (2) A document that describes such an agreement.

contract administration

The process of ensuring compliance with contractual terms and conditions during contract performance up to contract closeout or termination.

contract closeout

The process of verifying that all administrative matters are concluded on a contract that is otherwise physically complete. Typically when the seller has delivered the required supplies or performed the required services, and the buyer has inspected and accepted the supplies or services.

contract fulfillment

The joint Buyer/Seller actions taken to successfully perform and administer a contractual agreement and meet or exceed all contract obligations, including effective changes management and timely contract closeout.

contract interpretation

The entire process of determining what the parties agreed to in their bargain. The basic objective of contract interpretation is to determine the intent of the parties. Rules calling for interpretation of the documents against the drafter, and imposing a duty to seek clarification on the drafter, allocate risks of contractual ambiguities by resolving disputes in favor of the party least responsible for the ambiguity.

contract management

The art and science of managing a contractual agreement(s) throughout the contracting process.

contract type
Refers to a specific characterization made on the basis of certain key terms, usually pricing, used for the performance of work under the contract.

contractor
The seller or provider of goods and/or services.

controversy
A litigated question. A civil action or suit may not be instigated unless it is based on a "justifiable" dispute. This term is important in that judicial power of the courts extends only to cases and "controversies."

copyright
A royalty-free, nonexclusive and irrevocable license to reproduce, translate, publish, use and dispose of written or recorded material, and to authorize others to do the same.

cost
The amount of money expended in acquiring a product or obtaining a service. The total of acquisition costs plus all expenses related to operating and maintaining an item once acquired.

cost of good sold (COGS)
Direct costs of producing finished goods for sale.

cost accounting standards
Federal standards designed to provide consistency and coherency in defense and other government contract accounting.

cost-plus-award fee (CPAF) contract
A type of cost-reimbursement contract with special incentive fee provisions used to motivate excellent contract performance in such areas as quality, timeliness, ingenuity and cost-effectiveness.

cost-plus-fixed fee (CPFF) contract
A type of cost-reimbursement contract that provides for the payment of a fixed fee to the contractor. It does not vary with actual costs, but may be adjusted if there are changes in the work or services performed under the contract.

cost-plus-incentive fee (CPIF) contract
A type of cost-reimbursement contract with provision for a fee that is adjusted by a formula in accordance with the relationship between total allowable costs and target costs.

cost-plus-a-percentage-of-cost (CPPC) contract
A type of cost-reimbursement contract that provides for a reimbursement of the allowable cost of services performed plus an agreed-on percentage of the estimated cost as profit.

cost-reimbursement (CR) contract
A type of contract that usually includes an estimate of project cost, a provision for reimbursing the seller's expenses and a provision for paying a fee as profit. CR contracts are often used when there is high uncertainty about costs. They normally also include a limitation on the buyer's cost liability.

cost-sharing contract
A cost-reimbursement contract in which the seller receives no fee and is reimbursed only for an agreed-on portion of its allowable costs.

cost contract
The simplest type of cost-reimbursement contract. Governments commonly use this type when contracting with universities and nonprofit organizations for research projects. The contract provides for reimbursing contractually allowable costs, with no allowance given for profit.

cost proposal
The instrument required of an offeror for the submission or identification of cost or pricing data by which an offeror submits to the buyer a summary of estimated (or incurred) costs, suitable for detailed review and analysis.

counteroffer
An offer made in response to an original offer that changes the terms of the original.

customer revenue growth
The increased revenues achieved by keeping a customer for an extended period of time.

customer support costs
Costs expended by a company to provide information and advice concerning purchases.

default termination
The termination of a contract, under the standard default clause, because of a buyer's or seller's material breach of one or more of the contract terms.

defect
The absence of something necessary for completeness or perfection. A deficiency relates to something essential to the proper use of a thing. Some structural weakness in a part or component that is responsible for damage.

defect, latent
A defect that existed at the time of acceptance but would not have been discovered by a reasonable inspection.

defect, patent
A defect that can be discovered without undue effort. If the defect was actually known to the buyer at the time of acceptance, it is patent, even though it otherwise might not have been discoverable by a reasonable inspection.

definite-quantity contract
A legally binding agreement that provides for a definite quantity of supplies or services to be delivered at some later, unspecified date.

delay, excusable
A contractual provision designed to protect the seller from sanctions for late performance. To the extent that it has been excusably delayed, the seller is protected from default termination or liquidated damages. Examples of excusable delay are acts of God, acts of the government, fire, flood, quarantines, strikes, epidemics, unusually severe weather and embargoes. See also forbearance and force majeure clause.

depreciation
Amount of expense charged against earnings by a company to write off the cost of a plant or machine over its useful life,

giving consideration to wear and tear, obsolescence and salvage value.

design specification

(1) A document (including drawings) setting forth the required characteristics of a particular component, part, subsystem, system or construction item. (2) A purchase description that establishes precise measurements, tolerances, materials, in-process and finished product tests, quality control, inspection requirements and other specific details of the deliverable.

direct cost

The costs specifically identifiable with a contract requirement, including but not restricted to, costs of material and/or labor directly incorporated into an end item.

direct labor

All work that is obviously related and specifically and conveniently traceable to specific products.

direct material

Items, including raw material, purchased parts and subcontracted items, directly incorporated into an end item, which are identifiable to a contract requirement.

discount rate

Interest rate used in calculating present value.

discounted cash flow (DCF)

Combined present value of cash flow and tangible assets minus present value of liabilities.

discounts, allowances and returns

Price discounts, returned merchandise.

dispute

A disagreement not settled by mutual consent that could be decided by litigation or arbitration. Also see *claim.*

e-business

Technology-enabled business that focuses on seamless integration between each business, the company and its supply partners.

EBITDA
Earnings Before Interest, Taxes, Depreciation and Amortization, but after all product/service, sales and overhead (SG&A) costs are accounted for. Sometimes referred to as Operating Profit.

EBITDARM
Acronym for Earnings Before Interest, Taxes, Depreciation, Amortization, Rent and Management fees.

e-commerce
A subset of e-business, Internet-based electronic transactions.

electronic data interchange (EDI)
Private networks used for simple data transactions, which are typically batch-processed.

elements of a contract
The items that must be present in a contract for it to be binding, including an offer, acceptance (agreement), consideration, execution by competent parties and legality of purpose.

enterprise resource planning (ERP)
An electronic framework for integrating all organizational functions, evolved from Manufacturing Resource Planning (MRP).

entire contract
A contract that is considered a single agreement and cannot be made severable.

e-procurement
Technology-enabled buying and selling of goods and services.

estimate at completion (EAC)
The actual direct costs, plus indirect costs allocable to the contract, plus the estimate of costs (direct or indirect) for authorized work remaining.

estoppel
A rule of law that bars, prevents and precludes a party from alleging or denying certain facts because of a previous allegation or denial or because of its previous conduct or admission.

ethics

Of or relating to moral action, conduct, motive or character (such as ethical emotion). Also, treating of moral feelings, duties or conduct; containing precepts of morality. Professionally right or befitting; conforming to professional standards of conduct.

e-tool

An electronic device, program, system or software application used to facilitate business.

exculpatory clause

Contract language designed to shift responsibility to the other party. A "no damages for delay" clause would be an example of one used by buyers.

excusable delay

See *delay, excusable.*

executed contract

A contract that is formed and performed at the same time. If performed in part, it is partially executed and partially executory.

executed contract (document)

A written document, signed by both parties and mailed or otherwise furnished to each party, that expresses the requirements, terms and conditions to be met by both parties in the performance of the contract.

executory contract

A contract that has not yet been fully performed.

express

Something put in writing, for example, "express authority."

fair and reasonable

A subjective evaluation of what each party deems as equitable consideration in areas such as terms and conditions, cost or price, assured quality, timeliness of contract performance and/or any other areas subject to negotiation.

Federal Acquisition Regulation (FAR)

The government-wide procurement regulation mandated by Congress and issued by the Department of Defense, the General Services Administration and the National Aeronautics and Space Administration. Effective April 1, 1984, the FAR superseded both the Defense Acquisition Regulation (DAR) and the Federal Procurement Regulation (FPR). All federal agencies are authorized to issue regulations implementing the FAR.

fee

An agreed-to amount of reimbursement beyond the initial estimate of costs. The term "fee" is used when discussing cost-reimbursement contracts, whereas the term "profit" is used in relation to fixed-price contracts.

firm-fixed-price (FFP) contract

The simplest and most common business pricing arrangement. The seller agrees to supply a quantity of goods or provide a service for a specified price.

fixed cost

Operating expenses that are incurred to provide facilities and organization that are kept in readiness to do business without regard to actual volumes of production and sales. Examples of fixed costs consist of rent, property tax and interest expense.

fixed price

A form of pricing that includes a ceiling beyond which the buyer bears no responsibility for payment.

fixed-price incentive (FPI) contract

A type of contract that provides for adjusting profit and establishing the final contract price using a formula based on the relationship of total final negotiated cost to total target cost. The final price is subject to a price ceiling, negotiated at the outset.

fixed-price redeterminable (FPR) contract

A type of fixed-price contract that contains provisions for subsequently negotiated adjustment, in whole or part, of the initially negotiated base price.

fixed-price with economic price adjustment

A fixed-price contract that permits an element of cost to fluctuate to reflect current market prices.

forbearance

An intentional failure of a party to enforce a contract requirement, usually done for an act of immediate or future consideration from the other party. Sometimes forbearance is referred to as a nonwaiver or as a onetime waiver, but not as a relinquishment of rights.

force majeure clause

Refers to major or irresistible force. A contract clause that protects the parties in the event that a part of the contract cannot be performed due to causes outside of their control and could not be avoided by exercise of due care. Excusable conditions for nonperformance, such as strikes and acts of God (e.g., typhoons) are contained in this clause.

fraud

An intentional perversion of truth to induce another in reliance upon it to part with something of value belonging to him or her or to surrender a legal right. A false representation of a matter of fact, whether by words or conduct, by false or misleading allegations or by concealment of that which should have been disclosed, that deceives and is intended to deceive another so that he or she shall act upon it to his or her legal injury. Anything calculated to deceive.

free on board (FOB)

A term used in conjunction with a physical point to determine (a) the responsibility and basis for payment of freight charges and (b) unless otherwise agreed, the point at which title for goods passes to the buyer or consignee. FOB origin – The seller places the goods on the conveyance by which they are to be transported. Cost of shipping and risk of loss are borne by the buyer. FOB destination – The seller delivers the goods on the seller's conveyance at destination. Cost of shipping and risk of loss are borne by the seller.

functional specification
A purchase description for the deliverable stated in terms of performance characteristics and intended use, including minimum performance attributes necessary to satisfy the intended use.

general and administrative (G&A)
(1) The indirect expenses related to the overall business. Expenses for a company's general and executive offices, executive compensation, staff services and other miscellaneous support purposes. (2) Any indirect management, financial, or other expense that (a) is not assignable to a program's direct overhead charges for engineering, manufacturing, material, etc., but (b) is routinely incurred by or allotted to a business unit and (c) is for the general management and administration of the business as a whole.

general accepted accounting principles (GAAP)
A term encompassing conventions, rules and procedures of accounting that are "generally accepted" and have "substantial authoritative support." GAAP have been developed by agreement on the basis of experience, reason, custom, usage, and to a certain extent, practical necessity, rather than being derived from a formal set of theories.

General Agreement on Tariffs and Trade (GATT)
A multi-national trade agreement, signed in 1947 by 23 nations.

gross profit margin
Net Sales minus Cost of Goods Sold. Also called Gross Margin, Gross Profit or Gross Loss

gross profit margin % or ratio
Gross Profit Margin divided by Net Sales.

gross sales
Total revenues at invoice value before any discounts or allowances.

horizontal exchange
A marketplace that deals with goods and services that are not specific to one industry.

imply

To indirectly convey meaning or intent; to leave the determination of meaning up to the receiver of the communication based on circumstances, general language used or conduct of those involved.

incidental damages

Any commercially reasonable charges, expenses or commissions incurred in stopping delivery; in the transportation, care and custody of goods after the buyer's breach; or in connection with the return or resale of the goods or otherwise resulting from the breach.

indefinite-delivery/indefinite-quantity (IDIQ) contract

A type of contract in which the exact date of delivery or the exact quantity, or a combination of both, is not specified at the time the contract is executed; provisions are placed in the contract to later stipulate these elements of the contract.

indemnification clause

A contract clause by which one party engages to secure another against an anticipated loss resulting from an act or forbearance on the part of one of the parties or some third person.

indemnify

To make good; to compensate; to reimburse a person in case of an anticipated loss.

indirect cost

Any cost not directly identifiable with a specific cost objective but subject to two or more cost objectives.

indirect labor

All work that is not specifically associated with or cannot be practically traced to specific units of output.

intellectual property

The kind of property that results from the fruits of mental labor.

Internet

The World Wide Web.

interactive chat
A feature provided by automated tools that allow for users to establish a voice connection between one or more parties and exchange text or graphics via a virtual bulletin board.

intranet
An organization-specific internal secure network.

joint contract
A contract in which the parties bind themselves both individually and as a unit.

liquidated damages
A contract provision providing for the assessment of damages on the seller for its failure to comply with certain performance or delivery requirements of the contract; used when the time of delivery or performance is of such importance that the buyer may reasonably expect to suffer damages if delivery or performance is delinquent.

mailbox rule
The idea that acceptance of an offer is effective when deposited in the mail if the envelope is properly addressed.

marketing
Activities that direct the flow of goods and services from producers to consumers.

market intelligence
Information on your competitors or competitive teams operating in the marketplace or industry.

market research
The process used to collect and analyze information about an entire market to help determine the most suitable approach to acquiring, distributing and supporting supplies and services.

memorandum of agreement (MOA)/ memorandum of understanding (MOU)
The documentation of a mutually agreed-to statement of facts, intentions, procedures and parameters for future actions and matters of coordination. A "memorandum of understanding"

may express mutual understanding of an issue without implying commitments by parties to the understanding.

method of procurement

The process used for soliciting offers, evaluating offers and awarding a contract.

modifications

Any written alterations in the specification, delivery point, rate of delivery, contract period, price, quantity or other provision of an existing contract, accomplished in accordance with a contract clause; may be unilateral or bilateral.

monopoly

A market structure in which the entire market for a good or service is supplied by a single seller or firm.

monopsony

A market structure in which a single buyer purchases a good or service.

NCMA CMBOK

Definitive descriptions of the elements making up the body of professional knowledge that applies to contract management.

negotiation

A process between buyers and sellers seeking to reach mutual agreement on a matter of common concern through fact-finding, bargaining and persuasion.

net marketplace

Two-sided exchange where buyers and sellers negotiate prices, usually with a bid-and-ask system, and where prices move both up and down.

net present value (NPV)

The lifetime customer revenue stream discounted by the investment costs and operations costs.

net sales

Gross sales minus discounts, allowances and returns.

North America Free Trade Agreement (NAFTA)
A trilateral trade and investment agreement, between Canada, Mexico and the United States ratified on January 1, 1994.

novation agreement
A legal instrument executed by (a) the contractor (transferor), (b) the successor in interest (transferee) and (c) the buyer by which, among other things, the transferor guarantees performance of the contract, the transferee assumes all obligations under the contract and the buyer recognizes the transfer of the contract and related assets.

offer
(1) The manifestation of willingness to enter into a bargain, so made as to justify another person in understanding that his or her assent to that bargain is invited and will conclude it. (2) An unequivocal and intentionally communicated statement of proposed terms made to another party. An offer is presumed revocable unless it specifically states that it is irrevocable. An offer once made will be open for a reasonable period of time and is binding on the offeror unless revoked by the offeror before the other party's acceptance.

oligopoly
A market dominated by a few sellers.

operating expenses
SG&A plus depreciation and amortization.

opportunity
A potential or actual favorable event.

opportunity engagement
The degree to which a company or its competitors are involved in establishing a customer's requirements.

opportunity profile
A stage of the Capture Management Life Cycle during which a seller evaluates and describes the opportunity in terms of what it means to its customer and its company, and what is required to succeed.

option

A unilateral right in a contract by which, for a specified time, the buyer may elect to purchase additional quantities of the supplies or services called for in the contract, or elect to extend the performance period.

order of precedence

A solicitation provision establishing priorities so that contradictions within the solicitation can be resolved.

Organizational Breakdown Structure (OBS)

A organized structure which represents how individual team members are grouped to complete assigned work tasks.

outsourcing

A contractual process of obtaining another party to provide goods and/or services that were previously done internal to an organization.

overhead

An accounting cost category that typically includes general indirect expenses necessary to operate a business but are not directly assignable to a specific good or service produced. Examples include building rent, utilities, salaries of corporate officers, janitorial services, office supplies and furniture.

overtime

The time worked by a seller's employee in excess of the employee's normal work week.

parol evidence

Oral or verbal evidence; in contract law, the evidence drawn from sources exterior to the written instrument.

parol evidence rule

A rule that seeks to preserve the integrity of written agreements by refusing to permit contracting parties to attempt to alter a written contract with evidence of any contradictory prior or contemporaneous oral agreement (parol to the contract).

payments
The amount payable under the contract supporting data required to be submitted with invoices, and other payment terms such as time for payment and retention.

payment bond
A bond that secures the appropriate payment of subcontractors for their completed and acceptable goods and/or services.

performance bond
A bond that secures the performance and fulfillment of all the undertakings, covenants, terms, conditions and agreements contained in the contract.

performance specification
A purchase description that describes the deliverable in terms of desired operational characteristics. Performance specifications tend to be more restrictive than functional specifications, in that they limit alternatives that the buyer will consider and define separate performance standards for each such alternative.

post-bid phase
The period of time after a seller submits a bid/proposal to a buyer; include source selection, negotiations, contract formation, contract fulfillment, contract closeout and follow-on opportunity management.

pre-bid phase
The period of time a seller of goods and/or services uses to identify business opportunities prior to the release of a customer solicitation.

pricing arrangement
An agreed-to basis between contractual parties for the payment of amounts for specified performance; usually expressed in terms of a specific cost-reimbursement or fixed-price arrangement.

prime/prime contractor
The principal seller performing under the contract.

private exchange

A marketplace hosted by a single company inside a company's firewall and used for procurement from among a group of preauthorized sellers.

privity of contract

The legal relationship that exists between the parties to a contract that allows either party to (a) enforce contractual rights against the other party and (b) seek remedy directly from the other party.

procurement

The complete action or process of acquiring or obtaining goods or services using any of several authorized means.

procurement planning

The process of identifying which business needs can be best met by procuring products or services outside the organization.

profit

The net proceeds from selling a product or service when costs are subtracted from revenues. May be positive (profit) or negative (loss).

program management

Planning and execution of multiple projects that are related to one another.

progress payments

An interim payment for delivered work in accordance with contract terms; generally tied to meeting specified performance milestones.

project management

Planning and ensuring the quality, on-time delivery, and cost of a specific set of related activities with a definite beginning and end.

promotion

Publicizing the attributes of the product/service through media and personal contacts and presentations, e.g., technical articles/presentations, new releases, advertising and sales calls.

proposal

Normally, a written offer by a seller describing its offering terms. Proposals may be issued in response to a specific request or may be made unilaterally when a seller feels there may be an interest in its offer (which is also known as an unsolicited proposal).

proposal evaluation

An assessment of both the proposal and the offeror's ability (as conveyed by the proposal) to successfully accomplish the prospective contract. Evaluations of competitive proposals should be based solely on the factors specified in the solicitation.

protest

A written objection by an interested party to: (a) a solicitation or other request for proposals, (b) the cancellation of a solicitation or other request, (c) an award or proposed award of a contract or (d) a termination or cancellation of a contract award, if the written objection contains an allegation that the termination or cancellation is based in whole or in part on improprieties concerning the evaluation or award.

punitive damages

Damages awarded to a plaintiff over and above compensatory damages. Unlike compensatory damages, punitive damages are based on an actively different public policy consideration, that of punishing the defendant or of setting an example for similar wrongdoers.

purchasing

The outright acquisition of items, mostly off-the-shelf or catalog, manufactured outside the buyer's premises.

quality assurance

The planned and systematic actions necessary to provide adequate confidence that the performed service or supplied goods will serve satisfactorily for the intended and specified purpose.

quotation

A statement of price, either written or oral, which may include: a description of the product or service, the terms of sale, delivery or period of performance and payment. Such statements are usually issued by sellers at the request of potential buyers.

reasonable cost

A cost is reasonable if, in its nature and amount, it does not exceed that which would be incurred by a prudent person in the conduct of competitive business.

request for information (RFI)

A formal invitation to submit general and/or specific information concerning the potential future purchase of goods and/or services.

request for proposals (RFP)

A formal invitation that contains a scope of work and seeks a formal response (proposal), describing both methodology and compensation, to form the basis of a contract.

request for quotations (RFQ)

A formal invitation to submit a price for goods and/or services as specified.

request for technical proposals (RFTP)

Solicitation document used in two-step sealed bidding. Normally in letter form, it asks only for technical information; price and cost breakdowns are forbidden.

revenue value

The monetary value of an opportunity.

risk

Exposure or potential for injury or loss.

sealed-bid procedure

A method of procurement involving the unrestricted solicitation of bids, an opening and contract award to the lowest responsive, responsible bidder.

selling, general & administrative (SG&A) expenses
Administrative costs of running business.

severable contract
A contract divisible into separate parts. A default of one section does not invalidate the whole contract.

several
A circumstance when more than two parties are involved with the contract.

single source
One source among others in a competitive marketplace that, for justifiable reason, is found most worthy to receive a contract award.

small business concerns
A small business is one that is independently owned and operated, and is not dominant in its field; a business concern that meets government size standards for its particular industry type.

socioeconomic programs
Programs designed to benefit particular groups. They represent a multitude of program interests and objectives unrelated to procurement objectives. Some examples of these are preferences for small business and American products, required sources for specific items and minimum labor pay levels mandated for contractors.

solicitation
A process through which a buyer requests bids, quotes, tenders or proposals orally, in writing or electronically. Solicitations can take the following forms: request for proposals (RFP), request for quotations (RFQ), request for tenders, invitation to bid (ITB), invitation for bids and invitation for negotiation.

solicitation planning
The preparation of the documents needed to support a solicitation.

source selection

The process by which a buyer evaluates offers, selects a seller, negotiates terms and conditions and awards a contract.

Source Selection Advisory Council

A group of people appointed by the Source Selection Authority (SSA). The Council is responsible for reviewing and approving the source selection plan (SSP) and the solicitation of competitive awards for major and certain less-than-major procurements. The Council also determines what proposals are in the competitive range and provides recommendations to the SSA for final selection.

source selection plan (SSP)

The document that describes the selection criteria, process, and organization used in evaluating proposals for competitively awarded contracts.

specification

A description of the technical requirements for a material, product or service that includes the criteria for determining the requirements have been met. There are generally three types of specifications used in contracting: performance, functional and design.

stakeholders

Individuals who control the resources in a company needed to pursue opportunities or deliver solutions to customers.

standard

A document that establishes engineering and technical limitations and applications of items, materials, processes, methods, designs and engineering practices. It includes any related criteria deemed essential to achieve the highest practical degree of uniformity in materials or products or interchangeability of parts used in those products.

standards of conduct

The ethical conduct of personnel involved in the acquisition of goods and services. Within the federal government, business shall be conducted in a manner above reproach and, except as authorized by law or regulation, with complete impartiality and without preferential treatment.

statement of work (SOW)
That portion of a contract describing the actual work to be done by means of specifications or other minimum requirements, quantities, performance date and a statement of the requisite quality.

statute of limitations
The legislative enactment prescribing the periods within which legal actions may be brought upon certain claims or within which certain rights may be enforced.

stop work order
A request for interim stoppage of work due to nonconformance, funding or technical considerations.

subcontract
A contract between a buyer and a seller in which a significant part of the supplies or services being obtained is for eventual use in a prime contract.

subcontractor
A seller who enters into a contract with a prime contractor or a subcontractor of the prime contractor.

supplementary agreement
A contract modification that is accomplished by the mutual action of parties.

technical factor
A factor other than price used in evaluating offers for award. Examples include technical excellence, management capability, personnel qualifications, prior experience, past performance and schedule compliance.

technical leveling
The process of helping a seller bring its proposal up to the level of other proposals through successive rounds of discussion, such as by pointing out weaknesses resulting from the seller's lack of diligence, competence or inventiveness in preparing the proposal.

technical/management proposal
That part of the offer that describes the seller's approach to meeting the buyer's requirement.

technical transfusion
The disclosure of technical information pertaining to a proposal that results in improvement of a competing proposal. This practice is not allowed in federal government contracting.

term
A part of a contract that addresses a specific subject.

termination
An action taken pursuant to a contract clause in which the buyer unilaterally ends all or part of the work.

terms and conditions (Ts and Cs)
All clauses in a contract, including time of delivery, packing and shipping, applicable standard clauses and special provisions.

unallowable cost
Any cost that, under the provisions of any pertinent law, regulation or contract, cannot be included in prices, cost-reimbursements or settlements under a government contract to which it is allocable.

uncompensated overtime
The work that exempt employees perform above and beyond 40 hours per week. Also known as competitive time, deflated hourly rates, direct allocation of salary costs, discounted hourly rates, extended work week, full-time accounting and green time.

Uniform Commercial Code (UCC)
A U.S. model law developed to standardize commercial contracting law among the states. It has been adopted by 49 states (and in significant portions by Louisiana). The UCC comprises articles that deal with specific commercial subject matters, including sales and letters of credit.

unilateral
See *bilateral contract.*

unsolicited proposal
A research or development proposal that is made by a prospective contractor without prior formal or informal solicitation from a purchasing activity.

variable costs
Costs associated with production that change directly with the amount of production, e.g., the direct material or labor required to complete the build or manufacturing of a product.

variance
The difference between projected and actual performance, especially relating to costs.

vertical exchange
A marketplace that is specific to a single industry.

waiver
The voluntary and unilateral relinquishment a person of a right that he or she has. See also *forbearance.*

warranty
A promise or affirmation given by a seller to a buyer regarding the nature, usefulness or condition of the goods or services furnished under a contract. Generally, a warranty's purpose is to delineate the rights and obligations for defective goods and services and to foster quality performance.

warranty, express
A written statement arising out of a sale to the consumer of a consumer good, pursuant to which the manufacturer, distributor or retailer undertakes to preserve or maintain the utility or performance of the consumer good or provide compensation if there is a failure in utility or performance. It is not necessary to the creation of an express warranty that formal words such as "warrant" or "guarantee" be used, or that a specific intention to make a warranty is present.

warranty, implied

A promise arising by operation of law that something that is sold shall be fit for the purpose for which the seller has reason to know that it is required. Types of implied warranties include implied warranty of merchantability, of title and of wholesomeness.

warranty of fitness

A warranty by the seller that goods sold are suitable for the special purpose of the buyer.

warranty of merchantability

A warranty that goods are fit for the ordinary purposes for which such goods are used and conform to the promises or affirmations of fact made on the container or label.

warranty of title

An express or implied (arising by operation of law) promise that the seller owns the item offered for sale and, therefore, is able to transfer a good title and that the goods, as delivered, are free from any security interest of which the buyer at the time of contracting has no knowledge.

web portals

A public exchange in which a company or group of companies list products or services for sale or provide other transmission of business information.

win strategy

A collection of messages or points designed to guide the customer's perception of you, your solution and your competitors.

Work Breakdown Structure (WBS)

A logical, organized, decomposition of the work tasks within a given project, typically uses a hierarchical numeric coding scheme.

World Trade Organization (WTO)

A multi-national legal entity which serves as the champion of fair trade globally, established April 15, 1995.

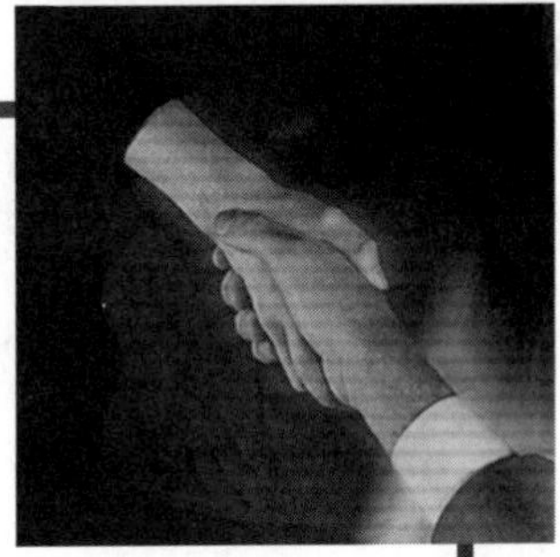

Bibliography

Amrhein, Tom, *Failure to Lead, Leads to Failure – The Art of Proposal Management,* Journal of the Association of Proposal Management Professionals, Spring/Summer 2002 (Association of Proposal Management Professionals).

Badgerow, Dana B., Gregory A. Garrett, Dominic F. DiClementi and Barbara M. Weaver, *Managing Contracts for Peak Performance* (Vienna, Va.: National Contract Management Association, 1990).

Bazerman, Max, and Margaret A. Neale, *Negotiating Rationally* (New York: The Free Press, 1992).

Binnendijk, Hans, ed., *National Negotiating Styles* (Washington, D.C.: Foreign Service Institute, U.S. Department of State, 1987).

Black, Henry Campbell, Joseph R. Nolan, Jacqueline M. Nolan-Haley, M.J. Connolly, Stephan C. Hicks and Martina N. Alibrandi, *Black's Law Dictionary,* 6th ed. (St. Paul, Minn: West Publishing Co., 1990).

Bockrath, Joseph T., *Contracts, Specifications, and Law for Engineers,* 4th ed. (New York: McGraw-Hill Inc., 1986).

Bruce, David L., Norby, Marlys and Ramos, Victor, *Guide to the Contract Management Body of Knowledge (CMBOK)* 1st Edition (Vienna, VA: National Contract Management Association, 2002).

Cavanaugh, Tom, *Computer Security from a Proposal Perspective,* Journal of the Association of Proposal Management Professionals, Spring/Summer, 2002 (Association of Proposal Management Professionals).

Clarkson, Kenneth W., Roger LeRoy Miller, Stephen A. Chaplin and Bonnie Blaire, *West's Business Law: Alternate UCC Comprehensive Edition* (St. Paul, Minn.: West Publishing Company, 1981).

Cohen, Herb, *You Can Negotiate Anything,* 1st ed. (Secaucus, N.J.: L. Stuart, 1980).

Corbin, Arthur L., *Corbin on Contract* (St. Paul, Minn.: West Publishing Company, 1993).

Coulson-Thomas, Colin, *Creating the Global Company,* (New York: McGraw-Hill, 1992).

Covey, Stephen R., *The Seven Habits of Highly Effective People* (New York: Simon and Schuster, Inc., 1989).

DiGiacomo, John and Kleckner, James, *Win Government Contracts for Small Business* (Chicago, CCH Incorporated, 2000).

Dobler, Donald W., David N. Burt and Lamar Lee, Jr., Types of Contracts and Ordering Agreements, in *Purchasing and Materials Management: Text and Cases,* 5th ed. (New York: McGraw-Hill Publishing Company, 1990).

Fisher, Roger, *Getting Ready to Negotiate: The Getting to Yes Workbook* (New York: Penguin Books, 1995).

Fisher, Roger, and Scott Brown, *Getting Together* (New York: Penguin Books, 1989).

Fisher, Roger, and William Ury, *Getting to Yes: Negotiating Agreement Without Giving In,* 2d ed. (New York: Penguin Books, 1991).

Fisher, Roger, Elizabeth Kopelman and Andrea K. Schneider, *Beyond Machiavelli: Tools for Coping with Conflict* (Cambridge: Harvard University Press, 1994).

Forsberg, Ph.D., Kevin, Mooz, Hal and Cotterman, Howard, *Visualizing Project Management* (New York: John Wiley & Sons, Inc., 1996).

Frame, J. Davidson, *Managing Projects in Organizations: How to Make the Best Use of Time, Techniques, and People* (San Francisco: Jossey-Bass, Inc., 1987).

Freed, Richard C., Romano, Joe and Freed, Shervin, *Writing Winning Business Proposals,* (New York: McGraw - Hill, 2003).

Garrett, Gregory A., *World Class Contracting: How Winning Companies Build Successful Partnerships in the e-Business Age* (Chicago, CCH Incorporated, 2001).

Gates, Bill, *Business @ The Speed of Thought: Using a Digital Nervous System* (New York: Warner Books USA, 1999).

Harris, Phillip R. and Robert T. Moran, *Managing Cultural Differences* (Houston: Gulf Publishing Company, 1996).

Hassan H. and Blackwell R., *Global Marketing* (New York: Harcourt Brace Publishing, 1994).

Hendon, Donald W. and Rebecca A. Hendon, *World-Class Negotiating: Dealmaking in the Global Marketplace* (New York: John Wiley & Sons, 1990).

Herond, David H., *Focus on Basics – Using Red Teams Effectively,* Journal of the Association of Proposal Management Professionals, Fall 2000 (Association of Proposal Managment Professionals)

Jacobs, Daniel M., Menker, Janice M. and Shinaman, Chester, P., *Solicitations, Bids and Proposals* (Vienna, VA: National Contract Management Association, 1990).

Kantin, Bob, *Sales Proposals Kit for Dummies* (New York: Hungry Minds, 2001).

Karrass, Chester L., *Give and Take: The Complete Guide to Negotiating Strategies and Tactics* (New York: Harper Collins Pubs., Inc., 1993).

Karrass, Gary, *Negotiate to Close: How to Make More Successful Deals* (New York: Simon and Schuster, 1985).

Kelman, Suzanne, *Proposal Production A Primer on Quality Drivers, Lead Times and Production Task Scope,* Journal of the Association of Proposal Management Professionals, Spring/Summer, 2002 (Association of Proposal Management Professionals).

Kirk, Dorthy, Managing Expectations, *PM Network Magazine,* August 2000 (Project Management Institute).

Koren, Leonard and Peter Goodman, *The Haggler's Handbook: One Hour to Negotiating Power* (New York: W.W. Norton & Co., Inc., 1992).

Lewis, James P., *Mastering Project Management: Applying Advanced Concepts of Systems Thinking, Control and Evaluation, Resource Allocation* (New York: McGraw-Hill, 1998).

McFarlane, Eileen Luhta, *Developing International Proposals in a Virtual Environment,* Journal of the Association of Proposal Management Professionals, Spring 2000 (Association of Proposal Management Professionals).

Monroe, Kent B., *Pricing: Making Profitable Decisions,* 2d ed. (New York: McGraw-Hill Publishing Company, 1990).

Moran, J. and Riesenberger M., *The Global Challenge* (New York: McGraw-Hill, 1994).

Newman, Larry, *Shipley Associates Proposal Guide for Business Development Professionals* (Shipley Associates, 2001).

Nash, Ralph C., Jr. and John Cibinic, *Formation of Government Contracts,* 3d ed (Washington, D.C.: The George Washington University & CCH Incorporated, 1998).

Nash, Ralph C., Jr. and John Cibinic, *Administration of Government Contracts,* 3d ed (Washington, D.C.: The George Washington University & CCH Incorporated, 1995).

Nash, Ralph C., Jr., Karen R. O'Brien and Steven L. Schooner, *The Government Contracts Reference Book: A Comprehensive Guide to the Language of Procurement,* 2d ed. (Washington, D.C.: The George Washington University & CCH Incorporated, 1998).

The National Contract Management Association, *The Desktop Guide to Basic Contracting Terms,* 4th ed. (1912 Woodford Road, Vienna, Virginia 22182, 1994).

Nierenberg, Gerard, *The Art of Negotiating* (New York: Penguin Books, 1989).

O'Connell, Brian, *B2B.com: Cashing-in on the Business-to-Business E-commerce Bonanza* (Holbrook, Massachusetts: Adams Media Corp., 2000).

Ohmae, Kenichi, *The Borderless World: Power and Strategy in the Interlinked Economy* (New York: Harper Collins Pubs., Inc., 1991).

Ohmae, Kenichi, *The Evolving Global Economy* (Boston, MA: Harvard Business School (HBS) Press, 1995).

Project Management Institute Standards Committee, *A Guide to the Project Management Body of Knowledge* (Upper Darby, Pa.: Project Management Institute, 2001).

Pugh, David G., *A Bidder's Dozen: Golden Rules for Winning Work,* Journal of the Association of Proposal Management Professionals, Spring/Summer 2002 (Association of Proposal Management Professionals).

Rhea-McKenzie, Denise, *Proposal Security 101: The Basics of Managing Competition Sensitive Data,* Journal of the Association of Proposal Management Professionals, Spring/Summer 2002 (Association of Proposal Management Professionals).

Reichheld, Frederick F., *The Loyalty Effect* (Boston: Harvard Business School Press, 1996).

Shannon, Rebecca, *Government Proposals: Cutting Through the Chaos* (McLean, VA: Management Concepts, Inc., 2002).

Tepper, Ronald, *How to Write Winning Proposals For Your Company or Client* (New York: John Wiley & Sons, 2nd Edition, 1990).

Ury, William, *Getting Past No: Negotiating Your Way from Confrontation to Cooperation* (New York: Bantam Books, 1993).

Vivian, Kaye, *Winning Proposals: A Step-By-Step Guide to the Proposal Process* (New York: American Institute of Certified Public Accountants, 1993).

Walker, Danielle, Walker, Thomas and Schmitz, Joerg, *Doing Business Internationally* (New York: McGraw-Hill, 2003).

Webster' Dictionary, The New Lexicon of the English Language (New York: Lexicon Publications, Inc., 1989).

Weiss, Kenneth D., *Building An Import/Export Business* (New York: John Wiley & Sons, Inc., 2002).

Whalen, Tim, *Writing and Managing Winning Technical Proposals* (McLean, VA: Management Concepts, Inc., 1998).

Wilson, Greg, *Developing In-House Proposal Tools,* Journal of the Association of Proposal Management Professionals, Spring/Summer 2002 (Association of Proposal Management Professionals).

Wilson, Greg, *Proposal Automation Tools,* Journal of the Association of Proposal Management Professionals, Spring/Summer 2001 (Association of Proposal Management Professionals).

Index